Re-reading Household Relationships Christologically

Biblical Hermeneutics Rediscovered

The Series as the name suggests will focus on Biblical Hermeneutics, i.e., literary works concerned with methods of interpreting the Old and New Testaments of Bible via different stream of topics like Literature & Poetry, Indigenous Philosophizing, Ethical response towards Ecology, Health & Healing, Science & Technology, Feminist Theology, Sociological approach towards Human Rights, Law & Politics, Arts, History of Ideas, Ancient Civilizations, Cultural Contiguity, Religious Cosmologies & Mysticism, Appraisal of various Theologians, World Peace & Harmony, Global Capitalism, Network Marketing, Cybertheology, Population & Demographics, Epigraphic Studies, Contextualized Education, and many others. We welcome a Mss. on any topic/s mentioned, whether they are original works, scholarly monographs, collections of conference papers, revised dissertations, or translations of historical documents. Through the Series we, the Publishers, are striving to put forward published works that may help Institutions, Academic Bodies, Researchers, Scholars and the World at large in furthering their respective knowledge and understanding on the concerned subject. We welcome your comments on our efforts and further suggestions on how we can enshrine new ray of analysing & explaining the written Texts through our upcoming books.

Biblical Hermeneutics Rediscovered - 4

Re-reading Household Relationships Christologically

Ephesians, Empire and Egalitarianism

Jayachitra Lalitha

CWI

Christian World Imprints™

First Published in 2017 by

Christian World Imprints™
Christian Publishing & Books from India
H-12 Bali Nagar, **New Delhi-110015**
info@christianworldimprints.com
www.ChristianWorldImprints.com
Phone: +91 11 25465925

ISBN 13: 978-93-5148-189-8 ISBN 10: 93-5148-189-1

Cataloging in Publication Data--DK
Courtesy: D.K. Agencies (P) Ltd. <docinfo@dkagencies.com>

Lalitha, Jayachitra, 1974- **author.**
Re-reading household relationships christologically : Ephesians, empire and egalitarianism / Jayachitra Lalitha.
pages cm. -- (Biblical hermeneutics rediscovered ; 4)
Includes bibliographical references.
ISBN 9351481891
ISBN 9789351481898

1. Households--Religious aspects--Christianity--Biblical teaching. 2. Spouses. 3. Man-woman relationships--Religious aspects. 4. Bible. New Testament.--Criticism, interpretation, etc. I. Title. II. Series: Biblical hermeneutics rediscovered ; 4.

BV4526.3.L35 2017 DDC 261.83581 23

Printed in India.

Dedicated to

Pranay, my son and Rohan, my husband, who have been continually inspiring to make an egalitarian home possible!

Contents

Foreword

Among the three pairs of relationships mentioned in the household codes, the wife-husband relationship poses a greater challenge to New Testament scholarship, especially when it is viewed against the backdrop of the gender egalitarianism of early Christianity and contemporary feminist hermeneutics ~Jayachitra

There has been a rising interest in the nature of the household in recent times, motivated and provoked by feminist perspectives which envisage the household as a major and significant institution, in which and through which gender relations are arranged, prescribed and perhaps disputed. Examining the nature of the household has enhanced our understanding of its particularities, leading to the awareness that there is variation in the manner in which relationships are forged between members within the household and between the household and the society, all influenced by context, space and time. Households were in all likelihood internally differentiated. How we analyse and understand these variations and diversities are in turn dependent upon our understandings of patriarchies. The possibility and the need for wide-ranging analyses of the household are therefore essential.

The Indian *grha* or household has always been recognized as a basic unit of society and its health and success was crucial to the life and the well-being of the society and the State. The Indian tradition therefore contains within it several such codes found, for example, within the *śāstric* traditions – the *Manusmṛti, the Arthaśāstra and the Kāmasūtra.* These codes continue to sway influence on the Indian household, irrespective of caste, class or religion and govern relationships amongst its members, particularly between men and women. One cannot therefore ignore their influence and relevance in today's Indian context, in spite of the eras that separate us from the time when they were composed or compiled. What a juxtaposed reading of these *śāstric* traditions and the household codes (*haustafel)* within the New Testament might produce remains to be seen.

The *haustafel* found within the New Testament and their interpretations over the many centuries have impacted and influenced the Indian Christian household. In many ways, the uncritical interpretations of these codes and a prescriptive use of these along with the Indian cultural traditions which relegate women to a subservient position within family and society have reinforced women's subordination and subjugation with the Christian household and the Church. The extent to which these prescriptions are followed remains enigmatic. Changing social circumstances have led to the questioning, to modifications, sometimes abandonment and other times reversals as well.

The importance of the questioning of Ephesians 5 and its interpretations for Indian women cannot be undermined. The text, a favorite in marriage rituals, has often been used prescriptively to encourage married women to be submissive and to buttress male superiority and domination; female inferiority and submission. But, that there is a huge gap between such sexist interpretations and what the text might actually be suggesting has been highlighted by several scholars both men and women. Ephesians 5:21-33 reflects a revolutionary idea - a re-conceptualized relationship between a man and a woman in the context of marriage. But does it really? Let Jayachitra tell us.

This book by Jayachitra's makes a welcome contribution to existing research on the topic in terms of identifying the manner in which certain interpretations of the text might impinge on women's lives in India which are already battered due to a cultural and social system that views women as inferior. Her contribution to the discussions on this text is twofold:

First, with insights derived from postcolonial thinkers, she asserts and affirms the colonized identity of the Ephesian church and its use of colonial language and mimicry to impart what one might consider subversive messages.With the use of the postcolonial optic and a feminist hermeneutical lens, she traces and highlights the Greco-Roman influences on the household code in Ephesians and notes how the Ephesian community in their status as the colonized, "mimic" the then dominant Roman Society and its practices regarding the household. A closer study of these codes as adopted by the Ephesian community reveals that inherent within them are modifications of the Roman code based on both Jewish and Christian values, resulting in "a third space of enunciation" (Bhabha).

She writes,

> It may seem that the Ephesian Church is imitating the dominant imperial social ideologies, however, an in-depth analysis unravels the overlapping identities, which in turn pose threats to the dominant ideologies.

Jayachitra argues and concludes that inherent within the Ephesian household code are two opposing notions – submission and mutuality which are in tension. With the inclusion of Gen 2:24, the author of Ephesians mitigates this tension, with an emphasis on the idea of "one flesh" which expresses the equality of their union and the unity of humanity. That the Genesis text implicitly shapes the whole of this marriage section in the Ephesian household code has been suggested by several NT scholars and has received scholarly consensus. Sarah J. Tanzer in her commentary on this text maintains that the

> Genesis quotation encourages the idea of marriage expressed in these verses: marriage (between Christ and Church and between husband and wife) creates a new, single entity and strives for unity as the ideal. The quotation of Gen 2:24 is not an afterthought, but rather informs this entire first section of the Ephesian household code ["Ephesians" in E. S. Fiorenza ed., *Searching the Scriptures: A Feminist Commentary,* Vol. 2, (New York: Crossroad, 1994) 339].

In recognizing the strengths of such an interpretation we can move towards a fuller understanding of both a woman's and a man's place within the household.

Second, the book calls attention to the manner in which traditional interpretations of the text might impinge on women's lives in India which are already battered due to a cultural and social system that views women as inferior. Jayachitra writes,

> Wives are ideally expected to obey their husbands in 'everything' and this eventually calls for a silent bearing of all the atrocities inflicted upon them. Women remain silent mainly because the social system forces them to ignore domestic violence in order to save the honor of their families. This kind of attitude is enhanced by the shame-honor binaries of ethical living in many societies

Addressing such issues requires that we challenge texts and established traditions in order to foster change. In one of his essays, entitled, "The Play's The Thing," – Amartya Sen writes, "Voice is important, in demanding redress, in arguing forcefully, in insulting nicely and for conversing and contradicting…" [*The Country of First Boys*, edited by Antara Dev Sen and Pratik Kanjilal (New Delhi: Oxford, 2015), 40].

Although Sen is referring to voice in play, I do believe that what he says can be applied to women's participation in the crusade against sexist interpretations of the Bible. Voices of women and their insights are essential in order to redress, contradict, demand, argue, converse and reshape our current and oppressive understandings of the Biblical text. I hope that what Jayachitra has started here will encourage and engender voice among other women both within and outside the academy.

Monica Jyotsna Melanchthon
Associate Professor, Hebrew Bible/Old Testament Studies
Pilgrim Theological College, University of Divinity
Melbourne, Australia.

Preface

This book, originally submitted as a doctoral dissertation to the Senate of Serampore College (University), is an attempt to analyze the household marital relation in the letter to the Ephesians as a site for postcolonial theological formulations. Since, Ephesus itself is a colonized city and a prominent centre of Christianity in the first century Roman imperial era, there might have been direct impact of Greco-Roman religion, ideology and ethics on the Christian living in its early stages of development. The Church at Ephesus would probably have struggled to negotiate its existence amidst other dominant ideologies. The letter to the Ephesians exhibits hybridized nuances from its multicultural setting of Judaism, Greco-Roman religions and Christianity and therefore, portrays a narrative ambivalence as a literature. Thus, a reader might encounter anti-imperial strategies not in an explicit manner, but in a subtle way in the form of hybridity and colonial mimicry.

The epistle to the Ephesians reflects overtones of imperial ideology as it struggles to keep the pressures from the colonial environment at a check. As far as the author is concerned, God's empire is in the heavenly realms with all the spiritual blessings (1:3), which in fact becomes the starting point for narrating the whole theology against the colonial backdrop. The empire of God's spiritual/heavenly realm is now incarnated into the household of God (2:19), where no one remains foreigner or alien but everyone is a fellow citizen with God's people. A study on the ethnic, religious and linguistic groups in the multicultural Rome in first century CE supports that the Jewish and

Christian communities were treated as 'foreign' to Roman culture and social life.[1] But, in the epistle to the Ephesians, the empire is replaced by the household, while retaining the other political terms. A household in a Roman society plays a significant role in that the social order is being established beginning from the smallest unit of the society. The concept of the household of God comprising all the members of Ephesian church links to the author's intention of making God's empire very much relevant for the church in a colonial environment.

Unless the Ephesian church is a colonized community in itself, the thrust of the letter will not make sense to the readers.[2] It also should be noted that in the process of creating a counter-empire, the Ephesian church tends to become imperial by mimicking the strategies of the imperial power. The author's inclination to use Greco-Roman terminologies and concepts like Household, ecclesia, powers, authorities and the imagery of army/ soldier in the letter to the Ephesians attests to this.

Christian household codes in general and Ephesian household codes in particular exhibit possibilities of a hybrid formulation of the prevalent household duties practiced from the time of Aristotle till Roman captivation. The author of Ephesians, by asking the husbands to love their wives, is actually setting a resistant tone to the then prevailing Greco-Roman household codes. It was by no means conventional in the imperial Roman society to expect of husbands to love their wives. The marriage relationship is generally viewed as a contractual bond, which can be broken legally at any time by divorce. Since, wives continued to live under the patriarchal control of their fathers even after their marriage, the husbands were actually not enjoying much legal control over their wives in Roman society. In such a conventional Roman society, it would be radical and revolutionary to demand from husbands love toward their wives. It raises the question whether such an exhortation challenges the patriarchal domination safeguarded by the imperial powers.

1 Beryl Rawson, "'The Roman family' in Recent Research: State of the Question" *Biblical Interpretation,* vol. 11, no. 2 (2003): 131.

2 Margaret MacDonald, "The Politics of Identity in Ephesians," in *Journal for the Study of the New Testament,* vol. 26 (2004): 422.

Despite the conventional understanding of patriarchal domination in the Ephesian passage, it nevertheless exhibits a kind of constant resistance to the norms of the world outside the Church.

It is the paradoxical status of wives and husbands in Eph. 5:21-33 that highlights the 'almost the same, but not quite' portrayal of the marital bond. The new paradoxical status in Christ challenges the patriarchal and imperial notions embedded in the Roman household norms. The husband is expected to love his wife as her head just like Christ loves the church. Christ's headship is characterized by the power of love, which is paradoxically revealed in the weakness of his sacrificial death. Similarly, the mutual submission expected of all believers in v. 21 continues to remain applicable for husbands as well, even though they are metaphorically equated to Christ. Further, a husband's headship is evaluated by the amount of love manifested in his sacrificial attitude to his wife. Therefore, the Ephesian household code, and especially the marital gender norms continuously negotiate with the power structures of the Roman marital codes, by which the passage remains resistant to the imperial power notions of the hegemony of Roman imperialism.

This book is divided into six chapters, of which the first one introduces the postcolonial feminist methodology used in this book to examine the close link between Ephesian household codes and Empire. The second chapter deals with the origin and background of Christian household codes in the early Church against the background of Jewish and Greco-Roman religions and cultures. The third chapter highlights how marital relationships were understood in ancient Mediterranean religions and cultures in order to establish socio-cultural and religio-political background to Ephesian wife-husband relationship. The fourth chapter is a postcolonial feminist reading of the Ephesian text. The fifth chapter, which is the defining chapter of this book, attempts to Christologically evaluate the patriarchal and imperial nuances embedded in the Ephesian household code especially in relation to wives and husbands. The sixth, which is the final chapter, recapitulates the findings of a postcolonial feminist appraisal of Eph 5:21-33.

Chapter 1

Ephesian Household Codes and Empire

In the New Testament, household codes are found in Col. 3:18-4:1, Eph. 5:21-6:9, 1 Tim. 2: 8-15; 6:1-10, Tit. 2:1-10, and 1 Pet. 2:18-3:7. They are also used in the writings of apostolic fathers or early Christian teachers.[1] It was Martin Luther, who proposed the term, *haustafel* (household code), which means 'a list of rules for the household.' These household codes are supposed to be formulated to oversee the behavioural patterns of households.[2] The household codes denote the responsibilities of three pairs of relations such as wives-husbands, children-parents and slaves-masters. The general format consists of a paraenetic form containing an addressee and a command followed by the motive for obeying the command. The first party addressed is in a lower rank and is expected to submit to the second.[3] When one tries to understand the role of household codes in New Testament writings, s/he invariably encounters the apparent tension between the concepts of equality of persons and

1 Didache 4:9-11, Barnabs 19:5-7, 1 Clement 1:3, 21:6-9, *Ignatius*, *Polycarp* 4:1-6:2, *Polycarp*, Philippians 4:2-6:1.

2 Peter T. O'Brien, *The Letter to the Ephesians* (Leicester: Apollos, 1999), 405.

3 O'Brien, *Ephesians,* 405., Bonnie Thurston, *Reading Colossians, Ephesians, and 2 Thessalonians: A Literary and Theological Commentary* (New York: Crossroad, 1995), 56.

the functional hierarchy embedded in the various relationships. Among the three pairs of relationships mentioned in the household codes, wife-husband relationship poses a greater challenge to the New Testament scholarship, especially when it is viewed against the backdrop of the gender egalitarianism of early Christianity and the contemporary feminist hermeneutics.

The household codes appear in later writings of the New Testament (Col. 3:18-4:1, Eph. 5:21-6:9, 1 Tim. 2:8-15; 6:1-10, Tit. 2:1-10, and 1 Pet. 2:18-3:7), while they are significantly absent in major Pauline epistles. Does it indicate a development in the post-Pauline period? The wife-husband relationship as mentioned in Eph. 5:21-33 projects a hierarchical familial situation, which is different from the gender equality advocated by Paul in Gal. 3:28. If so, what could have been the intentions or motivations of the author? While the author of Ephesians mention about mutual submission of all believers in v. 21 (including wives and husbands), there is specific emphasis on the wife's obligation to be submissive to the husband (vv. 22-24). Reading this obligation against the background of first century Judaism and Greco-Roman political rule, where the household was modeled on a patriarchal pattern, one could imagine that the Ephesian wife-husband relationship code is a Christian reinstatement of the prevalent code of conduct. If this observation were to be correct, then the wife-husband relationship mentioned in Ephesians could be viewed as a step-back from the Pauline emphasis of gender equality. All these concerns provide sufficient rationale to study this topic.

In both, Greek and Roman households, *oikos* was the basic concept of the citizenry. Both householders and their wives came from the citizen ranks and it was only in such a fully legal conjugal union that citizen children could be born. In the Greco-Roman society, the household was structured as a patriarchal institution, whose male head exercised authority over the other members including wives. Plutarch's marriage rule states, "women are to be praised if they subordinate themselves to their husbands."[4] In this societal set up,

4 E. W. Stegemann and W. Stegemann, *The Jesus Movement: A Social History of its First Century,* translated by O. C. Dean, Jr. (Minneapolis: Fortress Press, 1995), 372.

one could notice various levels of social interactions. At one level, wives in both Greek and Roman societies were subjected to a sexual double standard that demanded from them strict chastity, while their husbands enjoyed extensive sexual freedom.[5] The traditional Jewish household was also a patriarchal one, yet it had its own distinctive social features based on their religion. At the level of interaction among women, Jewish women were making comparatively more public appearances than Greek women, but did not have the freedom of Roman women.[6] However, as Hellenistic Judaism developed, the Jewish households in the cities of Hellenistic-Roman Diaspora became undistinguishable from others.[7]

In the first century CE, there existed social tension in connection with the wife's role within the family. The notion that women possessed intellectual and moral capacities equal to that of men could receive a hearing in the basically conservative Roman setting. The idea that husbands and wives should be held accountable to a single standard of sexual behaviour was also gaining acceptance.[8] At the same time, gender roles based upon strict patriarchal domination continued to have great hold to the extent that the traditional patriarchal household and conventional sex roles had come to be associated with the preservation of an orderly and stable society.[9] Amidst such positive shifts from patriarchal household to a more liberated perspective of marriage and family in the Greco-Roman cities, the early Christian church also underwent tremendous social modification. The newly found freedom in Christian faith would have probably provoked the Christians to question the oppressive social norms and thus created social tension in the church.

James E. Crouch proposes that the household codes are primarily the conservative response to a sort of Christian enthusiasm, widely prevalent in the early church that confronted established social

5 David C. Verner, *The Household of God. The Social World of the Pastoral Epistles* (Chicago: Scholars Press, 1983), 79.

6 Everett Ferguson, *Backgrounds of Early Christianity* (Grand Rapids: William B. Eerdmans Publishing Company, 1993), 71.

7 Verner, *The Household of God,* 80.

8 Verner, *The Household of God,* 80.

9 Verner, *The Household of God,* 81.

conventions, especially in the case of wives. Thus, Crouch views them as a response to social tension in the church.[10]

It is interesting to note that the gender is the determining factor in establishing the domination-subjugation order of the familial relationship in the Christian household code. The wife-husband relation here is compared to the Church-Christ analogy. The gender roles assigned to wives in this passage are that of submission to their husbands as to the Lord (5:22) and in everything as the church submits to the Lord (5:24). Further, they are exhorted to fear their husbands (5:33). Originally, Eph. 5:22 does not contain the verb 'be subject to' (*hupotasso*), but it is carried over from v. 21. Similarly, the verb *hupotasso* in the v. 24b is understood as implemented for wives from v. 24a. Coming to the gender norms delegated to husbands, they are commanded thrice to love their wives (vv. 25, 28, 33) just as 'Christ loved the church and gave himself up for her' (v. 25), just as 'they love their own bodies' (v. 28) and just as 'they love themselves' (v. 33). This exhortation may sound quite radical in the sense that a sacrificial love similar to that of Christ is envisioned here. However, some feminist interpreters have raised the question as to whether the church-Christ imagery used to interpret the wife-husband relation has seemingly reinforced "the inferior position of the wife Christologically."[11] Furthermore, non-reciprocal duties assigned to wives-husbands seem to contradict the mutual submission intended of all in v. 21.

The modern scholarly consensus on the origin of household code draws back to Aristotle's *Politics* (1.1253b.1-14), which was also found in Hellenistic discussions in Josephus' apologetic discourse (*Against Apion* 2.199-216). According to them, domestic harmony

10 James E. Crouch, *The Origin and Intention of the Colossian* Household code (Gottingen: Vandenhoek, 1972), 9, 19-22, 122ff.; David Balch, *Let Wives be Submissive: The Domestic Code in 1 Peter* (Chicago, CA: Scholars Press, 1981), 132-36.

11 Carolyn Osiek and David L. Balch. *Families in the New Testament World. Households and House Churches* (Loiseville: Westminister John Knox Press, 1997), 121.; Elisabeth Schussler Fiorenza. *In Memory of Her. A Feminist Theological Reconstruction of Christian Origins* (London: SCM Press Ltd., 1983), 270.

is linked to national harmony and model citizenship.[12] Carolyn Osiek and David L. Balch are of the opinion that even though the structured household code has its origin in Aristotle, it was historically reinforced by emperor Augustus. The imperial ideology, which structured Roman society, had treated household as the basic microcosm of the large macrocosm of Roman society.[13] Historians on Roman family highlight the speeches of emperors and various political rhetoricians and moralists to recognize the concord of the married couple as encoding the political stance of the community. In this connection, the church in Ephesian passage is projected as the one who stands purified and united with/to her one true husband Christ and manifestly distinct from a corrupt society.[14]

Against the backdrop of Greco-Roman imperial ideology, an analysis of the Ephesian household code raises the following questions: Was the author conceiving a radical change in the then prevalent social structure? Or was the author presenting a Christian model of household code as an apologetic to avoid confrontation with the imperial social norms? What were the pressing issues that led to adapting household code into Christian community in Ephesus? How does the Christian adaptation of marital gender norms in Eph. 5:21-33 vary from those practiced in the Greco-Roman communities? Does the Christ-Church analogy aim to challenge the patriarchal pattern of Greco-Roman household code? If so, to what extent, does the Ephesian household code contribute towards establishing a more egalitarian familial situation in Ephesus?

As stated earlier, the problem lies in the way submission is demanded from wives while mutual submission is a major concern of the passage. While there is something radically new as far as husbands are exhorted to love their wives as Christ loved the church (v. 25) and as he loves his own body (v. 28), how can the exhortations to wives to submit to husbands be justified? The scope of the present research is that it could reveal the intention of the author and the

12 Margaret Y. MacDonald, "The politics of Identity in Ephesians," in *Journal of the Study of New Testament 26.4 (2004):* 443.

13 Osiek and Balch, *Households and House Churches,* 119.

14 MacDonald, *The Politics of Identity,* 441.

findings could be helpful to provide a critique on the Ephesian wife-husband relationship.

The present research woks on a hypothetical framework based on two fundamental aspects: firstly, the Ephesian household code has drawn heavily from the Greco-Roman household codes, which may have been mediated through Hellenistic Judaism to early Christian communities. The imperial ideology based on hierarchy, patriarchy and competition might have crept into the Christian familial structure as household was treated as the basic unit to establish a stable and uninterrupted Roman society. For the Greek speaking Christians, who were Roman citizens, the familial rules of Rome could have been applicable despite their new religious identity. Secondly, Eph. 5:21-33 contains exhortations to wives and husbands on the basis of Church-Christ analogy that seem to challenge the patriarchal pattern of traditional household codes and set up an egalitarian relation between wives and husbands.

There have been many researches to study the household codes, which have mainly focused on their origin, nature and purpose. The recent researches heavily depend on the Greco-Roman background of the household codes. The Roman imperial ideology has strongly influenced the ethical living of the Church in the early centuries of Christianity. This raises questions regarding how the Christian church maintained its identity amidst growing influences of the socio-political environment. Can we understand the household code as a "dialogue of early Christianity with its wider environment and therefore the (cultural) struggle of the early Christian movement in defining its own identity?"[15] Since the letter to the Ephesians deals primarily with the "household of God" (2:19), can it be proposed that the household codes are an effort to define the new identity of Christianity amidst Roman political pressures? How do the marital norms pertaining to wives and husbands in Eph. 5:21-33 promote the unity of the household of God? Do these norms question the patriarchal customs of the then prevalent household codes and if so, how? These concerns are not adequately treated in the

15 Tet-Lim N. Yee, *Jews, Gentiles and Ethnic Reconciliation: Paul's Jewish Identity and Ephesians* (Cambridge: Cambridge University Press, 2005), 224.

previous researches. The point of departure of the present research on Ephesian household code is that it aims to explore whether the Christian adaptation of marital gender norms in Eph. 5:21-33 was able to challenge the then prevalent male-privileged familial norms and contribute towards establishing egalitarian wife-husband relationship.

A postcolonial feminist approach is quite relevant to critique the portrayal of wife-husband as binary opposites in Eph. 5:21-33 and the way such biblical passage and interpretation have been used to legitimize subjugation of wives in families under the mask of faith perspectives. A postcolonial feminist biblical hermeneutic helps to analyze the larger cultural and political contexts in which the Christian household code negotiated with the patriarchal social norms of Judaism and Hellenistic culture under the gaze of the Roman Empire.[16]

To define postcolonial feminist hermeneutics, it is important to start with postcolonialism and its entry into Biblical studies. Musa W. Dube, a postcolonial African feminist biblical scholar, uses the term postcolonial to denote literary theories, which could be used to analyse the Bible's literary role in the institution of imperialism. For her, the formation of biblical literature denotes a constant struggle whether to endorse or resist imperial powers.[17] She identifies biblical texts as propounding "values that are compatible with imperialistic tendencies. Historical evidence of modern imperialism thus categorizes the biblical texts as imperializing texts: texts that

---

16 Kwok Pui-lan, "Postcolonialism, Feminism and Biblical Interpretation," in *Scripture, Community and Mission*, edited by Philip L. Wickeri (Hong Kong: CCA & CWM, 2002), 277. Elisabeth Schussler Fiorenza. *Wisdom Ways. Introducing Biblical Interpretation* (Maryknoll, New York: Orbis Books, 2001), See Musa W. Dube, *Postcolonial Feminist Interpretation of the Bible* (St. Louis, Missouri: Chalice Press, 2000); Kwok Pui-lan, *Postcolonial Imagination and Feminist Theology* (Louisville: WJK, 2005); R. S. Sugirtharajah, *Postcolonial Criticism and Biblical Interpretation* (Oxford: Oxford University Press, 2002); R. S. Sugirtharajah, *Postcolonial Reconfigurations. An Alternative Way of Reading the Bible and Doing Theology* (London: SCM Press, 2003).

17 Dube, *Postcolonial Feminist Interpretation*, 48.

authorize the imposition of foreign institutions on one nation by another."[18]

Biblical narratives are evolved from the people's colonial experiences, whether it is Egyptian, Assyrian, Babylonian, Persian or Greco-Roman.[19] Empire building and colonialism have shaped biblical texts, canonization and interpretation. Until late 19th century, empire was considered to be "a humanitarian enterprise where an amiable form of civilization was pressed upon the hapless and ignoble races."[20] The predatory nature of imperialism/colonialism became vividly clear as economical and political propaganda began to unfurl in the colonized territories. Postcolonial theory originally initiated as a resistance discourse of the colonized to interrogate dominant knowledge systems of the colonizers and the neo-colonizers.

R. S. Sugirtharajah, comments that postcolonial biblical interpretations emerging from the once colonized peoples highlight the historical and cultural reality of colonialism, the effects of colonization and colonial ideals on interpretative works, the possibilities of reconstructive readings from the perspective of postcolonial concerns, and the dubiousness of not only the colonial past but also the dubiousness of the contemporary world order in the form of globalization and its neo-colonizing tendencies.[21] In a contemporary situation of biblical interpretation, which is detached from the problems of the contemporary world, the ineffectuality is evident, as it has failed to work towards social change. In such a scenario, postcolonial criticism could act "as life-enhancing and constitutively opposed to every form of tyranny, domination, and abuse, its social goals are noncoercive knowledge produced in the interests of human freedom."[22]

---

18 Dube, *Postcolonial Feminist Interpretation,* 129.

19 Kwok Pui-Lan, "Postcolonialism, Feminism and Biblical Interpretation" in *Scripture, Community and Mission,* edited by Philip L.Wickeri (Hong Kong: CCA & CWM, 2002), 271.

20 R. S. Sugirtharajah, *Postcolonial Criticism and Biblical Interpretation* (Oxford: Oxford University Press, 2002), 24.

21 Sugirtharajah, *Postcolonial Reconfigurations,* 103.

22 Sugirtharajh, *Postcolonial Criticism and Biblical Interpretation,* 14.

Postcolonial criticism itself being a product of hybridity enhances interaction between the colonizing countries and the colonized.[23] Hybridity, a postcolonial analytical concept with its accent on mixed cultural legacies and fruitful cross-pollination of cultures challenges the western inclined portrayals of insular, monocultural perspectives. Therefore, this concept of hybridity could "challenge and resist fictitious notions of cultural purity and authenticity claimed for biblical cultures by speaking of texts, culture, race and history as fluid and amalgamated."[24] This will in turn disentangle biblical and theological narratives from binary divisions.

As Bhabha suggests, hybridity acts as an 'in-between space' in which the colonized translate or undo the binaries imposed by the colonial project. When narratives or discourses are analysed from this in-between space, metanarratives like cultural authenticity and sovereignty (supremacy, autonomy, hierarchy) become less significant 'values' than an awareness of the hybrid conditions of inter-cultural exchange.[25]

Sugirtharajah reiterates further:

> In the face of more coercive discourses which insist on a single truth, single world view and single history, the postcolonial mode of hybridization can be seen as more pliable and accommodative and more willing to incorporate dissent... What hybridity, as a discursive practice, does is to shift the conceptualization of identity. Rather than seeing identity as a stable reference point, it switches to a different 'epistemological paradigm in which it is liminality, instability, impurity, movement and fluidity that inform the formation of identities.'"[26]

---

23 R. S. Sugirtharajah, "Charting the Aftermath: A Review of Postcolonial Criticism" in *The Postcolonial Biblical Reader* (Oxford: Blackwell Publishing Ltd., 2006), 16. Sugirtharajh, *Postcolonial Criticism and Biblical Interpretation,* 23.

24 Sugirtharajah, *Postcolonial Reconfigurations,* 109.

25 Homi K. Bhabha, *The Location of Culture* (London and New York: Routledge, 1994), cited by Sugirtharajah, *Postcolonial Criticism and Biblical Interpretation,* 22.

26 Sugirtharajah, *Postcolonial Reconfigurations,* 125.

In this way, postcolonial hermeneutics can empower the colonized to take control of their identities by rectifying the misinterpretations of the colonialists.[27]

Here comes to limelight another catchword of postcolonialism, i.e., hyphenated or multiple identities, which in turn call our attention to multiplicity of meanings and truths as well. While attempting to do a reconstructive reading of the text, Postcolonial critics highlight the struggles and resistance in different colonial contexts. Their goal is to unearth the voices of subalterns such as women and colonized and in this process, they try to be sensitive to postcolonial concerns such as hybridity, deterritorialization, and hyphenated or multiple identities.[28]

The postcolonial concept of hybridity creates transcultural spaces of mutual cultural exchange nullifying hierarchical purity of cultures. Dube resonates a similar idea in identifying hybridity as a form of resistance, "for it dispenses with dualistic and hierarchical constructions of cultures, which are used to claim the superiority of colonizing cultures, and shows that cultures grow and are dependent on borrowing from each other."[29] Sugirtharajah adds that hybridity does not dissolve the differences, but renegotiate the power notions built on differences. It involves two way interactions of both colonizers and the colonized towards creating something new,[30] in Homi Bhabha's words, a "third space of enunciation."[31]

In continuity with hybridity, another postcolonial analytical term calls for attention. That is colonial mimicry, which highlights the "desire for a reformed, recognizable Other, *as a subject of a difference*

27 Sugirtharajah, *Postcolonial Criticism and Biblical Interpretation,* 17.

28 Kwok Pui-lan, "Making the Connections: Postcolonial Studies and Feminist Biblical Interpretation," in *The Postcolonial Biblical Reader,* edited by R. S. Sugirtharajah (Oxford: Blackwell Publishing Ltd., 2006), 46. R. S. Sugitharajah, The Bible and the Third World: Precolonial, Colonial and Postcolonial Encounters (Cambridge: Cambridge University Press, 2001), 251-3.

29 Dube, *Postcolonial Feminist Interpretation,* 51.

30 R. S. Sugirtharajah, *Postcolonial Criticism and Biblical Interpretation* (Oxford: Oxford University Press, 2002), 22, 191.

31 Bill Ashcroft, Gareth Griffiths and Helen Tiffin, *Key Concepts in Post-Colonial Studies* (London: Routledge, 2004), 118.

that is almost the same, but not quite."[32] In the process of mimicking the colonizer, the colonized attempts to imbibe colonizer's cultural habits, assumptions, institutions and value and the outcome would be a 'blurred copy' or camouflage' of colonizer's traits, marking the disruption of the very same.[33] Thus, colonial mimicry reveals the limitation in the authority of colonial discourse, "almost as though colonial authority inevitably embodies the seeds of its own destruction. The threat inherent in mimicry, then, comes not from an overt resistance but from the way in which it continually suggests an identity not quite like the colonizer."[34] In Bhabha's own words, it makes perfect sense as "almost the same, but not quite."[35]

It becomes imperative now to see how postcolonialism and feminism jointly function as a hermeneutical framework. The uniting/coinciding factor between Postcolonial criticism and feminism is their resistance to any form of oppression. "They seek to uncover the subjugation of both men and women in colonial texts, and the modes of resistance of the subjugated, and expose the use of gender in both colonial discourse and social reality."[36] Postcolonial feminism points to the impact of western imperialism on women's identity formation in their particular socio-cultural location. Initially, patriarchy and imperialism are approached as two parallel systems of oppression rather than constructing an integrated system of analysis.[37]

In such preliminary discussions, three issues were identified in the postcolonial feminist discourse:[38] firstly, male-centered postcolonial discourse overlooks and underplay gender differences and women's concerns (held by feminists of both developed and developing

32 Bhabha, *The Location of Culture,* 86.

33 Simon Samuel, *A Postcolonial Reading of Mark's Story of Jesus* (London and New York: T & T Clark, 2007), 27.

34 Sugirtharajah, *Postcolonial Criticism and Biblical Interpretation,* 191.

35 Bhabha, *The Location of Culture,* 86. Ashcroft, *Post-Colonial Studies*, 118, 139-141.

36 Sugirtharajah, *Postcolonial Criticism and Biblical Interpretation,* 29.

37 Elisabeth Schussler Fiorenza, *Wisdom Ways. Introducing Feminist Biblical Interpretation* (Maryknoll, New York: Orbis Books, 2001), 62-63.

38 Sugirtharajah, *Postcolonial Criticism and Biblical Interpretation,* 29.

countries); secondly, feminists of developing countries in solidarity with male counterparts question the male colonial tendencies of developed world biblical scholarship. Thirdly, developing world feminists have complained that the developed world feminists have overlooked the colonial contexts of biblical texts and compromised with the colonial agenda embedded in them. However,

> there have been vigorous debates in a number of colonized societies over whether gender or colonial oppression is the more important political factor in women's lives. This has sometimes led to division between Western feminists and political activists from impoverished and oppressed countries; or alternatively, the two are inextricably entwined, in which case the condition of colonial dominance affects, in material ways, the position of women within their societies. This has led to calls for a greater consideration of the construction and employment of gender in the practices of imperialism and colonialism."[39]

In such a complex methodological situation, the argument of Pilcher and Whelehan advances this line of thought further,

> (a) feminist perspective not only facilitates a re-evaluation of the way 'third world women' have been homogenized in postcolonial discourse, but also "…reviews the relationships of power between women as colonizers and colonized. Feminists' concern with issues such as sexuality and the body have yielded important analyses of the eroticisation of women's bodies and the projection of illicit desires into the space of the colonized.[40]

Categorically, in recent researches, feminism and postcolonialism along with their distinct methodological features are treated in an eclectic manner to analyze the intricate web of the hegemony of oppressive forces such as patriarchy and colonialism. Any gender

39 Ashcroft, *Post-Colonial Studies,* 101-102.

40 Jane Pilcher and Imelda Whelehan, *Fifty Key Concepts in Gender Studies* (London: Sage; 2004), 103.

category in a colonial worldview could analyze how women act in favor of and against colonialism in such an eclectic approach. To quote the words of Trinh T. Minh-Ha, "pitting of anti-racist and anti-sexist struggles against one another allows some vocal fighters to dismiss blatantly the existence of either racism or sexism within their lines of action, as if oppression only comes in separate monolithic forms."[41] The rationale for postcolonialising feminist hermeneutics is well attested in the fact that

> post-colonial theory from a feminist perspective could in fact facilitate further analysis of difference as well as investigations into how women have historically wielded power over other women within the logic of colonialism. The language of borders, margins and spaces where the post-colonial critic denies her identity as marginal or encompassed by the mainstream speaks eloquently to the ways in which feminists have articulated female identity and resistance to male power.[42]

History has revealed that imperialism comes as a package of political, economic, and cultural impositions of social institutions of the dominant nation over the other. While we read the New Testament against the backdrop of the imperial setting of first century CE, the wife-husband relationship in Eph. 5:21-33 is closely linked with the overall *sitz im leben* of the letter to the Ephesians. In this connection, the Ephesian passages that offer insight into the *ekklesia*'s political response to the *Pax Romana* (imperial propaganda for Roman Rule) shed light on the kind of marital relations and gender norms prevailed in the social context of the church at Ephesus. Furthermore, the growing awareness of the socio-political impact of marriage ideals among ancient historians working on the Roman family strengthens the case for viewing the marriage teaching of Ephesians as an

41 Trinh T. Minh-ha, "Writing Postcoloniality and Feminism," in *The Post-Colonial Studies Reader,* edited by Bill Ashcroft, Gareth Griffiths and Helen Tiffin (London: Routledge; 1995), 268; Trinh T. Minh-ha quoted by Pilcher and Whelehan, *Fifty Key Concepts*, 103.

42 Pilcher and Whelehan, *Fifty Key Concepts,* 103.

important socio-political statement.[43] This, in turn, raises questions regarding the kind of political dynamics involved in Roman empire which might have imposed socio-cultural norms upon its subjugates' understanding of marriage.

Dube, while critiquing the categorization of 'woman' as a homogeneous entity in the western feminist discourses, highlights a danger in allotting superiority of western women over non-western, predominantly Asian and African women.[44] She argues,

> The failure of Western feminists to recognize and to subvert imperialist cultural strategies of subjugation means that their advocacy for women's liberation has firmly retained the right of the West to dominate and exploit non-Western nations. ... most two-thirds world women are alienated from participating fully in the articulation of women's liberation precisely because they recognize their counterparts to be jealously guarding their imperialist traditions.[45]

Here, she warns of the overarching impact of the Roman empire which controlled the formation of early Christian literature in collaboration with patriarchal culture. In general, colonial discourses were prominent during the colonial period as a means of propagation of knowledge, producing texts that were invariably "colonialist" in their endorsement and thus demanding conformity to the existing dominant imperial ideologies. These texts represented the social existence of colonial relations, which were shaped by dominant imperial notions of hierarchy, competency and absolute power and had the supreme target of consolidating the unity of the empire/imperialism.

---

43 Carolyn Osiek and Margaret Y. MacDonald with Janet H. Tulloch, *A Woman's Place: House Churches in Earliest Christianity* (Minneapolis: Fortress Press, 2006), 119-120.

44 Chandra Mohanty, "Under Western Eyes," in *Colonial Discourse and Postcolonial Theory: A Reader,* edited by Patrick Williams and Laura Chrisman (New York: Columbia University Press, 1994), 213.

45 Dube, *Postcolonial Feminist Interpretation,* 26.

> In the light of the above mentioned postcolonial feminist analytical concepts, developed from the methodologies of Bhabha, Sugirtharajah and Dube, a few questions are fundamentally raised to the Ephesian passage in discussion: Does the Ephesian passage mimic the political imperialism of its time? Does the Ephesian passage employ gender and divine representations to construct relationships of subordination and domination?[46] How does the imperial environment influence the Christian identity of the Ephesian church as far as household norms regarding wife-husband relationship are concerned? How does the Ephesian household code reveal the possibilities of multiple identities, influenced by Jewish, Greco-Roman and Christian socio-cultural and religio-political influences?

To summarize, the aims of this book, primarily, it is to analyze wife-husband relationship in Eph. 5:21-33 in the light of Gal. 3:28 to see whether the text moves away from the egalitarian gender relations in the early Christian church. Secondly, the Ephesian text will be evaluated over against the Roman imperial background to establish whether the gender norms of Christian household differed from those practiced in the surrounding Greco-Roman religions and cultures. Thirdly, this book aims to investigate whether the unity expected from the wife-husband relationship in Eph. 5:21-33 links directly to the unity of the household of God in Eph. 2:19. Fourthly, this book explores whether the Christian theological elements in the marital gender norms pose any threat to the then common male privileged institution of family and bring about any change in their understanding of the same. Fifthly, along with critiquing the portrayal of wife-husband as binary opposites in Eph. 5:21-33, it will also look into the possibilities of deriving any contribution towards establishing wife-husband relationship on egalitarian terms.

46 Dube, *Postcolonial Feminist Interpretation,* 129, 201.

Chapter 2

Household Codes in New Testament Jewish or Greco-Roman or Christian?

There has been much effort undertaken in New Testament scholarship to explore the original source of the household codes. It seems natural for the newly emerging Christian community in the first century CE, adhering to certain rules to establish their specific religio-social and political identity in a surrounding Greco-Roman society. The question that arises here is about the extent to which the Greco-Roman imperial environment might have influenced the formation of Christian household codes. And to what extent have they retained the Jewish and Christian ethics in formulating the household codes? In understanding the origin and background of New Testament household codes, one finds no consensus among scholars and researchers on a common background to the Christian household codes.

It is Ernst Lohmeyer, who has made a significant research on Jewish background of household codes, bases his study on the literary style of the Colossian household codes and proposes that they are in fact pre-Christian paraenetic material, which would have originated from Judaism.[47] The appeal to 'the fear of the Lord' (Col 3:22) as

47 Ernst Lohmeyer, *Briefe an die Kolosser und an Philemon (Kitisch-Exegetischer Kommentar uber das Neue Testament, IX)* cited by James E. Crouch, *The Origin*

the motive for ethical obligations is an exclusive Jewish term, and the term, 'Lord' refers to God than to Christ. Therefore, he suggests that the original household code was Jewish, which had used the term, 'Lord' as an integral element. In this way, his thesis certainly affirms that the New Testament households are predominantly of Jewish cultural orientation than of anything else, especially the Hellenistic.[48]

Lohmeyer highlights the Jewish resources where women, children and slaves were treated as religiously inferior. These groups of people had never enjoyed rights or responsibilities of adult, free, male members of the household. And in many instances, they are collectively addressed as inferior members.[49] Since they do not have any cultic obligations, Lohmeyer thinks that, there would have been simple Jewish codes of conduct for them. For him, the Colossian code is one such, which had included the duties of husbands, masters and Fathers much prior to the formation of Christian household codes in general.[50] Many scholars of his time and later did not receive Lohmeyer's thesis well since his pre-Christian Jewish code remained a theoretical construction.[51] There is no evidence for a Jewish code mentioning the duties of these groups of people. The available literature[52] rather indicates cultic than social duties of women, slaves and children toward their husbands, masters and fathers.[53] It could be commented here that the New Testament household codes might have been influenced by Jewish ethical does of living, however, it

---

and Intention of the Colossian Haustafel (Gottingen: Vandenhoek, 1972), 23. (Hereafter, *Colossian Haustafel*).

48 Crouch, *Colossian Haustafel,* 23-24.

49 Lohmeyer, *Briefe an die Kolosser,* cited by Crouch, *Colossian Haustafel,* 104.

50 Lohmeyer, *Briefe an die Kolosser,* cited by Crouch, *Colossian Haustafel,* 24.

51 Lohmeyer, *Briefe an die Kolosser,* cited by Crouch, *Colossian Haustafel,* 24.

52 *Berakoth 3:3* reads: "Women and slaves and minors are exempt from reciting the Shema and from wearing phylacteries, but they are not exempt from saying the Tefillah, from the law of the Mezuzah or from saying the Benediction after meals."

Berakoth 7:2: "Women or slaves or minors may not be included for the Common Grace."

Sukkah 2:8: "Women, salves and minors are exempt from the Sukkah."

53 Crouch, *Colossian Haustafel,* 105.

would be unreliable to state that Jewish women, children and slaves were religiously inferior and therefore such kind of codes emerged.

Crouch studies the Hellenistic Jewish writings of Philo and Josephus and highlights the inferior position attributed to women in them. The exhortation that women are inferior and are to be submissive to their husbands in the household codes reflects the influence of Hellenistic Judaism and not of Stoicism.[54] He comments that,

> The rigid attitude of Hellenistic Jews in this respect was due to their reaction against Hellenistic religiosity and against the license allowed women in the cults of Dionysus, Isis and Cybele. So, the New Testament household codes resulted of tension between Jewish morality, which the codes mirror and Hellenistic religiosity, which found expression within some Christian circles through a stress on Gal 3:28…, a stress which caused unrest among Christian slaves and women who desired emancipation.[55]

Crouch agreed with Schroeder that the Colossian *haustafel* was to address "the excesses created by an overemphasis on the equality created by the Spirit."[56] He identifies "the clash between Hellenistic and Jewish forms of religiosity or, more specifically, between enthusiastic and nomistic tendencies in Hellenistic Christianity. The *haustafel* itself was formulated in nomistic circles to combat what was regarded as the growing danger posed by enthusiastic excesses."[57] Primarily, the original concern of such codes was to exhort the subordinate members such as slaves and women. Gradually as they became more formalized, children were also included. It was the

54 Crouch, *Colossian Haustafel,* 109, 111, 119.

55 Crouch, *Colossian Haustafel,* 119, cited by David L. Balch, *Let Wives be Submissive: The Domestic Code in 1 Peter* (Chicago, CA: Scholars Press, 1981), 9. See Crouch, *Colossian Haustafel,* 144 (with n.108), 149, 122-145 esp. 126 on Gal 3:28.

56 David Schroeder, *Die Haustafeln des Neuen Testaments. Ihre Herkunft und ihr Theologischer Sinn* (Dissertation: Hamburg, 1959), cited by Crouch, *Colossian Haustafel,* 141.

57 Crouch, *Colossian Haustafel,* 157.

Jewish-Oriental influence that motivated Christian household codes later on to include instructions to husbands, fathers and masters. Originally the reciprocity of duties in household codes finds parallel with social duties in Egypt and Israel in antiquity, especially in the relationship between rich and poor.[58] But Balch critiques that "it is a very broad jump from the reciprocal relations of rich and poor in society to the reciprocal relations of husband and wife in a household."[59] Crouch's argument sounds male-biased since the early Christian egalitarianism could only provide more liberative space for women and slaves and in turn have furthered Christianity.

Another scholar who contributed significantly to the same line of scholarship was Eduard Schweizer, who held the basic contention that the Hellenistic patterns have reached the New Testament mediated by Hellenistic Judaism. He identifies some remarkable differences between Hellenism and Hellenistic Judaism.[60] Firstly, in Hellenistic practices, an adult free male is instructed to act over against his wife, children and slaves, but in the Hellenistic Jewish tables, (e.g. Philo) an adult male has to side with the weak, the minor and the slave. Secondly, while the aim of the Greek ethical rules was the self-perfection of the individual who ought to have a right attitude to inferiors and their needs, the Hellenistic Judaism focused on protection of the weak and the helpless. While dealing with Col. 3:18-4:1, Schweizer highlights that all the members of household are ethically responsible to do "what is fitting in the Lord." Rather than living in conformity with the socio-cultural practices, they have to live under the lordship of Christ and in conformity with his will.[61] Therefore, hellenistic ethical codes might have influenced Christianity through the early converts from Hellenistic Jewish background. However, by the time of the

58 Crouch, *Colossian Haustafel,* 144-5.

59 Balch, *Let Wives be Submissive,* 8.

60 Eduard Schweizer, "Traditional Ethical Patterns in the Pauline and Post-Pauline Letters and their Development (Lists of Vices and Housetables)," in *Text and Interpretation,* edited by E. Best and R. M. Wilson (Cambridge: Cambridge University Press, 1979), 201-202.

61 O'Brien, Peter T., *Colossians, Philemon. Word Biblical Commentary, Volume 44* (Dallas, Texas: Word Books, 1998), CD-ROM. (Hereafter, *Colossians*).

end of first century, there were large numbers of Christians from Greco-Roman background and they seemed to have outnumbered the Jewish or Hellenistic Jewish Christians.

William Lillie also attests to the Hellenistic Jewish background that Greeks and later Roman Stoics practiced giving good advice to subordinates including wives.[62] People like Paul who lived in the Hellenistic culture might have been familiar with "the conventional views of morality prevailing in the Hellenistic world and the Old Testament [*sic*] and Jewish traditions that any educated Jew would possess."[63] Yet, the hierarchical nature of the Christian household codes is not adequately substantiated by the combined influences of Hellenistic and Jewish socio-cultural milieu. Further, New Testament literature that is produced in the end of first century does not fall under that of Pauline authorship.

Martin Dibelius (1926) followed by Karl Weidinger (1928) attribute the origin of household codes to Hellenistic household ethic. They both highlight the fundamental parenetic origin of Christian household codes. Hellenistic Judaism and late stoicism share similar codes, which have been incorporated into Christian household codes. Dibelius' study on Colossian household codes suggested that they were Christianized version of a Stoic code.[64] The phrases like 'fitting' in Col 3:18 and 'well pleasing', in Col 3:20 denote key concepts in Stoic literature. In Col 3:20, the phrase, 'in Christ' does not fit appropriately and hence it looks like a Christian addition to the common social value. The more natural expression might be *to Christ.*[65] According to Dibelius, a waning interest in an imminent Parousia and a growing recognition by Christians that they needed to come to terms with the world were the reasons for the Christian

---

62 W. Lillie, "The Pauline House-Tables." *Expository Times,* 86 (1975): 180. (Hereafter, *House-Tables*).

63 Lillie, *House-Tables,* 181.

64 Martin Dibelius, *Geschichte der Urchristlichen Literatur* (Berlin – Leipzig, 1926), 67ff, cited by Crouch, *Colossian Haustafel,* 18 and Harold W. Hoehner, *Ephesians: An Exegetical Commentary* (Grand Rapids, MI: Baker Academic, 2002), 721.

65 Dibelius, *Geschichte der Urchristlichen Literatur,* 67ff, cited by Crouch, *Colossian Haustafel,* 19.

adoption of such a schema.[66] Alfred Juncker critiques Dibelius meticulously that Hellenistic sources do not provide very substantial similarities with Christian *Haustafeln*. In fact, the differences are more considerable.[67] Further he finds Dibelius' comment on waning eschatological interest not convincing enough, instead he highlights the emphasis placed on the duties of the subordinate members, which had in fact played the impulse of the household tables.[68]

Karl Weidinger (1928), a student of Dibelius, also thinks that the Christian household codes are essentially based on the Stoic concept of duty. According to him, there is no essential difference among Stoic, Hellenistic Jewish and Christian forms of the Stoic schema. Only the Christian elements made the Christian household codes vary from their non-Christian parallels.[69] For Weidinger, the need to regulate the inner life of the church on a nonenthusiastic, noneschatological basis was the cause behind such an adoption.[70]

For Crouch, the dibelius-Weidinger thesis helps to identify household codes as traditional, paraenetic material with universally human rather than specifically Christian concerns.[71] If they are not uniquely composed in Christian communities, then certainly, one would accept the remarkable similarities between the Christian household codes and their hellenistic parallels. Eduard Lohse approves Dibelius-Weidinger thesis citing Phil 4:8 that Christianity would have borrowed from whatever is just, pure, virtue worthy of praise in the Hellenistic paraenesis.[72]

---

66 Dibelius, *Geschichte der Urchristlichen Literatur,* 72, cited by O'Brien, *Colossians*, CD-ROM.

67 Alfred Juncker, *Die Ethik des Apostels Paulus, II* (Halle a. S., 1919), 205ff, cited by Crouch, *Colossian* Haustafel, 21.

68 Juncker, *Die Ethik des Apostels Paulus,* 205ff, cited by Crouch, *Colossian Haustafel,* 22.

69 Karl Weidinger, *Die Haustafeln: Ein Stuck Urchristlicher Paranese* (Leipzig: 1928), 4f, cited by Crouch, *Colossian Haustafel,* 19.

70 Weidinger, *Die Haustafeln,* 6, cited by O'Brien, *Colossians*, CD-ROM.

71 Crouch, *Colossian Haustafel,* 20-21.

72 Balch, Let Wives be Submissive, 5., See Eduard Lohse, A Commentary on the Epistles to the Colossians and to Philemon (Hermeneia, Philadelphia: Fortress, 1971), 154-63.

Nevertheless, Crouch feels that the Dibelius-Weidinger thesis projects an inner tension as there is contradiction in believing the early Christian usage of non-Christian material. He believes that there would not have been any need to borrow from Hellenistic environment, rather the Jewish Christians would have followed their Jewish ethic, including Hellenistic Jewish ethic.[73] Weidinger fails to note certain unique factors in the Hellenistic Jewish usage of the stoic schema. Hellenistic Jewish Codes differ from Stoic in presenting social duties in reciprocal terms and making the distinction between subordinate and superior persons. Furthermore, exhortations to women and slaves conform neither to the concerns of the Stoic schema nor to the presuppositions of Stoic philosophy.[74]

It is further unconvincing that the early Christians opted for the Hellenistic ethic due to the delay of *Parousia.* And it is not that only the Christian motivations make the Christian household codes different, for "there is considerable variety among the Christian *Haustafeln* with regard both to the persons addressed and to the form and content of the exhortations."[75] Even though, there are similarities, it seems to indicate that the Christian household codes had their own independent approach in being incorporated into Christian communities.

David L. Balch proposed the link between Christian household codes and Greco-Roman governing rules. Primarily, he agrees with Crouch to rule out any relation between Christian household codes and Stoic laws. He identifies a type or a model of set of governing rules on household management practiced in the early years of Greco-Roman imperial rule in Palestine. Categorically, this set of rules deals with the relationships between husband-wife, parent-child, and master-slave in the Greco-Roman society.[76] In the writings of Plato and Aristotle, there are references to large traditional topos on the State rules. They seemed to have influenced their moral social codes as late as the fourth century CE. They have fundamentally

73 Crouch, *Colossian Haustafel,* 23.

74 Crouch, *Colossian Haustafel,* 147-8.

75 Crouch, *Colossian Haustafel,* 23.

76 Balch, *Let Wives be Submissive,* 132-134.

encouraged good citizenship and were strong apologetic means to suppress the foreign religious groups (like the Cult of Isis and Judaism), which disturbed the smooth running of the established political order.[77]

A very good example of topos 'concerning household management' is found in Aristotle's Politics I. In Politics I 1253 b 1-14, Aristotle mentions that every state is composed of households and household management is important when it comes to analyse the state management. Aristotle treats three pairs of relationships such as master-slave, male-female and parents-children in a framework of ruler and the ruled (cf. Politics I 1260 a 9-14).[78] This code is found in three rhetoricians who trained Roman governors to enforce the ethic (Dionysius, Arius Didymus, and Seneca), and, correspondingly, every household code found in early Christian literature is in a context exhibiting high tension with the Roman state.[79] This topos was widely known in the Hellenistic Roman world

77 Balch, *Let Wives be Submissive,* 134-136. Foreign cults like those devoted to Dionysus, Isis, Yahweh and Christ Jesus were suspect in Greco-Roman society." The dominant Greco-Roman society exerted powerful pressure on the devotees of the foreign, Egyptian Isis, on the worshipers of the Palestinian Yahweh, and on the disciples of the crucified Christ to conform to the Roman "constitution."

78 Aristotle cited by Margaret Y. MacDonald, *The Pauline Churches: A Socio-Historical Study of Institutionalization in the Pauline and Deutero-Pauline Writings* (Cambridge: Cambridge University Press, 1988), 106.

79 David L. Balch, "Household Codes." In *Greco-Roman Literature and the New Testament,* edited by David. E. Aune (Atlanta, GA: Scholars Press, 1988), 29. The Greek historian Dionysius lists "slanders" against Rome (*Rom. Ant.* I. 89.1-4) and immediately responds to them by presenting the virtuous, laudable *politeia* of the Romans. Husbands are to rule their wives, and the wives are to be obedient in all things to their husbands (*Rom. Ant.* II. 25.4-5). Children are to honor and obey parents in all things (*Rom. Ant.* II.26.1-4); in fact Romulus gave "greater power to the father over his son than to the master over his slaves" (*Rom. Ant.* II.27.1). In the first century BCE, Aristotle's structured discussion of "household management" was summarized in a popular handbook by the Stoic Arius Didumus, Augustus Caesar's court philosopher. In his handbook summary of Peripatetic ethics, Arius Didymus presents these three pairs when outlining the "constitution" (*politeia*), the proper form of authority, in the house: "the relationship (*koinonias to schema*) to (of) parents to children is monarchic, of husbands to wives aristocratic, of children to one another ...

and most probably it would have been adapted into the Jewish homes and later the Christian homes as well.

Even though the structured household code has its origin in Aristotle, emperor Augustus historically reinforced it during his reign. The imperial ideology, which structured Roman society, had treated household as the basic microcosm of the large macrocosm of Roman society. It was due to the overarching power of the Roman Empire that persons and groups including early Christian community internalized the components of Augustus' politics such as competition, hierarchy, and patriarchy.[80] This, in fact, happened simultaneously in the course of repressing the deviant social behaviour of the devotees of minority religious communities including Christians.

David Verner agrees with Balch that the Greco-Roman *topos* is reflected in the household codes in Colossians and Ephesians.[81] However, certain recurrent features especially syntactical features are not accounted by this *topos*. Verner feels that the individual exhortations of the various Christian *Haustafeln* follow a predictable schema which is not associated with the household management topos anywhere except in the *Haustafeln* themselves.[82] But Balch feels

---

is democratic (II.148,16-19). …Unlike the NT household codes, this is not ethical exhortation, but is practical philosophical ethics. Later in the summary, Didymus argues that the patriarch rules this household because his deliberative faculty is superior to those of wives, children and slaves (II.149, 5-8). See Balch, *Household Codes,* 28., MacDonald, The Pauline Churches, 107.

80 Carolyn Osiek and David L. Balch, *Families in the New Testament World: Households and House Churches* (Loiseville: Westminister John Knox Press, 1997), 119.

81 Here not only do the three pairs of relationships – wives-husbands, children-parents, and slave-masters – appear together, but they are also treated expressly as relationships of subordinate to superior. …Thus, the traditional domestic morality represented by the household management topos *(sic)* is here taken over uncritically. See David C. Verner, *The Household of God: The Social World of the Pastoral Epistles* (Chicago: Scholars Press, 1983), 85.

82 Verner, *The Household of God,* 86. The schema has primarily to do with the structure of the individual exhortations and secondarily with the way in which these exhortations are characteristically linked. The elements of the schema may be outlined as follows: Firstly, there is an address (usually in the plural) to a group of persons representing a certain social station *(*aiJ gunai`ke", OiJ dou`loi, etc.). Secondly, there is an imperative, variously expressed with

that Verner's definition of schema is ambiguous in addressing the several possibilities of grammatical forms in household codes.[83] What Verner proposes, in fact, is a combination of *topos* and schema.[84] Here Verner takes revised position of Crouch that the household codes represent a combined product of external and internal influences to the church.[85] However, Balch fears that such characterization of the *topos* as an external influence and the schema as internal Christian development may overemphasize the uniqueness of the latter.[86]

Dieter Luhrmann also contends Stoic origin of household codes, instead he suggests "a totally different tradition which can be subsumed under the title *oikonomia* or *ho oeconomicus*," citing parallels from Xenophon's *Oeconomicus*, the first book of Aristotle's

---

imperative proper, infinitive or participle, and often accompanied by an object in the appropriate case. Thirdly, there is an amplification, which is typically expressed as a prepositional phrase, although other forms are used as well, especially the form mh; (ouj) ... ajlla; ... The amplification either defines the imperative more fully (typically as an adverb of manner) or provides a general motivation for it. Finally, there is a reason clause providing motivation, theological justification, etc., which is typically introduced by gavr, o{ti, or eijdovte" o{ti. The reason clause may be expanded into a paragraph. ... Secondarily, the schema is characterized by the fact that the exhortations which belong to it do not appear alone, but in series with other exhortations of the same type. See Verner, *The Household of God,* p. 87.

83 Balch, *Household Codes,* 36-7.

84 On the one hand, then, the *Haustafeln*, especially those of Colossians and Ephesians, have been shaped by the *topos* "concerning household management." This fact makes it likely that the original thrust of the *Haustafeln* was indeed toward relationships within the households of Christians. On the other hand, the *Haustafeln* have been shaped according to a schema which appears both to have originated and to have experienced development within the early church. See Verner, *The Household of God,* 90.

85 To elaborate the same point, it thus appears that the literary-traditional influences upon the *Haustafeln* were of two kinds: (1) influences (associated with the household management topos) which were essentially external to the early church and which exerted influence on the various *Haustafeln* independently, and (2) specific inner Christian influences (associated with the station code schema) which gave to the *Haustafel* form the status of a schema which underwent a traceable evolutionary process in the history of the early church. See Verner, *The Household of God,* 90.

86 Balch, *Household Codes,* 37.

Politics, the fragmentary *Oikonomia* of Philodemos of Gadara, the selection of Hierocle's *Oikonomikos peri oikon*, and Senecca's Epistle 94.[87] In the *Oikonomia*, the relationships within a household are given due importance.[88]

Luhrmann thinks that the household codes in the post-Pauline letters are reflections of continuing socio-religious issues in the Christian community.[89] The household played a significant role in establishing the new identity and integrity of Christianity as a new sectarian movement. All the New Testament household codes highlight a common Christian concern to establish their communal identity and integration of the Christian movement. In this way, they accomplish this constructive task amidst the destructive forces both inside and outside the Christian Church.[90]

Luhrmann and Elliott concur on the study of household codes in 1 Peter that 'identity' and 'integration' form the major social components of the sectarian Christian community and their literature and social strategies. Further, the household played the pivotal role in enhancing the Christian adaptation of conventional household

---

87 Dieter Luhrmann, "Wo man nicht mehr Sklave oder Freier ist: Uberlegungen zur Struktur fruhchristlicher Gemeinden," in *Wort und Dienst,* edited by H. Kramer (Jahrbuch der Kirchlichen Hochchule Bethel NF 13, 1975), 76, cited by John. H. Elliott, *A Home for the Homeless: A Social-Scientific Criticism of 1 Peter, Its Situation and Strategy* (Philadelphia: Fortress, 1981), 214.

88 This fundamental feature of the *oikonomia* tradition corroborates the accuracy of Rengstorf's observation concerning the specifically household character of the New Testament household codes.

89 Comparing the form and content of the *Haustafeln* with such Pauline passages as Gal. 3:28, 1 cor. 12:13 and 7: 21-24 and the letter to Philemon, he notes that the common point at issue is the stimulus which the new Christian vision of salvation provides for new forms of social and relationships. That which Christianity offered ancient society with its antiquated and objectionable forms of social differentiation was "new possibilities of identification which become concrete in social community" (au.). The proclamation of a communal rather than individual salvation grounded in an identification with the crucified Christ served not as a legitimation of social revolution but indeed as a lasting impulse for the creation of new traditions and forms of Christian social life. See Luhrmann quoted by Elliott, *A Home for the Homeless,* 218.

90 Luhrmann quoted by Elliott, *A Home for the Homeless,* 219.

codes and developing the Christian concept of 'the household of God' constituting the entire Christian community.[91]

K. H. Rengstorf (1953) and David Shroeder (1959) attributed household codes to Christian origin.[92] Rengstorf argues that the early Christian interest in the family is the primary impulse for forming household code. The father, as the head of the entire household, is expected to love all other members, which is purely a teaching of Jesus. He contends that the relations are not based on sexual differences or distinctions in rank even though the emphasis is laid on the role of the fathers.[93] For him, submission expected of wives is uniquely Christian in origin.

The essential Christian nature of the concerns of the house-tables may be compared with the similar elements in the infancy narratives of Lk.1& 2, where the home life of John the Baptist and Jesus are described. Particularly, he draws similarities with the use of *hupotassetai* (root meaning, 'to sumit') in Lk. 2:51 and the role of Joseph and Zechariah as heads of their respective families.[94] Is there anything specifically Christian about the family life of Jesus and John the Baptist? In fact, their families were set against Jewish background. Positioning father at the center of household lacks support as performing same duty to all other members is not very convincing. However, it could be agreed with Rengstorf that household codes refer to explicit and emphatic Christian notions of regulating familial relationships for the well-being of all members of the Christian community.

Crouch comments that Rengstorf's emphasis on *oikos* as the impulse for Christian household code lacks direct evidence. "In reality, however, our N. T. texts nowhere claim to be *Haus-Tafeln*. The *oikos* (*house/home*) concept which Rengstorf finds decisive for our understanding of the origin of the *Haustafeln* is not to be found

91 Elliott, *A Home for the Homeless,* 219.

92 Crouch, *Colossian Haustafel,* 24-31., Ben Witherington III, *Women in the Earliest Churches* (Cambridge: Cambridge University Press, 1988), 43.

93 K. H. Rengstorf, *Mann und Frau im Urchristentum* (Koln: Opladen, 1954), 32ff, cited by Crouch, *Colossian Haustafel,* 25.

94 Rengstorf, *Mann und Frau,* 22, cited by O'Brien, *Colossians,* CD-ROM., Crouch, *Colossian Haustafel,* 25.

in any of the haustafeln nor in their immediate context."[95] But Elliott thinks differently that Rengstorf is not given due appreciation, perhaps due to his remark on the unique Christian origin of the household codes. According to him, what should be highlighted is Rengstorf's contribution to address household codes as "an early Christian formation" or "a genuine Christian creation."[96]

David Schroeder subjects the Dibleius-Weidinger thesis to extensive criticism and thinks that the Christian *Haustafel* owes neither its form nor its content to Stoicism. "Nor does he see any basic connection between the *Haustafel* and Hellenistic Judaism, although he concedes that some material in Philo offers closer similarities to the Christian *Haustafel* than does the Stoic ode."[97] Schroeder makes a comparison of first century Hellenistic Judaism (Philo's The Decalogue 165) and Stoic Philosophy and makes certain observations:

> (1) the order of the Colossians and Ephesians codes - wife, children, slaves – occurs in Philo but not in Stoicism, (2) the duties are mentioned in pairs – wives and husbands, children and parents, slaves and masters – in Philo but not in Stoicism, and (3) Philo is concerned that one member of each of these pairs is to be subordinate to the other member of the pair, a concern absent from and even alien to Stoicism.[98]

---

95 Crouch, *Colossian Haustafel,* 104.

96 Elliott, *A Home for the Homeless,* 212. For Rengstorf, the peculiarity of the new Testament *Haustafeln* is marked by the choice and sequence of the subject matter which in its *comprehensiveness* manifested the household dimension of the thus explicitly household codes. This observation concerning the peculiar formation and emphasis of the Christian codes, however, has been mistaken as an assertion of the unique Christian origin of these codes.

97 David Schroeder, *Die Haustafeln des Neuen Testaments: Ihre Herkunft und ihr Theologischer Sinn* (Dissertation: Hamburg, 1959), cited by Crouch, *Colossian Haustafel*, 26.

98 Schroeder, *Die Haustafeln des Neuen Testaments*, cited by Balch, *Let Wives be Submissive,* 6.

It would be reliable if Hellenistic Judaism is believed to have developed this ethic out of the Decalogue (Exod 20:12, "Honor your father and your mother...") coupled with Leviticus 18-19. The special stress on submission in the later New Testament writings indicates the writer's opposition to a social actualizing of Gal 3:27-28.[99]

Schroeder believes that household code is created by Paul to address the problem that emerged from his own preaching of the equality of all in Christ (Gal 3:28). According to him, slaves and women (wives) were overemphasizing the Christian freedom at the stake of neglecting their social responsibilities. It was created in a Greek setting, but intended for the Christians who were overenthusiastic about the newly found equality in Christ. The exhortations to the superior members could be a later development.[100]

Schroeder identifies the exhortations to the subordinate members as the oldest elements of the household codes. For him, any study on household code will be adequate only if it seriously analyses the explicit emphasis given to the norms of subordinate members. He acclaims Jewish nature of the codes, which have originally been instructed by Jesus and carried over to Paul through Apostolic tradition.[101] Schroeder's opinion that the norms of subordinate members were originally derived from Jesus has called for wider scholarly disagreement.

Crouch strongly feels that Schroeder's attempt to exegete the household code as specifically of Christian origin disregard sound principles of exegesis. Crouch highlights the way Schroeder has exegeted wife-husband relationship. Schroeder justifies the submission of wives in the context of the love expected of husbands.[102]

---

99 Balch, *Let Wives be Submissive,* 6.

100 Schroeder, *Die Haustafeln,* cited by Elliott, *A Home for the Homeless,* 209, Crouch, *Colossian Haustafel,* 27, O'Brien, *Colossians,* CD-ROM.

101 Schroeder, *Die Haustafeln,* 151-153, cited by Crouch, *Colossian Haustafel,* 27-29.

102 Crouch, *Colossian Haustafel,* 31. Admittedly, the relationship between a husband and a wife will exhibit a superior quality if the husband loves his wife. Such a quality does nothing, however, to alter the *content* of an exhortation to the wife to submit herself to her husband...The exhortation to the wives is to

Another argument in favor of Christian impact on household codes comes from Wolfgang Schrage's proposal that "the household codes express an "offensive" and not simply a "defensive" Christian position."[103] The household codes were fashioned in such a way that it will encourage an active involvement in the social practices rather than withdrawing from the world. According to Schrage, the purpose of the *Haustafeln* was to enjoin Christians to practice their obedience to the Lord 'not in a ghettoized sphere isolated from the world… not in pure inwardness or solely in a churchly conventicle but also in the social sectors of society."[104]

Scholars who hold on to the unique Christian influences on the formation of household codes mostly relate to the practical struggles that the early Christians went through to establish their Christian identity in a hostile world. But the very fact that they were kept in tension with the surrounding Greco-Roman environment could have led them to incorporate the ethical codes of their neighbors.

To sum up, it is very hard to draw a clear line between Judaism and Hellenism in the New Testament era, as "what may on the surface appear to be a 'Greek' element in a particular passage may, in fact, reflect an indebtedness to a Judaism that had been influenced earlier on by the spread of Hellenism."[105] It is also impossible to draw a fixed household code from which the New Testament authors were depending on. However, there are many parallel ethical discussions found in the Jewish, Hellenistic and Greco-Roman periods. Even though Balch comments that the scholars have come to a consensus on the Hellenistic discussions, it may be appropriate to say that the Christian household codes are a hybrid formulation of the prevalent household duties practiced from the time of Aristotle till Roman captivation.

---

be interpreted in light of the reciprocal duty of the husband. The wife's duty in turn, however, has no bearing on the duty of the husband. Such exegesis admittedly makes more acceptable the exhortations of the *Haustafel*, but it hardly commends itself as sound methodology.

103 Schrage, "Haustafeln," 5, cited by Elliott, *A Home for the Homeless,* 209.

104 Schrage, "Haustafeln," 5, cited by Elliott, *A Home for the Homeless,* 210.

105 Martin Hengel, *Judaism and Hellenism, 2 Vols.* (Philadelphia: Fortress, 1974), cited by Witherington, *Women in the Earliest Churches,* 43.

The imperial ideology of Roman government especially from the time of Augustus had implemented competition, hierarchy and patriarchy in the households as part of the larger Roman society.[106] It is possible that the New Testament authors have initiated the household pattern as we find it in the post-Pauline letters, drawing on a host of ethical material inherited both from their Jewish heritage and possibly from their wider Greco-Roman milieu.[107] The Hellenistic Judaism might have probably played a major role in the transport of household codes from Hellenism down through Roman imperialism to the Christian literature. The relation between the household codes and the household character of the Christian community in which and for which they are employed highlights the adaptive nature of the early Christian movement.[108] Since the household was viewed as the basic component of the Roman State, it was expected of all to manage household properly. Therefore, household management was a crucial socio-political concern and "any upsetting of the traditional hierarchical order of the household could be considered a potential threat to the order of society as a whole."[109]

Basic Purposes of Household Codes

Scholars' different approaches to the origin and background of household codes have given rise to a number of opinions regarding the functions performed by such codes in the early Christian community. Dibelius and Weidinger commonly felt that the household codes are general ethical duties not addressed to any particular situation. However, Dibelius identified that a waning interest in an imminent Parousia and a growing recognition by Christians that they needed to come to terms with the world were the reasons for the Christian adoption of such a schema.[110] For Weidinger, the need to regulate the inner life of the church on a nonenthusiastic, noneschatological basis

106 Osiek and Balch, *Families in the New Testament World,* 119.

107 Witherington, *Women in the Earliest Churches,* 47.

108 Elliott, *A Home for the Homeless,* 211.

109 Andrew T. Lincoln, *Ephesians. Word Biblical Commentary, Volume 42* (Dallas, TX: Word Books, 1990), 358.

110 Dibelius, *Geschichte der Urchristlichen Literatur,* 72, cited by O'Brien, *Colossians,* CD-ROM.

was the cause behind such an adoption.[111] Balch strongly criticizes that even though the household codes are paraenetic in nature, "the traditional Greek ethic is intended to have a specific – apologetic – function in a problematic situation in certain provinces of Asia Minor in the last third of the first century."[112]

Rengstorf argues that the early Christian interest in the family is the primary impulse for forming such ethical codes.[113] Schroeder believes that they are created by Paul to address the problem that emerged from his own preaching of the equality of all in Christ (Gal 3:28). It was created in a Greek setting, but intended for the Christians who were overenthusiastic about the newly found equality in Christ.[114] Crouch also argues in the same line that the household codes were formulated by the nomistic tendencies in the Hellenistic Christianity so that the growing danger posed by enthusiastic excesses will be regulated.[115] Nevertheless, there is no indication in the post-Pauline epistles that either the slaves or the wives were drastically attempting to expand their social roles equal to that of masters or husbands.[116]

Among the varying opinions on the purpose of the household codes, Balch and Elliott raise a major debate on the basis of their study of Greco-Roman influences. Balch believes that the Christian

111 Weidinger, *Die Haustafeln*, 6, cited by O'Brien, *Colossians*, CD-ROM.

112 Balch, *Let Wives be Submissive*, 106. Balch thinks that the code has an apologetic function as this paraenesis is given in the light of outside criticism. Persons in Roman society were alienated and threatened by some of their slaves and wives who had converted to the new, despised religion, so they were accusing the converts of impiety, immorality, and insubordination. As a defense, the author of 1 Peter encouraged the slaves and wives to play the social roles which Aristotle had outlined; this, he hoped, would shame those who were reviling their good behavior (3:16, 2:12). The conduct of the slaves was not expected to convert masters. However, the author hoped that the wives would convert their husbands by laudable behavior. See Balch, *Let Wives be Submissive*, 109.

113 Rengstorf, *Mann und Frau*, 22, cited by O'Brien, *Colossians*, CD-ROM., Crouch, *Colossian Haustafel*, 25.

114 Schroeder, *Die Haustafeln*, cited by Elliott, *A Home for the Homeless*, 209, Crouch, *Colossian Haustafel*, 27, O'Brien, *Colossians*, CD-ROM.

115 Crouch, *Colossian Haustafel*, 157.

116 Balch, *Let Wives be Submissive*, 107.

household codes are explicitly apologetic in function. The dominant Greco-Roman society was suspicious that the foreign cults would cause sedition and insubordination. Therefore, it exerted pressure on the devotees of the foreign cults such as those of Egyptian Isis, Palestinian Yahweh, and the crucified Christ to conform to the Roman government. So, Balch identifies that every household code found in the New Testament is in a context exhibiting high tension with the Roman authorities.[117] For him, the function of household code is to reduce tension between Roman society and the church. "Christians must conform to the expectations of Hellenistic society, so that society will cease criticizing the new cult."[118]

Elliott contends that the social conformity and assimilation, which Balch highlights, are precisely the dangers that the household codes intend to discourage.[119] Basing his argument on the sectarian Petrine community, Elliott comments that the household codes try to avert external forces of social disintegration by reinforcing the distinctive identity of the Christian community and of its socio-religious cohesion. The Petrine strategy of stressing upon the household identity of the Christian community and its God-pleasing maintenance of familial integrity would avert the "disintegrative dangers of despair, renunciation of the faith, and the return of converts to their previous Jewish or pagan associations."[120]

Balch further argues against Elliott that the household codes in Petrine letter promote integration into Greco-Roman society. He adopts anthropological theories of "selective acculturation" and suggests that "A receiving culture selectively adapts cultural traits from a donor culture, which sometimes includes "a model of its family life," although "the family configuration is certain to be refracted" by the "filter of traditional and idiosyncratic perception" of the receiving culture."[121] It must be noted at this point that the household codes in the New Testament share a common focus of both the internal and the external relations of the addressees.

117 Balch, *Household Codes,* 29.

118 Balch, *Let Wives be Submissive,* 230.

119 Elliott, *A Home for the Homeless,* 218.

120 Elliott, *A Home for the Homeless,* 217.

121 Balch, *Household Codes,* 33.

Luhrmann advances the discussion that the household codes strengthen the social bonds of the Christian households upon which the life of the early Christian movement depended heavily for its existence. Therefore, such codes aim to concretize the communal implications of the early Christian proclamation of salvation by establishing the communal identity and integration within the households.[122] Elliott concurs with Luhrmann that the household played a central role within the Christian movement that the Christian adaptation of household codes from the Greco-Roman society further established the believing community as the household of God.[123]

Conclusion

Having done a critical analysis of the origin and background of household codes, it becomes unacceptable to attribute the complete validity to any one of the different theses proposed by the various scholars. However, there has been certain kind of consensus during the last two decades that the household codes in the early Christian literature including the New Testament have tremendously drawn materials from the Greco-Roman society. The New Testament writers have seemingly not given up the influences from their Jewish background while adopting such Hellenistic influences in Christian writings. The findings of this chapter lead further to narrow down the focus on the relationship between wives and husbands in the household codes especially in Ephesians 5:21-33. In order to do justice to the study of Ephesian passage, an initial probe into the wife-husband relationship in antiquity is essential and therefore the same will be undertaken in the following chapter.

122 Luhrmann, "Wo man nicht mehr Sklave oder Freier ist," 82-83, cited by Elliott, *A Home for the Homeless,* 218-9.

123 Elliott, *A Home for the Homeless,* 219.

Chapter 3

Wife-Husband Relationships Intersecting Judaism, Greco-Roman Religions and Christianity

Any study in the New Testament literature requires a clear understanding of the socio-cultural and religio-political contexts in which the events of New Testament had taken place. The Jesus Movement and the early Christianity existed in the colonial era of the Roman empire, thus distinctly marking the impact of the dominant colonialist cultures upon them. Since household codes have originated from the time of Aristotle and reinstated by the Roman emperors like Augustus in their colonies, it is inevitable to critically analyze how the household management was perceived and practiced in the different cultures that co-existed in the antiquity. Cultures owe to religions in formulating identities of individuals and communities. Marriage, being the core institution of any community, demands a critical evaluation of how religions have influenced the cultures that determine marital norms.

Here in this chapter, the focus is on the ancient Mediterranean religions through a time span of 100 BCE to 200 CE. Nonetheless, a still earlier religion like Judaism and its Scriptures are taken into account since Christianity can only be perceived as nothing but an offshoot of Judaism. However, both Judaism and Christianity thrived independently in the Roman Empire, which became a distinctive feature especially after the destruction of the Jerusalem temple in 70 CE. Furthermore, early Christian church could never be categorized exclusively as of Jewish or gentile Christians, rather as of mixed Jewish-gentile believers. Against the backdrop of these thoughts, in the first part of the chapter, a study on the concepts like marriage, divorce, and marital gender norms in Hebrew Scriptures, Judaism with an additional reference to Hellenistic Judaism, Greek and Roman imperial religions is undertaken. In the second part, the study is focused on the Christian adaptation of the same concepts to assess how the surrounding cultures have influenced the early Christianity. Particularly, Jesus' sayings on marriage and divorce and the household tables in the other New Testament writings (excluding Ephesians) are reviewed in search of the common background for wife-husband relation in the Ephesian household codes. The household codes in the early Christian literature are also surveyed to understand the interpretation of New Testament household duties of wives and husbands and the ramifications of such interpretation in the Christian ethic on marital relation.

I. Wife-Husband Relationship in Judaism

Jewish Papyri scrolls provide documentary evidences "to illustrate and open up for discussion areas of social history which bear on the history of the early church and the study of the NT in particular."[124] Even though Hebrew Scriptures are not primarily historical documents, but faith conceptualizations, they are useful in verifying the historical documents like Jewish Papyri scrolls. Further, first century historians like Philo and Josephus provide information on marital relations as lived out and as expected by the Jewish law and customs in the Roman imperial society. The hellenization of Jewish culture and living in Diaspora indicate the high intensity with which

124 S. R. Llewelyn, and R. A. Kearsley, *New Documents Illustrating Early Christianity. A Review of the Greek Inscriptions and Papyri Published in 1980-81* (Australia: The Ancient History Documentary Research Centre, Macquarie University, 1992), i.

the Greco-Roman imperial strategies have captured the minds of elite aristocratic Jews toward cultural assimilation. In this section, marriage and marital relation between wives and husbands in Hebrew Scriptures, Judaism and the Hellenistic Judaism (literature of Philo and Josephus) are reviewed.

A. The Hebrew Scriptures (The Old Testament)

In Gen. 1: 27-28, God creates male and female in God's image and commands them to "Be fruitful and multiply, and fill the earth and subdue it." Procreation was meant as part of human life right from the beginning of creation in the Hebrew scripture. God found man alone and wanted to create a helper as his partner. Since Adam could not find a suitable partner among the animals, God created a woman from the rib taken from man's body and she became the wife of the first man. It is in Gen. 2:23-24 that the concept of marriage is introduced. V. 24 ("Therefore a man leaves his father and his mother and clings to his wife, and they become one flesh.") indicates the union of the first couple in marriage as a continuation of God's creation of the first woman. However, it does not seem to be the practice of husband moving to wife's house, but rather wife moving to her husband's patrilocal residence.[125]

The Hebrew understanding of marriage is summed up in the two words, "one flesh."[126] The second creation story seems to indicate monogamy and a loving husband-wife relationship. Polygamy was strictly prohibited, especially in the case of kings (Deut. 17:17). If

125 Jennie R. Ebeling, *Women's Lives in Biblical Times* (London & New York: T & T Clark International, 2010), 81.

126 "Genesis 2:24 makes two points in connection with the 'one-flesh-ness' of true marriage. First, in marrying, a man is to leave his father and his mother. Although, the father and mother give a man his very life out of themselves, and although a man's early emotional attachment is to his parents, a married man's primary loyalty is to be directed elsewhere. Secondly, a married man is to cling to his wife. This is the positive complement of leaving his parents. The language suggests a profound union of husband with wife, so that his primary identification in all of life is with her. The outcome is that the man and woman become 'one flesh'." See R. C. Ortlund, Jr., "Marriage," in *New Dictionary of Biblical Theology,* edited by Alexander, T. Desmond and Brian S. Rosner (Downers Grove, Illinois: InterVarsity Press, 2000), CD-Rom.

polygamy was not allowed for privileged kings, then it also might have been prohibited to commoners. Nevertheless, polygamy was rampant in ancient Israel, as evident from the Hebrew Scriptures. Perhaps, this would have led to separation in marriage demanding for laws on divorce and remarriage.[127]

Even though there is no specific age mentioned for marriage in the Hebrew Scriptures, the Hebrew boys and girls got married at a younger age. There are historical evidences for girls getting betrothed at an age of 12 years.[128] Josephus writes about Agrippa I betrothing his two daughters at the age of 10 and 6.[129] As in Gen. 24:1-4 and Judg. 14:1-3, endogamous marriage is encouraged and marriage with foreigners is strictly prohibited.

In Jewish marriages is that the bridegroom has to pay *mohar* (bride price, cf. Gen. 34:12; Exo. 22:16-17; 1 Sam. 18:25) and the bride or the wife brings dowry (*shiluchim*) or property into marriage by way of inheritance or gift from father's house (cf. Gen. 31:15; Hos. 15:18-20; 1 Kings 9:16). Once the bridegroom pays the bride price he was said to have acquired his wife (cf. Ruth 4:5,10) and in certain cases, this transaction was considered as a sale (cf. Gen. 31:15). On the basis of such a deal, the husband was treated as the master of his wife (Gen. 20:3; Deut. 21:13, 22:22, 24:1). She could be possessed as husband's property along with his servants and animals (cf. Exo. 20:17). Bride price could also be paid in the form of service rendered to the bride's family, military service or conquering a city (Gen. 29:16-30; Josh. 15:16; Judg. 1:12; 1 Sam. 18:17-27; Hos. 12:12).

In the prophetic literature, marriage imagery is used to denote the covenant relation between Yahweh and Israel. An analysis of

---

127 The Genesis narrative recounts subsequent abuses: the violence, egotism and polygamy of Lamech (4:19, 23–24); the cowardice of Abram (12:10–20; 20:1–18) and Isaac (26:6–11); the rivalry and heartache of Sarai in relation to Abram and Hagar (16:1–6); the deceiving of Isaac by Rebekah and Jacob (27:5–29); Shechem's rape of Dinah (34:1–31); and Judah's disgraceful relations with his daughter-in-law Tamar (38:13–18).

128 Joachim Jeremias, *Jerusalem in the Time of Jesus* (Philadelphia: Fortress, 1969), 365.

129 *Antiquities* 19.354.

this imagery sheds light on the significance given to marriage in the Hebrew Scriptures. For instance, Ezek. 16:8-14 deals with a holy marriage, in which the bridegroom cleanses his bride by washing with water and makes her beautiful and pure.[130] This marriage imagery is self-explanatory for the virginity or fidelity expected of wives in Hebrew marriages.

Even though the marital practices indicate male authority, there are a few cases of women's role in decision making. For instance, Gen. 24:5, 57-58, there are references for refusal of the proposal by a girl or for the girl to have a say on the decision. Moreover, here in Gen. 24, Rebekah's mother Bethuel is active in her daughter's marriage arrangements (Gen. 24:28, 55). The daughters of Zelophehad (Num. 36: 6) could marry whom they think best provided the bridegroom is from a clan of their father's tribe. In Judg. 1:14-15, Achsah, Caleb's daughter demands for a marriage present from her father. Bathsheba plays a role in asking for a Shunammite wife for Adonijah in 1 Kings 2:13-25, even though the plot ends with the tragic death of Adonijah. There are also references to love marriages as in the cases of Jacob and Rachel (Gen. 29:18-20) and Samson and Delilah (Judg. 16:4). There is an initiative on the part of Michal (Saul's daughter) in her marriage with David (1 Sam. 18:20).

Therefore, in general, there are many different practices as far as different narratives in Hebrew Scriptures are taken into account. It seems to be that the socio-economic status of a woman determined to a large extent, her active role in marriage. Phyllis Bird comments that the daughter of a rich and powerful man could expect a better treatment in her husband's family compared to a poorer man.[131]

Deut. 24:1-4 denotes the Mosaic law on divorce and remarriage. If a man finds anything objectionable-if not virgin at the time of marriage (cf. Deut. 22:13-21)- about his wife, he can divorce her by writing a certificate of divorce. In case, the divorced woman marries

---

130 J. Paul Sampley bases his research on the traditional materials in Eph. 4:21-33 on Ezek. 16:8ff to affirm the Jewishness of Ephesian Haustafel. See *'And the Two shall become One Flesh' A Study of Traditions in Ephesians 5:21-33* (Great Britain: Cambridge University Press, 1971), 34-50.

131 Phyllis Bird, *Missing Persons and Mistaken Identities: Women and Gender in Ancient Israel* (Minneapolis: Fortress Press, 1997), 38.

another and is again divorced, the first husband is not allowed to remarry her, lest he commits abhorrence to the Lord Yahweh (v. 4). There is no mention about the possibility for a woman to initiate divorce. Nonetheless, there are certain restrictions on husbands concerning abusing the provision for divorce in the law. In Deut. 22:13-19, husbands are prohibited to bring false accusations on the virginity of the newly wedded wives and in such cases, divorce is not granted. Another case of protection of women from similar unlawful divorce practice is found in Deut. 22:28-29. Here, if a virgin is violated sexually and they are caught in the act, the man should pay a penalty of fifty shekels of silver to the girl's father and take her as his wife. In such marriages, man is not allowed to divorce her at all.

The first reference to different gender roles for husbands and wives appears in Gen. 3:16-19. As a result of eating the forbidden fruit, both the woman and the man were cursed by God. The notion of husband's authority over wife is first mentioned in Gen. 3:16 in the words, "and he shall rule over you." Women had to endure great pain during childbirth. Her desire would be attached her husband. The curse on the man led to his hard working in the fields, which later on linked to men working outside homes. It is very interesting to note that the Hebrew word used for 'wife' is same as the word for woman (isha) and a wife addresses her husband as 'Lord' (ba 'al). This might indicate a subordinate role of wife in relation to husband in his household. Bird comments that in such a context, a married woman might continue her loyalty to her father's home and kinsmen.[132]

It was the Hebrew custom that first-born son would succeed the head of the family. The eldest son would arrange all marriages for the family members. He could usually divorce his wife (Deut. 24:1; cf. 22:19, 29). "In the patriarchal period the head of the household had a theoretical power of life and death over family members, though he might choose not to exercise it and even to

132 Bird, *Missing Persons and Mistaken Identities,* 39.

defer to them"[133] Lot and Jephtah in the Hebrew scriptures narrate the absolute power exercised by fathers to decide the destiny of their daughters (Gen. 19:1-8; Judg. 11:29-40).

The Decalogue (Exo. 20:17; Deut. 5:21) treats wife as the property of husbands. If a betrothed woman is violated sexually, it is treated as violating his neighbour's wife. This clearly indicates the impersonal approach toward women in general. Barrenness of women was normally considered as a curse and having children as a blessing from God. Motherhood was esteemed highly and therefore the barren women were looked down upon in the society. Sons were given preference over daughters (Gen. 29:32; 30:24).

As far as the Mosaic Laws on man-woman equality are concerned, there are ambiguities in the Hebrew Scriptures. Some laws exercise equality in their approach to men and women. For instance, in Exod. 20:12, both father and mother are to be honored (cf. Lev. 20: 9; Deut. 5:16, 27:16). In Exod. 21:28–32, both men and women are protected against the violence of ox. In the laws regarding violation of rules and consequent punishments, both men and women are addressed (see Lev. 13:29, 38, 15–16; Num. 5:6, 6:2; Deut. 17:2–5, 29:18), However, in the laws of purification of woman giving birth, there are disparities in determining purification as evident in Lev. 12:1–5. If a woman gives birth to a baby boy, she will be ceremonially unclean for seven days and her time of blood purification will be thirty three days. But if she gives birth to a baby girl, she will be ceremonially unclean for two weeks and her time of blood purification will be sixty six days.

The patriarchal culture of Ancient Israel did not attach validity to the vows made by women. The pledges made by young daughters and wives could be invalidated by her father or husband respectively (Num. 30:1–16). But the vows made by widows and divorced women were binding upon them (v. 9). And yet such a patriarchal society expresses concern over property inheritance of daughters in case there are no sons in the family (Num. 27:1–11). Women's

133 J. W. Drane, "Family," in *New Dictionary of Biblical Theology,* edited by Alexander, T. Desmond and Brian S. Rosner (Downers Grove, Illinois: InterVarsity Press, 2000), CD-Rom.

issues were given special attention (Exo. 22:16; Deut. 21:10–14). A married woman is entitled to receive food, clothing and sexual gratification (cf. Exo. 21:10).

It was father's responsibility to protect the virginity of his unmarried daughters. If a betrothed woman is raped, it was considered as a violation of the honor and power of her father. Like Exo. 22:16-17 suggests, the rapist had to pay penalty to the girl's father. It was absolutely within the prerogative of the father whether to give the rape victim in marriage to the same man or not. Further women's interests are taken into account in exempting a newly married man from military duty to remain happy with his wife (Deut. 24:5). There are special provisions for safeguarding the rights of the firstborn of the disliked wife (Deut. 21:15–17). In case of death of the husband, the Levirate system legally sanctioned the widows to remain with the deceased husband's family. Her husband's brother was expected to marry her and give her a son to continue the name of her past husband among the Israel. In case, he did not prefer to marry the widow of his brother, he was humiliated publicly by the elders of the community (Deut. 25:5-10).

Drawing attention to the Wisdom literature, one would certainly identify powerful imageries of blissful marriage. Prov. 5:15-20 deals especially with the pressing need to maintain marital fidelity by expressing marital love and family unity. The husbands are exhorted to be satisfied with their own wives, lest his own life is liable to be used by other men or that his wife may become promiscuous.[134] Prov. 6:20-35 explains the distinction between a man approaching an unmarried woman, who is a prostitute and a married woman, who commits adultery. Here penalty is severely inflicted upon the male offender since prostitutes involve in sexual acts for their survival. However, the adulterous women were considered as an evil to be avoided.[135]

In Prov. 31:10-31, a prudent wife is praised as a trustful partner; she does good to her husband; hard working, enterprising,

134 Abraham Pezhumkattil, "Husband-Wife Relationship in the Wisdom Literature," *Bible Bhashyam,* XX/2 (June, 1994): 79.

135 Pezhumkattil, *Husband-Wife Relationship,* 82.

a successful merchandiser, mindful of the needs of her family; she brings honor to her family and her husband and children admire and praise her. Similarly, the book of *Song of Songs is totally dedicated to glorify the married love and the love relationship between husband and wife.*

Such a powerful feminine imagery points to the socio-cultural shift that was taking place in the Jewish community during the post-exilic period. It was a positive shift from a centralized bureaucracy of kingship to a family oriented community.[136]

All Jewish men, women, children and resident aliens were included in the assembly of 'all Israel' gathered in front of Moses to hear the law (Deut. 29:1-10,17-18; 21:1,12). It was further noted that all the family members including husbands and wives were gathered in the assemblies of Joshua, Nehemiah and Ezra (Josh. 8:35; Neh. 8:2f, 10:28f; cf. 1 Esdras 9:40f.). In the Midrash, the wives mentioned in Deut. 29 were there just to hear, even if they did not understand. In the same manner, Deut. 31:12 mentions that men were convoked to learn or teach, but women just to hear.[137] Both husbands and wives were excluded from the temple under circumstances of physical impurity in Mosaic Law (Lev. 15:31; Num. 5:3), however, the restriction were heavier upon women due to menstruation and childbirth (Lev. 15:19-24; Lev. 12 respectively). There are some references for women ministering in the assembly of Israel (Exo. 38:8, cf. 1 Sam. 2:22).

B. Judaism

Marriage was regarded as a divine ordinance since the Jews believed that the world was created with God's intention of procreation (Gen.1:26; cf. Isa. 45:18 and Gen. 2:18).[138] Marriage was preferred

---

136 Anthony R. Ceresko, *The Old Testament: A Liberation Perspective* (Bombay: St. Paul's, 1993), 381.

137 William Horbury, "Women in the Synagogue," in *The Cambridge History of Judaism Vol. 3. The Early Roman Period*, edited by William Horbury, W. D. Davies and John Sturdy, reprint (Great Britain: Cambridge University Press, 2001), 377-8.

138 George Foot Moore, *Judaism. In the First Centuries of the Christian Era: The Age of the Tannaim, volume II,* 6th reprint (Cambridge: Harvard University Press,

over remaining single and having children was valued highly among the Jewish women. Jewish Papyri documents indicate that Jewish marriages had signed a written prenuptial contract (*Ketubbah/ Kethubah),* though it was not widely practiced.[139] Jewish women entered married relationship fairly at an early age, possibly between twelve and eighteen. As far as the eligible age of men are concerned, there was no fixed age, but usually at the age of sixteen or seventeen, but certainly before twenty provided that they should be able to support their spouses.[140] This required a Jewish young man to finish his studies before he got married, however, there are evidences of men marrying during their studies as well.[141]

The woman became legally the man's wife by the act of betrothal. The Hebrew term, *Kiddushin,* indicates religious significance of betrothal as an act of consecrating the woman for the husband, in other words, setting apart for him exclusively.[142] Categorically, it was the father who gave his daughter in betrothal (Gen. 34:12; Exo. 22: 16-17; 1 Sam. 18:25). While *Kethubah* was addressed as a unilateral proposal by the groom to his bride, betrothal was more of an agreement between them.[143]

Since the first marriages of women were normally to older men, the cases of them becoming widows at younger age were common in Jewish society. There were also tendencies of women dying early from childbirth. In case of widowhood, they were expected to remarry. "First marriages were regularly a matter of family arrangements, often negotiated between the couple's fathers or between the bride's father and her future husband. Subsequent marriage arrangements might often involve more active participation by the woman, particularly

1950), 119.

139 Ross S. Kraemer, "Jewish Women and Women's Judaism(s) at the Beginning of Christianity,' in *Women and Christian Origins,* edited by Ross Shepard Kraemer and Mary Rose D'Angelo (Oxford: Oxford University Press, 1999), 57.

140 Alfred Edersheim, *Sketches of Jewish Social Life,* 3rd Print (U.S.A: Hendrickson Publishers, 1996), 136.

141 Moore, *Judaism,* 120. See note 1.

142 Moore, *Judaism,* 122.

143 Llewelyn and Kearsly, *New Documents Illustrating Early Christianity,* 12.

when her father was no longer alive."[144] As far as the Jewish slave women are concerned, they "could not contract licit marriage with either one another or free persons... Enslaved Jewish women owned by non-Jews would almost certainly have routinely found themselves required to provide sexual services for their owners and, doubtless, sometimes would have borne children to those owners."[145]

Certain Papyri documents indicate the change from paying bride price to the bride's father to an obligation to pledge an assured payment of an agreed sum (also called kethubah) on divorce or death. This could be a cultural adaptation from the Egyptian marriages to Judaism of Diaspora.[146] There were Greek influences on Jewish practices, especially as found in the earlier Jewish practice of keeping account of the property of both husband and wife separately. Later it was changed that the property of wife was recorded either in the kethubah or as an additional document and included in the husband's property. While on divorce, this property or equivalent amount was returned to her.[147]

Chastity and fidelity were treated as high morals among the Jewish women.[148] Especially at the first marriage women were strictly expected to be virgins and the fathers were expected to guard their daughters' virginity.[149]

Polygamy and divorce were quite rampantly practiced in the first century, though predominantly among the learned and wealthy.[150] "The great mass of the people, indeed, lived in circumstances which precluded polygamy. The rabbinical institution of the marriage contract and settlement operated not only as a check upon the

---

144 Kraemer, *Jewish Women and Women's Judaism(s),* 58.

145 Kraemer, *Jewish Women and Women's Judaism(s),* 57.

146 Llewelyn and Kearsly, *New Documents Illustrating Early Christianity,* 13.

147 Llewelyn and Kearsly, *New Documents Illustrating Early Christianity,* 13.

148 C. C. Kroeger, "Women in Greco-Roman World and Judaism," in *Dictionary of New Testament Background,* edited by Craig A. Evans and Stanley E. Porter (Illinois: InterVarsity Press, 2000), 1277.

149 Kraemer, *Jewish Women and Women's Judaism(s),* 59.

150 Raphael Loewe, *The Position of Women in Judaism* (London: S.P.C.K, 1966), 22.

freedom of divorce but upon plural marriages."[151] A legitimate divorce could be sought by the husband giving his wife a document (*get*) which could terminate the prenuptial agreement, the *Ketubbah*. Only after getting formal divorce can the wife enter into another licit marriage. However, Jewish men could take another wife without divorcing the existing marriage because of the privileges guaranteed by the practice of polygamy.[152]

The causes for the justification of divorce were a matter of lively rabbinic debate. "The school of Shammai insisted that it was possible only in cases of adultery, while the school of Hillel maintained that there might be a myriad of reasons, such as spinning in the street, talking with a stranger, a spoiled dinner, a dog bite that did not heal or finding another woman who was more attractive."[153] Jewish law did not sanction a woman divorcing her husband, but she could take legal action for divorce in the courts. That would require him to give her a bill of divorce. But she could do that only on the basis of certain causes: "impotence, denial of conjugal rights, unreasonable restriction of her freedom of movement, such as keeping her from going to funerals or wedding parties, loathsome ailments, or nasty occupations such as tanning."[154] This was a later development in the post-biblical or inter-testamental era.

The Jewish father was responsible for educating sons of Law and Commandments. His duties toward sons are manifold: he must circumcise, redeem (the first born son), teach him a trade and get him a wife.[155] The daughters were not given much opportunity for accessing education. Generally, they were trained in household arts. Law was taught to them especially the purity laws pertaining to women.[156] Yet, rarely the young girls were taught by their fathers or husbands to read Hebrew so that they could read the Scriptures.[157]

---

151 Moore, *Judaism,* 122.

152 Kraemer, *Jewish Women and Women's Judaism(s),* 59.

153 Kroeger, "Various, *Dictionary of New Testament Background* (Downers Grove, IL: InterVarsity Press) 2000. See also Moore, Judaism, 123-4.

154 Moore, *Judaism,* 125.

155 Moore, *Judaism,* 127.

156 Kroeger, *Women in Greco-Roman World and Judaism,* 1275.

157 Moore, *Judaism,* 128.

They were mostly bound to household and farm responsibilities. The unmarried women were not allowed to enter any other area except the women's quarters in a household and the married women can proceed to the front door or even go out freely.[158]

Jewish law demanded mutual obligations between husband and wife. Certain papyri documents on *Kethubah* show that the wife was legally expected to honor and serve her husband and could not avoid her duties by making any vow. The husband was expected to take care of her physical needs and to honor her.[159] To elaborate this further, in the domestic arena, a Jewish woman was involved in cooking and house-keeping apart from spinning, weaving and sewing garments for the family. Her main work outside house was fetching water from the village well, collecting firewood, working in the farms, selling produces in the markets, taking care of the animals etc. Some women worked as midwives or nurses.[160]

Even though early Palestinian Judaism did not restrict women's movement the way classical Greek culture did, the wife's standard duties were largely domestic like grinding wheat, cooking, washing, nursing and sewing (cf. *m. Ketub.* 5:5.).[161] But if the women had brought female slaves with her to the husband's house, then she would find some relief from the entire heavy load of work, nevertheless, complete idleness was perceived to be perilous to her moral dignity.[162] Wives were expected to love their husbands and to remain chaste. In the first century Jewish women of Roman empire expressed willingness to die with one's husband, which was considered as an ideal virtue.[163]

The early Rabbinic Judaism also provided women some rights not common in broader Mediterranean culture. For instance, the legal rights of the Jewish women-to sue at courts without the assistance of a guardian, to file a sue initiating divorce, to own and manage property independently of their husbands (but not free to

158 Kroeger, *Women in Greco-Roman World and Judaism,* 1276.

159 Llewelyn and Kearsly, *New Documents Illustrating Early Christianity,* 14.

160 Kroeger, *Women in Greco-Roman World and Judaism,* 1278.

161 Keener, Marriage CD-ROM.

162 Moore, *Judaism,* 127.

163 Keener, Marriage, CD-ROM.

dispose property), to recover a portion of their dowry after divorce or death of husband- were unknown to traditional Greek and Roman women.[164]

The husband was bound by the marriage contract to support his wife by providing food and clothing. Classical Athenian law urged husbands to provide intercourse with their wives three times a month especially to fulfill the duties of procreation. If a husband abstained from intercourse with his wife for more than one or two weeks, the Pharisees felt that he was obligated to grant her a divorce. Husbands should also love their wives, which involves more than merely sexual union.[165] Women acquired property in accordance with a statutory sum of amount assured by the bridegroom at the time of marriage. In this way, the Jewish law in general required husbands to provide their wives with expected comforts. Yet, to dispose the property she needed the acquiescence of the husband.[166]

The wife's role in Judaism was mainly to keep laws intact in a household. They had to recite the prayers (Tefillah, the Eighteen Prayers) and the table blessings, and to maintain the Mezuzah on the doors of houses. Further, certain responsibilities such as the separation of the Hallah - apportioning dough from every baking for the priest - and the lighting of the Sabbath lamp with the proper benediction were assigned to wives. Whereas the husbands were bound to the religious obligations like the recitation of the Shema, and the wearing of Phylacteries on the head and left arm (Tefillin).[167] This highlights the religious confinement of Jewish women in the domestic realm.

---

164 David C. Verner, *The Household of God. The Social World of the Pastoral Epistles* (Chico, California: Scholars Press, 1983), 45.

165 C. S. Keener, "Marriage" in *Dictionary of New Testament Background,* (Downers Grove, IL: InterVarsity Press), 2000.

166 Raphael Loewe, *The Position of Women in Judaism* (London: S. P. C. K., 1966), 34.

167 Moore, *Judaism,* 129-130.

C. Hellenistic Judaism

From as early as 4th century B.C.E.[168] is concerned, hellenization - in the form of accepting Greek language, education, culture, philosophy, religion and life style – was assimilated by Jews in Diaspora in view of improving their social status and acquiring the prosperity of Greeks. Their attempts to conform initially to the Greek and later on to the Roman patronized Hellenistic civilization, in a way, enabled them to claim equality guaranteed by the Greek and Roman imperial civic rights.[169] Significantly, Jews of Diaspora assimilated many customs regarding household management from the Greco-Roman society.

Verner highlights some of the differing customs of Jews of Diaspora: the Egyptian Jews had not practiced levirate marriage by he time of Philo, which is evident from the absence of the same in Philo's *Special Laws*; Alexandrian Jews followed the Greek form of marriage contract; Jewish women filed suits for divorce in Greek courts with the assistance of their guardians; Jewish women inherited property as per Greek laws; and unlike Palestinian Jewish women, they lived in seclusion from the public sphere in households.[170] There were patronesses and women office holders found in the Synagogues of Diasporan Jews, which is clear adaptation of better living standard of their Hellenistic counterparts. This would have been facilitated by the fact that "the inheritance of earlier Judaism survived in a continuing emphasis on women's presence in the assembly."[171]

It becomes quite clear from the aforementioned features that the Jews in hellenistic-Roman Diaspora had acquiesced certain predominant Hellenistic cultural elements. However, they also struggled to retain their particular identity different from the surrounding "pagan" *Sitz im Leben.* So, there was an attempt to

---

168 Jewish slaves from 4th century B.C.E. adapted Greek culture and assimilated into gentile environment. Similarly, upper class Jews had intermarriages with Greeks in order to get into civil services.

169 Martin Hengel, "The Interpenetration of Judaism and Hellenism in the Pre-Maccabean Period," in *The Cambridge History of Judaism, vol. 2. The Hellenistic Age,* edited by W. D. Davies and Louis Finkelstein, reprint (Great Britain: Cambridge University Press, 1989), 186.

170 Verner, *The Household of God,* 46-7.

171 Horbury, *Women in the Synagogue,* 401.

practice a higher ethical living than the surrounding non-Jewish people. As John Collins highlights, the common ethic in Hellenistic Jewish tradition projected to the surrounding elite gentiles, the appealing Jewish laws such as monotheism, prohibition of idolatry, various sexual laws forbidding adultery, homosexuality, rape of virgin, and abortion.[172] So, even upon the sweeping impact of Greco-roman civilization, the Diasporan Jews safeguarded their position in the foreign dominant land by preserving a "theocratic alien element" and a "third nation" between Greeks and Romans.[173] Therefore, in general, the attitude of Diasporan Jews toward Romans was an ambivalent one, both accommodating and abrogating Greco-Roman imperial pressures, thus creating a third space of trans-cultural space.

Philo and Josephus provide information on the hellenization of Jewish marital relationships and especially of the gender roles in marriage influenced by the practices in Greco-Roman society. As far as Philo is concerned, women are with little sense by nature and the opposite of masculine rationality. Philo believes that Moses' law enjoins wives to serve and obey their husbands (*De Hypothetica.* 7.3). The servitude expected from wives should not be imposed by violent ill treatment. However, such subservience would be good for women for women are less rational than men (*Quod Omnis Probus Liber Sit* 18. 117).[174] His use of feminine imagery connotes women's inferiority by nature, which reflects Jewish understanding in a broader pattern of Greco-Roman thought. The difficulties of bearing and rearing children also necessarily subject the wife in obedience to her husband (*De Opificio Mundi* 60.167). Further he is of the opinion that the

172 John Collins, *Between Athens and Jerusalem: Jewish Identity in the Hellenistic Diaspora* (New York: Crossroad, 1983), 142, cited by Carolyn Osiek and David L. Balch, *Families in the New Testament World. Households and House Churches* (Louisville, Kentucky: Westminister John Knox Press, 1997), 104.

173 Martin Hengel, "The Interpenetration of Judaism and Hellenism in the Pre-Maccabean Period," in *The Cambridge History of Judaism, Vol. 2. The Hellenistic Age,* edited by W. D. Davies and Louis Finkelstein, reprint (Great Britain: Cambridge University Press, 1989), 186.

174 Philo, *De Hypothetica. 7.3* and *Quod Omnis Probus Liber Sit 18. 117,* cited by Kraig S. Keener, *Paul, Women & Wives. Marriage and Women's Ministry in the Letters of Paul* (U.S.A: Hendrickson Publishers, 2007), 163.

masculine rules the feminine and wife is equated to slaves when it comes to her service toward husband.[175]

In *De Hypothetica* 7.14, Philo deals with the duties of the head of the family. The husband must teach Law to wives, master to the slaves and father to the children. James E. Crouch attributes the presence of these pairs in Philo's writings as a direct literary influence of Hellenistic Judaism to New Testament household codes. He identifies that neither Hebrew Scriptures nor Rabbinic Judaism have similar duty schemes.[176] Philo's advice to parents in *Spec. Leg.* ii. 228 to inculcate good virtues is clearly in line with Hellenistic terms.

Josephus affirms the presence of women, children and slaves in the assembly of Israel (*Antiquities* iv. 209; 309). Nevertheless, he also views women as inferior in moral character to men (*Antiquities of the Jews* 4.8.15 & 219). Because women are inferior in all things, the law prescribes the husband's authority and wife's submission for the wife's own good (Josephus *Against Apion* 2.25, 200–201). Here the God given authority to husbands is not for wives' humiliation, but for deriving direction in their lives. Josephus believed that God punished both Adam and Herod Antipas for being so weak as to have heeded their wives (*Antiquities of the Jews* 1.1.4 , 49; 18.7.2, 255).[177]

As it was noted earlier, the Hebrew Scriptures provide evidences for women ministering in the assembly of Israel, for instance, there is a reference in Exo. 38: 8 (cf. 1 Sam. 2:22) that "the ministering women who ministered at the door of the tent of meeting." Interestingly, the word used for ministry in this verse was replaced by 'fasting' in Septuagint and 'praying' in Targums and Peshitta overshadowing the

175 Philo, *De Opificio Mundi 60. 167,* cited by Keener, *Paul, Women & Wives,* 164-65.

176 Crouch, *Colossian Haustafel,* 106.

177 Josephus may have felt personal existential reasons for his opinions; although he later found a wealthy Jewish woman he believed to be of nobler character than most other women (Josephus *Life* 76 §427), he divorced another wife, displeased with her behavior (Josephus *Life* 76 §426). Yet he was hardly alone in his opinions; negative views of women predominate in Sirach (e.g., Sir 42:13) and probably the *Testament of Job*, though positive pictures appear in Tobit (Sara; Edna; Anna) and Pseudo-Phil. Samaritan marriage contracts require full obedience from the wife.

official priestly function.[178] Such contrast between original Hebrew text and interpretation in the Hellenistic period seem to indicate that Jewish women's religious involvement was probably restricted in the Greco-Roman period.[179] However, the recent scholarship affirms women's leadership in ancient synagogues as "synagogue heads" and "mothers of the synagogue."[180] The Jewish women in Diaspora were active in synagogues. However, in the later synagogues, they were not counted to form a quorum for public worship in the synagogues, for which ten adult males were needed. In certain cases, they were allowed to be part of the seven to read the Sabbath lessons.[181]

Categorically, the misogynic opinions of Philo and Josephus indicate that the Hellenistic Jews responded to the moral freedom of the Hellenistic culture by tightening the restrictions on women. Their opinions are very different from the more egalitarian contemporary Stoic Philosophers like Plutarch and Musonius. Since women were viewed inferior, they were forced to remain submissive to their husbands. Crouch proposes that the Hellenistic Jewish version of Mosaic Law insisted on the inferiority of woman and her submission to her husband, which had later on influenced the Christian household codes.[182] But he fails to note that this kind of modification was a necessary evil for Jewish men in Diapora due to the heavy pressure from the Greco-Roman imperial environment of Stoic and popular philosophy.

II. Wife-Husband Relationship in Greco-Roman Cultures/ Religions

In any study undertaken in the New Testament, it is indispensable that the socio-cultural and political influences of Greco-Roman society upon Judaism and Christianity are taken seriously into account. Especially, the Greek and Roman empires of the first century B.C.E. through the second and third centuries CE have

178 Horbury, *Women in the Synagogue,* 379.

179 Horbury, *Women in the Synagogue,* 381.

180 Yamaguchi, *Mary & Martha,* 45.

181 Moore, *Judaism,* 131.

182 Crouch, *Colossian Haustafel,* 111.

tremendously influenced the socio-religious developments of both Judaism and Christianity. There is some continuity in the cultural elements prevalent in Roman society from the Hellenistic ethos, which makes the history of Greco-Roman society a unified phenomenon. The Greco-Roman world of the last century B.C.E. and the first century CE was comprised of people of diverse cultures, religions and demographic composition that it is difficult to limit the study to a handful of elite spokespersons, who wrote down the history. Very often, early Greek literature has been adapted in the Roman society in such a way that "certain attitudes about women that governed their actual lives, as well as helped to shape their images, preserved throughout classical antiquity."[183] Yet the Greco-Roman society witnessed upward mobility of women in the course of socio-political changes of different empires. It would be appropriate to analyse the progression of changes in the socio-cultural realms of both Greek and Roman societies especially in relation with marriage and marital gender norms.

The Greek woman was married when she was very young. There are historical evidences of Athenian citizen women marrying at an age of fifteen or sixteen.[184] Due to high maternal death rate and the practice of exposing daughters, there was shortage of marriageable women in Hellenistic culture. The sexual exploitation of Greek women is evident from their classification in early Greek literature: "courtesans for companionship, concubines for the daily pleasure of the master of the house and wives to bear legitimate children and keep the house."[185]

Marriages were legally valid only if it took place between citizens and the daughters of citizens. The betrothal was basically an agreement between the bridegroom and the bride's father. The father pledges his daughter by specifying the dowry and the bridegroom

183 Judith P. Hallett, 'Women's Lives in the Ancient Mediterranean," in *Women and Christian Origins,* edited by Ross Shepard Kraemer and Mary Rose D'Angelo (New York/Oxford: Oxford University Press, 1999), 20.

184 Ben Witherington III, *Women in the Earliest Churches,* Society for New Testament Studies Monograph Series (Cambridge: Cambridge University Press, 1988), 6.

185 Kroeger, *Women in Greco-Roman World and Judaism,* 1278.

accepts it. "The prospective bride was not a party to the contract at all, but only its object."[186] Marriage marked her transfer from the lordship of her father to that of her husband. Legally, Greek culture allowed monogamy, nevertheless, married men owned concubines and many wives. The dinner parties (which men indulged), where legitimate wives could not appear, were characterized by the presence of courtesans. They were generally slave girls who were exposed as infants and reared for helping as sexual partners.[187] But only the children of legal marriages were treated as citizen children.[188]

Since every household was a religious unit as well, marriage demanded the bride to accept the religion of her husband's household. The marriage ritual consisted of introducing the bride to the gods of her new household and submitting to the protection of them.[189]

In Sparta, a prominent city-State in Greece, marriages were solely meant to procure a first rate breed of men. Such conceptualization of marriage further stratified women on the basis of their potential to give birth to good breed of male progeny. This is evident from James Donaldson's words,

> The Spartans felt it necessary to educate and train women to be strong, brave, and resolute so that their sons would have a similar character, ideal for military service. From the earliest times, Spartan women were involved in gymnastics, wrestling, festivals, rudimentary educational schemes, offering sacrifices, and, in general, they mingled freely and competed openly with men. This prepared not only to be good mothers, but also afforded the men an opportunity to choose a proper mate. The darker side of this selection process was that the weaker women would be detected in various contests and prevented from marrying for fear of weak children.[190]

---

186 Verner, *The household of God,* 31.

187 Kroeger, *Women in Greco-Roman World and Judaism,* 1278.

188 Verner, *The Household of God,* 32.

189 Verner, *The Household of God,* 28.

190 James Donaldson, *Woman: Her Position and Influence in Ancient Greece and Rome, and among Early Christians* (London: Longmans, Green and Co., 1907),

Here the Spartan men enjoyed a better social status on account of their maleness. On the contrary, in addition to their inferior status, women had to bear the extra burden to prove their sexual potential to give birth to male children.

A Greek man was allowed to divorce his wife on the basis of her infertility.[191] A woman could also initiate divorce in Greek culture, even though it was easier for men. A husband could decide to divorce his wife by sending her away from his household. But for a woman to divorce her husband, she had to persuade her husband or another male citizen to register her divorce with a magistrate.[192]

Plato and Aristotle had greatly influenced philosophically the social life of Greece. The male by nature is treated superior to women. Men are rulers and females are subjects to their rule.[193] For a man to be treated as brave in real sense, he should be brave beyond the bravery of women and women to be treated as modest, should live out modesty beyond the limits set for modesty of men. The household duties of husbands and wives were different: "his business is to get and hers to keep."[194]

The Greek household codes imposed severe restrictions on the activities and freedom of women. Their responsibility was mainly restricted to stay at home and supervise the household. If a woman did not have servants to do outdoor chores, she suffered social stigma. If a woman willfully and unnecessarily went out in public, then she was at the risk of her reputation as a faithful wife.[195]

The male head of the house, as master, husband and father, exercised tremendous power over slaves, wives and children. In general, the Greek women are treated as of less virtue than men and devoid of moral conscience. "Since women could not be trusted to make responsible choices, they might be compelled to remain within their own homes."[196] In Athens, married women lived in separate

26, cited by Ben Witherington, *Women in the Earliest Churches*, 9.

191 Verner, *The Household of God,* 29.

192 Verner, *The Household of God,* 32.

193 Aristotle, *Politics,* 1.2.12.

194 Aristotle, *Politics,* 3.2.10.

195 Verner, *The Household of God,* 31.

196 Kroeger, *Women in Greco-Roman World and Judaism,* 1276.

and guarded chambers.[197] They were forced to live under restrictive customs in their households, to the extent that "women neither slept nor ate nor discoursed with the men."[198] Conversation with males outside the family was completely forbidden. It is interesting to note that the husbands and wives also shared minimal verbal exchange.[199] In short, the dichotomy between domestic and public realms meant strict containment of Greek women's lives.[200]

In rearing children, the father was fully in charge in decision-making. In the antiquity, the father made the decision whether to rear a child or expose. Very often, daughters were exposed than the sons. The sons were moved to men's quarters at the age of seven and were trained in "philosophy, literature, science, politics and sports."[201] There were special slaves to take care of them. The girls were secluded in the women's quarters. They lived under the lordship of their fathers until their marriage. However, the girls were taught to read and write, "the remainder of their education having consisted in learning the traditional domestic skills such as spinning and weaving."[202]

Women were not treated as the full citizens of Greece and therefore, they could not inherit nor own property.[203] "Provision was made for married women, however, through their dowries. While the husband possessed the right to use the principal, he was obligated to support his wife from the income, for which a standard percentage was set by law. In addition the dowry was to be used for her support in the event of her divorce or the death of her husband."[204]

In the traditional Greek religion, women were denied of legitimate participation in blood sacrifices, consulting oracles, temple entrances and offering prayers. Women worshiped different

197 Witherington, *Women in the Earliest Churches,* 6.

198 Kroeger, *Women in Greco-Roman World and Judaism,* 1277.

199 Verner, *The Household of God,* 28.

200 Deborah F. Sawyer, *Women and Religion in the First Christian Centuries* (London and New York: Routledge, 1996), 15.

201 Kroeger, *Women in Greco-Roman World and Judaism,* 1277.

202 Verner, *The Household of God,* 31.

203 Verner, *The Household of God,* 29.

204 Verner, *The Household of God,* 32.

gods from men mostly on different days with different modes of worship in different temples.[205] There were women priestesses usually in the cults of goddesses and not gods. It is difficult to say whether such practices reveal women's autonomy and equality with men or their separation from men.[206] It may be true that the rituals and festivals of female deities provided women opportunities to have self-governance and solidarity among themselves, however, it would not have challenged the Greek patriarchal society in any way.

To elaborate this, a faith aspect can be highlighted: The triad of Greek female deities – Kore, Demeter, and Hecate – guarded the transition of free women from the stage of a daughter through motherhood and widowhood. Though their festivals were claimed to have intensified the mother-daughter bond beyond the separation by patriarchal marriages, they served only to conform to Greek male religious dominance.[207] Despite the limitations, the devotees to Dionysus – the Greek male deity from 5th century B.C.E. - felt spiritual and certain amount of social emancipation in their daily lives. It was mainly due to the elimination of socio-cultural binaries like male-female, young-old, and life-death among the devotees to Dionysus, which brought about social egalitarianism.[208]

III. Wife-Husband Relationship in Roman Empire

Roman empire considered the ideal marriage as "sacred conjugal union," which glorified "the union of male and female, a partnership (*consortium*) in all of life, the conjunction of human and divine law."[209] Various Roman popular literature, epitaphs, imperial propaganda and Stoic philosophy on marriage highlight that such ideal harmonious marriages were esteemed highly in public imperial ideology.[210]

---

205 C. C. Kroeger, *Women in Greco-Roman World and Judaism,* CD-ROM.

206 Witherington, *Women in the Earliest Churches,* 16.

207 Satoko Yamaguchi, *Mary and Martha. Women in the World of Jesus* (Maryknoll, New York: Orbis Books, 2002), 36.

208 Yamaguchi, *Mary and Martha,* 37.

209 Helen Rhee, *Early Christian Literature. Christ and Culture in the Second and Third Centuries* (London & New York: Routledge, 2005), 112.

210 Rhee, *Early Christian Literature,* 112.

Roman law attested as legal marriages only those, which are contracted by Roman citizens. This was similar to Greek practices. Although marriage involved legal implications, it was primarily a private act between free persons since the slaves could not contract legal marriage till the third century CE.[211] Marriage brought the bride under the authority of her husband. His power over her sanctioned him even to take away her life. The husband owned her body and her property.[212] Roman marriage did not demand a formal contract or ceremony, nevertheless, ceremonies of betrothal and marriage were often held.[213] As it was common in the ancient cultures to link marriage with procreation, Roman empire also regarded procreation as a civic duty and all Roman citizens were expected to fulfill this State responsibility.

In ancient Rome, the power relations between daughter-father/wife-husband are paramount in the procedures involved in marriage ceremonies. The father transferred the ownership of his daughter into the hands of the husband by a ceremony of 'selling' in the *coemptio* form of marriage.[214] Such ancient forms of Roman marriages demanded absolute submission of wives. The social unrest caused by such unequal partnership caused a drastic change in the marriage system of ancient Rome. By the time of 3rd century CE, "free marriage" was introduced with provisions for women to remain attached to her former family, to retain her property and to possess the freedom to divorce her husband.[215] In such marriages, *materfamilias* also exercised authority in the household since she was legally not under the authority of her husband, though by tradition remained subject to him.[216] During this period, the daughters

211 David G. Hunter, tr. & ed., *Marriage in the Early Church* (Minneapolis: Fortress Press, 1992), 6.

212 Verner, *The Household of God,* 32-33.

213 Hunter, *Marriage in the Early Church,* 6.

214 Witherington, *Women in the Earliest Churches,* 17.

215 Sawyer, *Women and Religion,* 19.

216 Carolyn Osiek, R. S. C. J., "The Family in Early Christianity: 'Family Values' Revisited," *CBQ* 58/1 (January, 2006): 10.

remained primarily under the control of their fathers, but a guardian or tutor was appointed after they reached the age 25.[217]

In the first century BCE, Rome witnessed a major change in its political system from republic to monarchy, which eventually led to a Roman coalition with Stoic philosophy for a conservative moral ethos of marriage, family and social order.[218] By the first century CE, due to the widespread influence of Stoic philosophy, Roman citizens were supposed to behave as good husbands giving due respect to their wives and marriage took different turn as friendship emphasizing the importance of harmony for an ideal, philosophical relationship. Musonius Rufus, a Stoic philosopher in the first century CE, writes on husband-wife relationship:

> They should regard all things as common between them, and nothing peculiar or private to one or the other, not even their bodies.... But in marriage there must be above all perfect companionship (*symbiosis*) and mutual affection (*kedemonia*) of husband and wife, both in health and sickness and under all conditions, since it was with desire for this as well as for having children that both entered upon marriage...Sexual intercourse is justified only when it occurs in marriage and is indulged in for the purpose of begetting children, since that is lawful, but unjust and unlawful when it is mere pleasure-seeking, even in marriage.[219]

However, the rhetorical sexual equality taught by Musonius remained inconsistent with the social practices. Another Stoic philosopher, Antipater believed in the Aristotelian phrase, "another like oneself", when he referred to a man's wife. Despite his willingness to accept wife as "similar" to her husband, he attributed her social position as subordinate to that of husband.[220] Hierocles was also inconsistent when he elaborated his Stoic philosophy. Though he

217 Witherington, *Women in the Earliest Churches,* 17.

218 Rhee, *Early Christian Literature,* 109.

219 Musonius cited by Hunter, *Marriage in the Early Church,* 8.

220 David L. Balch, "1 Cor 7:32-35 and Stoic Debates about Marriage, Anxiety, and Distraction," *JBL* 102/3 (1983): 437.

allocates rural, forensic and political duties to husbands and spinning wool, cooking and domestic duties to wives in general, he himself feels that such "division of roles is not fit, beautiful or pleasing."[221] Therefore, it could be evaluated that Stoic teachings provided pointers to gender egalitarianism, however they could not surmount the impact left by the hierarchical family living advocated by ancient philosophers like Plato and Aristotle in Greco-roman society.

Roman empire implemented the Augustan legislation on marriage known as the *Lex Iulia de Martandis Ordinibus* in 18 BCE and its revised document, the *Lex Papia Poppaea* in 9 CE. These legislations insisted on marriage as mandatory that all men of 25 to 60 years and women of 20 to 50 years must get married and produce legitimate children.[222] Only exception was made for the Vestal virgins and women over fifty.[223] Augustus prohibited marriages between senatorial class and persons of freed status to inculcate social and moral responsibilities in upper classes. Roman emperors valued marriage and family as indispensable for the continuation and welfare of empire.[224]

Suzanne Dixon's research on Roman family attests to the same that in upper class marriages, the spouses enjoyed friendship, mutual respect and affection and shared responsibilities in the maintenance of the household and the propagation of the family.[225] Even though the upper class women could initiate marriages, they were prohibited from reusing a marriage unless they proved the immorality of their fiancées. But it was a rare case as the girls of marriageable age were too young to decide upon this.[226]

Marriage in Roman culture was predominantly monogamous, however seeking extra-marital relationship was very common among

221 Balch, *1 Cor 7:32-35 and Stoic Debates...*, 438.

222 Rhee, *Early Christian Literature*, 109.

223 Witherington, *Women in the Earliest Churches*, 17.

224 Rhee, *Early Christian Literature*, 110.

225 Suzanne Dixon, "Sex and the Married Woman in Ancient Rome," in *Early Christian Families in Context. An Interdisciplinary Dialogue*, edited by David l. Balch and Carolyn Osiek (Grand Rapids, Michigan/Cambridge, U.K.: William B. Eerdmans Publishing Company, 2003), 128.

226 Witherington, *Women in the Earliest Churches*, 17.

the elite Roman men. Therefore, the Roman sexual affairs could be termed as polygynous, having many female sexual partners. Most of their partners were either slaves or freed women, but of lower social status.[227] Since marriage was permissible only between freed men and women, Roman slaves preferred to remain in such sexual relationships, which guaranteed them financial and emotional protection.[228]

In ancient Rome, husbands were authorized by the Roman law to divorce his wife, but not the wives. He was required to return only the dowry to her upon the divorce, but her property was retained by the husband.[229] Divorce was rampant among the upper classes, where alliances were intertwined with political and economical considerations. Both husbands and wives could dissolve their marriage unilaterally or by mutual consent. If they remained separated with the intention of divorce, it was not even necessary to notify the former spouse.[230] The emperor Augustus, along with his legislation on marriage, executed stricter procedures for initiating divorce. According to that procedure, a notification of divorce should be issued in the presence of seven witnesses.[231]

Along with formalizing divorce by requiring a formal letter and witnesses, Augustus banned extramarital relations and adultery. He declared them as public crimes liable to *accusatio publica.*[232] This was due to the influence made by Stoic philosophers like Musonius on the State ethic of the Roman empire. Musonius had severely condemned all extramarital sex including adultery, homosexuality and relations with slaves. He insisted on sexual chastity of both men and women and believed that indulgences in extramarital relations were signs of lack of self-control.[233] Augustus reinstated in *Lex Iulia de martandis Ordinibus* of 18 BCE (the marriage Legislation), the necessity of divorced women and widows within the age group between 20 and

227 Hallett, *Women's Lives in the Ancient Mediterranean,* 32.

228 Hallett, *Women's Lives in the Ancient Mediterranean,* 32.

229 Verner, *The Household of God,* 33.

230 Hunter, *Marriage in the Early Church,* 7.

231 Hunter, *Marriage in the Early Church,* 7.

232 Rhee, *Early Christian Literature,* 110.

233 Rhee, *Early Christian Literature,* 111.

50 years to remarry within 6 moths and a year respectively. When it was revised in 9 CE as *Lex Papia Poppaea,* the period of remarriage was extended to 18 months and 2 years respectively.[234]

The wealthy upper class women had considerable amount of financial leverage freedom in their marriages, especially because of their rights to divorce and to take back much of her dowry, together with her independent right of ownership.[235] Predominantly, financial and political incompatibilities led to divorces that life-long marriage became an exception rather than a rule among the aristocracy.[236]

The traditional Roman household (*familia*) was headed by *pater familias*, who exercised "almost unlimited power over wife, children, and slaves."[237] As an officially recognized domestic institution, *pater familias* was treated as a basic social unit at every level of Roman society, so much so that any change of headship for a family required a legal decree.[238] The *pater familias* had unlimited power of life and death over his children, subject only to religious and moral restraints, and, in later times, it was brought under the review of the censor.[239]

It is interesting to note that being part of Roman elite ensured high social status for both men and women in the society. In the first century CE, elite Roman women were well educated. Some of them were highly influential and enjoyed great social freedom.[240] "The men of their blood families-most notably their fathers, uncles, and brothers-served as their legal guardians before, and at times even after, they were married, arranged their marriages, funded their dowries, "took them in" when they were widowed or divorced, and played an active part in the education and acculturation of their children."[241] Romans viewed educating women not as an extravagance, but as a

234 Rhee, *Early Christian Literature,* 109.

235 Garnsey and Saller, *The Roman Empire,* 135.

236 Witherington, *Women in the Earliest Churches,* 17.

237 Verner, *The Household of God,* 33.

238 Sawyer, *Women and Religion,* 19.

239 Verner, *The Household of God,* 33.

240 James B. Hurley, *Man and Woman in Biblical Perspective: A Study in Role Relationships and Authority* (England: InterVarsity Press, 1981), 75.

241 Hallett, *Women's Lives in the Ancient Mediterranean,* 31.

due mode of enhancing their living.[242] They were given opportunities to study with the educated men usually hired to teach their brothers, and at times they had tutors of their own. They also enjoyed the freedom to dine and to socialize with the men of their families.[243] However it had its own specific power dynamics, which is evident from the research of Judith P. Hallett,

> Elite Roman Women's dependence on their male blood kin undoubtedly curtailed their personal autonomy, restricting their opportunities to make decisions for themselves and to act on these decisions. Yet, the elite roman women's situation appears to be an advantaged one if we compare their circumstances with those of women in lower social strata. For, unlike their less loftily positioned counterparts, women of elite family were able to rely on their male relations for protection and support of different sorts. Somewhat ironically, this state of dependence, this ability to rely on male blood kin for various kinds of support, also allowed elite Roman women a degree of independence in marriage unavailable to females lower on the social scale. Having male blood relations who had selected her husband and subsidized her dowry in the first place, who could intervene with her husband to protect her interests, and who might well be of aid in her child-rearing responsibilities, made it possible for an elite woman to avoid being totally subjected to her husband, to create her own "space" in a difficult marriage, or to exit-temporarily if not permanently- from an unendurable marriage.[244]

This suggests that, the gender-class nexus exhibited a powerful dynamic in routine affairs of Roman families and shaped the social mobility of the elite women at the cost of their independent identity. In fact, the female 'otherness' defined "women as a group altogether

242 Witherington, *Women in the Earliest Churches,* 18.

243 Hallett, *Women's Lives in the Ancient Mediterranean,* 32.

244 Hallett, *Women's Lives in the Ancient Mediterranean,* 31.

different from and inferior to men"[245] in Roman society. Roman women were prohibited from voting, holding public offices and serving in military.[246] Nevertheless, Roman wives had certain amount of political influences over their husbands and the male members of their families.

Early imperial historian Tacitus attests to the fact that women were "permitted to accompany husbands on tours abroad when the husbands were chosen to lead armies and govern provinces."[247] However, such acts of companionship were not taken place in terms of equality. It would be inappropriate for wives to influence their husbands in public affairs.[248] In this regard, they were not better off than slaves or freed men. If in private life, they provide moral support to their husbands, was considered praiseworthy.[249]

Since the household was the basic unit of Roman economic production, women, who constituted about the half population of the Roman empire, played a significant role in the empire economy. There existed "gendered division of spheres between female domestic work and male fieldwork with the plow and draft animals."[250] Such binary projection of men and women adversely affected the condition of both slave and freed women in Roman households. The *materfamilias* of the household enjoyed a privileged a position in the household economy as the guardian of property and financial resources. They had employed female servants to nurse and raise the children.[251]

As far as the work area of other women in the family is concerned, it included "'service' jobs (catering, prostitution); dealing, particularly

245 Hallett, *Women's Lives in the Ancient Mediterranean,* 18.

246 Witherington, *Women in the Earliest Churches,* 18.

247 Hallett, *Women's Lives in the Ancient Mediterranean,* 18.

248 Two exceptions in the Roman history were the wives of the Emperors, such as Augustus' Livia and Claudius' Messalina, who were very prominent in decision making on their own merit.

249 Garnsey and saller, *The Roman Empire,* 134.

250 Richard Saller, "Women, Slaves and the Economy of the Roman Household," in *Early Christian Families in Context. An Interdisciplinary Dialogue,* edited by David L. Balch and Carolyn Osiek (Grand Rapids, Michigan/Cambridge, U.K.: William B. Eerdmans Publsihing Company, 2003), 189.

251 Witherington, *Women in the Earliest Churches,* 18.

in foodstuffs; serving in shops; in certain crafts, particularly the production of cloth and clothes; 'fiddly' jobs such as working in gold-leaf or hair-dressing; certain luxury trades such as perfumery."[252] There was found complete absence of women in the work areas of banking, building, transportation and administration. Certain skilled services like that of barber, hairdresser, entertainer had been shared more or less equally by both men and women, however, the gendered patterns are followed here as well. There are evidences of wives working along with husbands in family trades, but on unequal terms in relation to the work distribution.[253] In the household economy, the Roman empire ideology of gender hierarchy was clearly attested to the extent of witnessing "less training of women, hence lower productivity and lower wages for women, hence less economic independence and possibly lower valuation of women in their families, and less growth in productivity for the economy as a whole."[254]

The *paterfamilias* had exercised complete right of proprietorship over all property held by all the members of the household. Despite a Roman woman's right to inherit property, she needed a legal guardian to deal with and dispose her property.[255] Even though adult sons could not own property in the full sense, they were granted a *peculium* (estate) to manage.[256] The intensity of such oppressive *patria potestas* had, in many occasions, created hostility between sons and fathers that parricide became a serious issue in Roman empire.[257] Daughters remained under the *potestas* until they got married and came under the headship of their husbands. But sons had to continue under the *potestas* of their *pater familias* indefinitely, till the time of his death, or until they were emancipated through legal means.[258]

---

252 Susan Treggiari cited by Saller, *Women, Slaves and the Economy of the Roman Household,* 193.

253 Saller, *Women, Slaves and the Economy of the Roman Household,* 194.

254 Saller, *Women, Slaves and the Economy of the Roman Household,* 195.

255 Hallett, *Women's Lives in the Ancient Mediterranean,* 18.

256 Verner, *The Household of God,* 34.

257 Peter Garnsey and Richard Saller, *The Roman Empire: Economy, Society and Culture* (U.S.A: University of California Press, 1987), 137.

258 Verner, *The Household of God,* 34.

Essentially, Stoic philosophy, regardless of its emphasis on ideal harmonious marriage, sanctioned a hierarchical relationship between husband and wife. For instance, Plutarch recommended that husbands could exercise authority over their wives as a guide, philosopher and teacher. But the wives must be submissive to their husbands. Pliny, the Younger proclaimed the supreme virtue of wife's loyalty to husband's interests and defense and compliance to him essentially to stabilize the empire. Wives were expected of virtues like *castitas*[259] (chastity) and *pudicitia*[260] (prudence) in maintaining ideal marriages and families.[261] Although men enjoyed extramarital relations, women were forbidden from such acts. Loyalty is highly valued toward their husbands.[262] Suzanne Dixon's comments on the sexual obligations of Roman couples reveal this in a better way: "Certainly Roman women as a group were not accorded the sexual freedom of their male equivalents, and were expected to comply with their husbands' sexual whims. As with fertility, the ultimate responsibility for sexual failure tended to be laid at their doors, and transgressive wives were gossiped about more intensively than errant husbands."[263] It is self-evident that the Roman ideal marriage preserves the fundamental social hegemony and conforms to the conventional gender roles. It is also a hierarchy that assumes a class structure prohibiting marriages between persons of senatorial and non-senatorial status.

It was expected of all the members of a Roman household to participate in the rituals of domestic religion. Both *paterfamilias* and *materfamilias* had to participate in daily, monthly, and other regular sacrifice together. Nonetheless, over against the conservative religious allegiance, the wives and other members were given freedom to

---

259 The complete sexual integrity and fidelity within marriage.

260 Conscience and scrupulousness that keep women from shameful actions in general and sexual conduct in particular.

261 Plutarch and Pliny, the younger cited by Rhee, *Early Christian Literature,* 113.

262 Hurley, *Man and Woman,* 76.

263 Dixon, *Sex and the Married Woman in Ancient Rome,* 128.

worship other gods along with those of the *paterfamilias*.[264] In order to enhance unity and conformity in worship as in everything else, Roman wives had embraced the religion of their husbands.[265]

Roman emperors, aiming at promoting socially desirable behaviour of married women, endorsed the religious cults advocating chastity, childbirth and strong familial bonds.[266] Even so, the Roman elite men always suspected the cult of Isis and Judaism as subverting the morals of virtuous Roman women.[267] The cult of Isis was a goddess of loving mercy with whom women could identify irrespective of class barriers. Since it benefited the low class women to experience equal status with aristocrat women, the cult of Isis challenged the social hegemony patronized by the Roman government.[268] The monotheistic faith of Judaism disturbed the religious conviction of Romans regarding polytheism. Yet the religions, that had ignored traditional roles of women, had greatly influenced women to improve their social status in households. The models of women who became socially powerful and independent encouraged other women to climb up the social ladder to the best of their capabilities.[269]

---

264 Carolyn Osiek, R.S.C.J., "The Family in early Christianity: "Family Values" Revisited," *CBQ* 58/1 (January, 1996): 15.

265 Plutarch advices brides to stop worshiping any other gods than those of her husband for he believed that no god encourages secret rituals done by a woman. Cf. Plutarch, *conj.praec.*19.

266 The goddess Fortuna Virginitis was patroness of young girls who, when they came of age, were expected to dedicate their togas to this deity. Fortuna Primigenia was patroness of mothers and child birth, as well as giver of virility and material success to men. There was the cult of Fortunata Muliebris for women married only once; and the cult of Venus, changer of hearts, dedicated to encourage women to marital fidelity. This latter cult began when several matrons were discovered to be adulterous and their husbands wanted to create a permanent warning against such infidelity. In contrast, Fortuna Virilis was a prostitutes' cult in which such women met in the men's baths to worship a god of sexual relations. See Witherington, *Women in the Earliest Churches,* 19-20.

267 Keener, *Paul, Women & Wives,* 141.

268 Witherington, *Women in the Earliest Churches,* 21.

269 Keener, *Paul, Women & Wives,* 143.

Greco-Roman Empire: A Transcultural Hybrid Space[270]

The Roman Empire established herself in the Mediterranean land in course of three to four centuries by means of adapting Greek language, religion, art and culture and through a series of political interventions and treaties with Hellenistic smaller kingdoms. Gradually Rome succeeded in ascertaining her military superiority and imperial ambitions primarily as a defender of Hellenic freedom. While Romans maintained an ambivalent relation with Greeks even though they adapted the Greek political and cultural interests, the native Greeks also treated Romans as both barbarians and saviors.[271]

The emperor Augustus' attempts also paved way for promoting mutual dependence between the colonial Romans and the colonized Greeks and other ethnic subjects in their colonial territories. The adaptation of Greek philosophy into the political administration and household management was a great means to achieve the same. The Stoicism of Roman imperial era along with Augustan marriage legislatures comprising legal, social and political acts became the ideological backbone of Greco-Roman society. There was a great significance attached to ideal marriage and sexual fidelity, which emphasized sexual moderation and restraints.[272] Especially, the Roman Empire believed in ideal households as inevitable for a stable State. In Greek society the dichotomy between domestic and public spheres meant strict containment of women's lives but in Roman society, many domestic occupations and interests crossed into the public sphere.[273] Nonetheless patriarchal hierarchy continued in Rome. A radical change in *paterfamilias* was a far cry of the imperial era.[274]

---

270 Simon Samuel uses "'transculturalism' in the sense of 'border-crossing' where the structures of power are deconstructed and decentered unlike in 'cross-culturalism' where they are often left untouched." See Simon Samuel, *A Postcolonial Reading of mark's Story of Jesus* (London: T & T Clark, 2007), 26, n.85.

271 Samuel, *A Postcolonial Reading…*, 54.

272 Rhee, *Early Christian Literature,* 111.

273 Sawyer, *Women and Religion,* 15.

274 Sawyer, *Women and Religion,* 20.

It is agreeable with Alcock that 'Greeks and Romans were engaged in a tense dialogue of "cultural mapping, of mutual self-definition and aggressive maintenance of boundaries."[275] Therefore, the Greco-Roman society could be understood, in the postcolonial term, a transcultural hybrid space where ambivalent responses like accepting and rejecting Rome and appreciating and disrupting native Greek culture was common among Greeks and Romans.

IV. Wife-Husband Relationship in New Testament Writings

A. Jesus' Sayings in Gospels

Jesus spoke relatively little about marriage and divorce. Yet, what he spoke was quite revolutionary to the norms and customs of his day. In Mk. 10:2-9, certain Pharisees raise the question regarding the lawfulness of divorce sanctioned by writing a certificate of dismissal as per the command of Moses. But Jesus points to the hardness of heart of the Jews, which forced Moses to write such a law for them. Then Jesus highlights the original intention of God in creation for the harmonious marriage by quoting Gen. 2:24. The words of Jesus very powerfully negate the divorce by stating that "what God has joined together, let no one separate' (v. 9). Further, he condemns the practice of divorce when he says to the disciples, "whoever divorces his wife and marries another commits adultery against her; and if she divorces her husband and marries another, she commits adultery" (Mk. 10:11-12). The husband who divorces his wife causes her to commit adultery because in the Jewish culture of Greco-Roman period, a single woman could hardly survive on her own, except through prostitution.[276] An additional nuance to this is added in Lk. 16:18 that "…and whoever marries a woman divorced from her husband commits adultery." In these two Gospel parallels, Divorce is strictly against the will of God and is not granted at all,

275 S. E. Alcock, "Greece: a Landscape of Resistance?", in *Dialogues in Roman Imperialism: Power, Discourse, and Discrepant Experience in the Roman Empire* (JRA Supp. Series, 23, Portsmouth: JRA, 1997), 109, cited by Samuel, *A Postcolonial Reading…*, 55.

276 Hagner, Donald A., *Matthew 1-13, Word Biblical Commentary, Volume 33a:* (Dallas, Texas: Word Books, 1998), CD-Rom.

thus overruling the Mosaic Law. Jesus' viewpoint presupposes the permanent character of the marriage bond, which divorce cannot alter. Therefore, in Jesus' teachings, divorce and remarriage are strictly ruled out. Such an outright ban on divorce would have certainly disturbed the Jewish religious inclinations and Roman State legal provisions.

The parallel passage found in Matthew's Gospel gears up a controversy due to a strange addition (mh; ejpi; porneiva/) in Mt. 19:9 (cf.5:32). Here a man may divorce his wife on the basis of her unchastity (infidelity/fornication) to him ("... whoever divorces his wife, except for unchastity, and marries commits adultery."). This addition may not be attributed to historical Jesus, but it may reflect how Jesus' teaching on divorce was applied in the Matthean Jewish Christian community quite long after Jesus' death and resurrection.[277] Probably, this alludes to rabbinic discussions on the legitimate causes of divorce in the first century CE,[278] or the political pressure from Roman government on Jews/Christians to accept the imperial law.

B. Pauline Literature

Paul was a child of his time, being a Diasporan Jew and having exposed to both Jewish religion and hellenization, embodies the characteristic tension faced by any learned person 'between local patriotism and the claims of the imperial order, between native culture and the allure of Greco-roman civilization, between Semitic languages and Greek, between pragmatic flexibility and committed sectarianism, between class loyalty and group loyalty."[279] His writings in the New Testament are classic examples narrating the impact of Jewish religion and Greco-Roman philosophy on him. It is very interesting to note how he borrows from the surrounding cultures to address the issues regarding marital relations of the Christians in the first century churches. In this section, a select set of Pauline passages

---

277 Liam Kelly. *Sacraments Revisited. What do they Mean Today?* (London: Darton, Longman and Todd Ltd., 1998), 154.

278 George Mangatt, "Jesus' Teaching on Marriage and Divorce," *Bible Bhashyam* (1994): 101.

279 Samuel, *A Postcolonial Reading*, 72.

dealing with marriage, divorce and marital obligations is evaluated to understand his theology.

Primarily, 1 Cor. 7 deals with Paul's response to various issues related to marriage raised by the members of the Corinthian church. Paul, in 1 Cor. 7: 2-4, approves the opinion of Stoic philosophers like Musonius and Plutarch that sexual relationships are to be with one's own partner performing due conjugal rights to each other. Musonius comments that a married couple should regard everything common including their bodies. In Plutarch's opinion, heterosexual marriages should base on friendship and not on procreation.[280] Paul applies Stoic friendship model to Christian marriage, accentuating mutuality in sharing sexual interests of both husband and wife. This prohibits the married (predominantly men) from extramarital relationships with slaves or prostitutes. As an exemption to this (v. 5), they may refrain from sex if they both agree together or for devoting to prayer, but not allowed to be separated for a longer period because of their vulnerability toward sexual temptations.

In 1 Cor. 7:10-16, the Pauline emphasis is on the issue of divorce. Primarily, Paul forbids separation/divorce in Christian families. The reference to separation of wives indicates the Corinthian preference for celibacy leading many to separate from their spouses. It is permitted only if the separated woman remains unmarried (or else she should be reconciled to her husband). This is an exceptional exhortation only for women who were longing for social or religious freedom to practice asceticism.[281] But divorce is strictly barred for husbands. In v. 12ff, the peculiar situation of having unbelieving partner is dealt with. If the unbeliever wants to remain in marriage, the believing spouses are not allowed to opt for divorce for it is their spiritual responsibility to lead them to Christian faith and salvation (v. 16). But in case, the unbeliever initiates divorce, the spouse can be free from the marriage (v. 15).

Paul returns to the issue of divorce in v. 39 again, here to reinstate Jewish religious binding on the wife to remain in marriage as long

---

280 Carolyn Osiek and David L. Balch, *Families in the New Testament World: Households and House Churches* (Louisville, Kentucky: Westminister John Knox Press, 1997), 115-6.

281 Osiek and Balch, *Families in the New Testament World,* 116.

as he lives for only the husband can initiate divorce (cf. Deut. 24:1). Only in case of his death, she is allowed to remarry, however, Paul prefers the widow to remain as she is (v. 40). This finds parallel in Rom. 7:2, where the same idea is expressed with an additional thought in v. 3 that if a married woman lives with another man, she will be called as an adulteress. The Greek term for adulteress, moicaliv" is found only in this verse in Pauline literature. It is also not attested outside the Judeo-Christian tradition, but appears several times in the LXX (cf. Prov 18:22a; 24:55; Ezek 16:38; 23:45; Hos 3:1; Mal 3:5). "Precisely because the husband had such authority over his wife in Jewish law and society the word contains a strong note of shame and guilt as denoting one who has been particularly disloyal and false."[282] But a widow can opt or remarriage and she will not be an adulteress. This particular teaching of Paul in 1 Cor. 7:39-40 and Rom. 7:2-3 regarding the marital gender norms fall more in line with Jewish or rather Hellenistic Jewish tradition because of the selection of words like moicaliv." Paul does not show any allegiance to Roman law[283] in his response to the Corinthian issues of marriage and divorce.

Another significant passage that sheds light on the wife-husband relationship appears in 1 Cor. 11:1-16. This is a controversial passage as it expresses Paul's inconsistency in portraying the husband-wife relationship. Vv. 3-10 narrates the hierarchy in husband-wife relationship, whereas vv. 11&12 deal with mutuality and interdependence of them.[284] In the descending hierarchy of God-

---

282 Dunn, James D. G., Romans 1-8, *Word Biblical Commentary, Volume 38a*: (Dallas, Texas: Word Books, Publisher, 1998), CD-Rom.

283 In Roman law, marriage could be brought to an end by the free will of either partner; and indeed by the time of the later republic divorce by common consent or at the wish of one had become common, "the normal course in matrimonial affairs". Moreover, in Roman law a woman was not freed from the law of her husband by his death, since she was obliged to mourn his death and to remain unmarried for twelve months; otherwise she would forfeit everything which had come to her from her first husband. See P. E. Corbett, *The Roman Law of Marriage*, reprint (Oxford: Clarendon, 1969), 249.; Dunn, Commentary on Romans, CD-Rom.

284 "Paul's two different attitudes are due to the context of Corinth and Corinthian Christian community. Corinth was the most licentious city in Greece. This was a strategic commercial center by its location on the high road from the East to

Christ-man-woman in 1 Cor. 11:2, each preceding member exercises authority over the latter as 'head' or 'source' (*kefalh;*). Therefore, 'man' or 'husband' (*janh;r*) is the image (*eijkw;n*) and glory/reflection (*dovxa*) of God, while woman (*gunh*;) is the glory (*dovxa*) of man (*ajndrov"*) as in v. 7. But it is to be noted that woman is not said to be of the image of man. By creating man first in the image of God, God set his own glory in man. And the woman is related to the man as his glory or reflection and therefore her lifestyle needs to be formulated in honour and respect to the man.[285] The authority of husbands over their wives is argued in vv. 8-9 that "Indeed, man was not made from woman, but woman from man. Neither was man created for the sake of woman, but woman for the sake of man." The symbol of his authority is the veil which women wear (v. 10) It seems to be that Paul disregards Gen. 2:18, in which the first man and woman were created for a relationship of mutuality and equality. Instead, he tries to approve that she was solely created for the sake of the man to serve him in obedience and submission.[286]

Irrespective of Paul's inconsistency in 1 Cor. 11:1-16, one may appreciate him for providing the hallmark egalitarian baptismal formula in Gal 3:28 (a pre-Pauline traditional formula), which

---

the West. Therefore Latins, Greeks, Syrians, Asiatic, Egyptians and Jews used to visit the city frequently and some even stayed in the city. Aphrodite temple with its thousand priestesses or cultic prostitutes was an example of Corinth's immorality. Women were active in some mystery religions and used excessive freedom. Corinth was one of the centers of Isis cult too. In this cultic worship women did not use veil. Besides, women having disheveled hair was typical in the cult. In some other mysteries like the cult of Dionysius also women participated without veil." See K. J. Mercy, "Mutuality and Interdependence of man and Woman: An Exegetical Study of 1 Cor 11, 11-12," *Bible Bhashyam* XXVI/3 (Sep.2000): 197-8.

285 C. K. Barrett, *The First Epistle to the Corinthians* (London: Adam & Charles Black, 1971), 252.; Gordon D. Fee, *The First Epistle to the Corinthians* (Grand Rapids: William B. Eerdmans Publishing Company, 1987), 515.

286 Virginia R. Mollenkott, *Women, Men and the Bible* (Abingdon: Nashville, 1977), 98.; Pauline Chakkalakal, "Paul a Friend or a Foe of Women?" in *Feminist Theology: Perspectives and Praxis*, edited by Prasanna Kumari (GSI: Madras, 1998), 410-411.; Mary Hayter, *The New Eve in Christ* (London: SPCK, 1987), 121.; Newsom, Carol A. and Sharon H. Ringe. *Women's Bible Commentary* (Louisville: Westminster John Knox Press, 1998), 417.

nullifies the socio-cultural discriminations existing in the woman-man relation in the first century CE.

C. Post-Pauline and Petrine Literature

The post-Pauline and Petrine churches had inherited the Aristotelian household rules, which were introduced as part of the hellenization process of Roman emperor Augustus.[287] This had adversely affected the pre-Pauline baptismal confession of egalitarianism found in Gal. 3:27-28. The household codes in Ephesians and Colossians are vivid examples of how hierarchical structures replacing the Christian proclamation of equality. Col 3:11 refers to "There cannot be Greek and Jew… slave, free", but the pair male nor female as already been vanished behind the Hegemonic religion.[288] Even though gender was and is never a criterion in the redemptive act of God, the Christian church could not withstand the socio-cultural patriarchal traits creeping inside the church.

The resemblances in the household codes of Colossians and Ephesians indicate the possibility of a common author or common literary source. Scholars are of the opinion that Colossian household codes are the most primitive form of all New Testament codes. Here it seems to be that the author is having in mind the Christian households unlike Petrine mixed religious households. In the Colossian household codes (3:18-4:1), relatively a small portion is assigned to deal with the wife-husband relationship, a verse each for each category. In Col. 3:18-19, wives are exhorted to submit to their husbands as is fitting in the Lord and husbands to love their wives and not to treat them harshly. The present tense, middle voice form of the verb, *hupotasso,* denotes that submission to husbands is a continual activity of wives, which they do voluntarily without the insistence from their husbands. The Christian rationale for the submission is drawn from the model of Christ ("as is fitting in the

287 Osiek and Balch, *Families in the New Testament World,* 120.

288 And in Col 3:22-4:1, the Christian slaves are exhorted to be obedient to their masters- immediately after the outstanding proclamation of "no more slave or free."

Lord"), thereby indicating Christianization of Stoic laws.[289] The exhortation to husbands to love is a concept unfamiliar to Hellenistic and Roman household literature.

The deutero-Pauline Pastoral Letters also share references to household tables (1 Tim. 2:8-15; 6:1-2 and Titus 2:1-10). Women are discouraged from remaining unmarried and are encouraged to adopt traditional gender roles (cf. 1 Tim. 4:3-5).[290] 1 Tim. 2:8-15 is a passage of ethical exhortation in which the story of Adam and Eve is used to support the guide of conduct set for women and men (particularly wives and husbands) in the church at Ephesus. The religious environment in Ephesus calls for attention as it was saturated with the "feminine principle" due to the Artemis cult and thus attitudes of female exaltation. This attitude continued among Greco-Roman women even after they turned to the Christian faith. The myths of Cybele and Attis, from which the Ephesian Artemis evolved, emphasized the creation of the goddess first, and then her male consort.[291] By stating the priority of Adam in creation (1 Tim. 2:13), the author might possibly be altering such an order of creation.

In the context of community worship, two activities of wives (or women in general) are criticized. Firstly, the apparel of women with outward adornments is criticized as not suiting to their Christian faith (1 Tim. 2:9). Secondly, they are not allowed to teach or to have authority over their husbands (1 Tim. 2:12). This second prohibition indicates that in the church at Ephesus, women were teaching men in the church. Adam and Eve are introduced to this passage to justify the refusal of teaching authority to women.

1 Tim. 2:13-14 exhibits clear dependence upon the Yahwistic creation story of Gen. 2-3. Adam and Eve are used as illustrative

289 Witherington, *Women in the Earliest Churches,* 52.

290 Margaret Y. MacDonald, "Rereading Paul. Early Interpreters of Paul on Women and Gender," in *Women and Christian Origins,* edited by Ross Shepard Kraemer and Mary Rose D' Angelo (New York/Oxford: Oxford University Press, 1999), 238.

291 Sharon H. Gritz, *Paul, Women Teachers, and the Mother Goddess at Ephesus. A Study of 1 Timothy 2:9-15 in Light of the Religious and Cultural Milieu of the First Century* (Lanham: University Press of America, 1991), 138.

models to affirm the roles of the authoritative patriarchal structure within the church and the family. Their lives are displayed as models of patriarchal power structure, so that the inter-relationship between husbands and wives will be appropriated according to Christian teaching. However, it becomes theologically and morally outrageous to argue that a woman "will be saved through childbearing" (1 Tim 2:15). Witherington suspects that the author is mimicking the words of emperor Augustus and of the Hellenistic medical doctor Soranus, who emphasized procreation as the primary purpose of marital sexual intercourse.[292]

Titus 2:4-8 deals with the marital duties assigned to young couples. Interestingly, here the wives are asked to love their husbands. Further they ought to love their children, be self-controlled, chaste, good managers of the household, kind, being submissive to their husbands" (Titus 2:4-5) The theological argument supporting this exhortation is that their exemplary behaviour may acclaim God's word (v. 5b). Even though the young men are given advices in general, there is no obligatory duty toward women or wives mentioned (cf. vv. 6-8).

1 Peter 3:1-7 deals with wife-husband relation in the Petrine household code. Here the context is of a mixed household of differing religious affiliations. Vv.1-5 are addressed to wives of non-Christian husbands to accept the authority of their husbands. The exemplary conduct of wives is appreciated for a missionary purpose, here, for the evangelization of their unbelieving husbands.

In Greco-Roman culture, wives, children, and slaves were expected to accept the religion of the male head of the household, the *paterfamilias*, and so religious groups that attracted women and slaves were particularly seen as potentially subversive of societal stability."[293] Nevertheless, there was religious freedom or tolerance provided the newly embraced faith did not interfere with the cultic practices of the household religion.

---

292 Witherington, *Women in the Earliest Churches,* 122. Soranus wrote *Gynecology*, a work exclusively concerned with women and with intercourse for childbearing. See Witherington, *Women in the Earliest Churches*, 104-107.

293 Lincoln, *Ephesians,* CD Rom.

Women in such a Petrine context were treated as "the perfect, modest, and discreet mediator between the church and the nonbelieving world (1 Pet. 3:1-6)."[294] They in fact risked their lives for the propagation of their new faith. The author encourages them strongly to exhibit marital fidelity through purity and reverence, by which their unbelieving husbands can be won over to Christian faith. Sarah's example from Hebrew Scriptures is drawn to inculcate obedience in wives toward husbands (v. 6).

Husbands are given a strange command to ""pay honour to the woman as the weaker sex" (v. 7). The Greek phrase *wJ" ajsqenestevrw/ skeuvei* (as somebody weaker) does not indicate weaker sex in a generalized sense. *skeu`o"* refers to human body in a metaphorical sense. *skeu`o"* in the sense of "body" refers here to a person, but not in such a way as to emphasize either personhood or sexuality."[295]

The notion about women as weaker was common in ancient Mediterranean cultures as we have references in Plato and Philo.[296] But the use of this notion to command respect for women is an innovation of the author. The theological underscoring is done for enhancing unity in prayer between believing couples, which proves that the husbands addressed are having believing wives unlike the case of wives.

As the study on the origin and background of household codes in the first chapter unravels, it is possible that the New Testament authors have initiated the household management pattern, drawing on a host of ethical material inherited both from their Jewish heritage and possibly from the wider Greco-Roman milieu.[297] The Hellenistic Judaism might have probably played a major role in the transport of

---

294 Margaret Y. MacDonald, "Was Celsus Right? The Role of Women in Expansion in Early Christianity," in *Early Christian Families in Context: An Interdisciplinary Dialogue*, edited by David L. Balch and Carolyn Osiek (Grand Rapids, Michigan/Cambridge, U.K.: William B. Eerdmans Publishing Company, 2003), 176.

295 Michaels, J. R., *1 Peter, Word Biblical Commentary, Vol. 49* (Dallas, Texas: Word Books, Publisher, 1998), CD-Rom.

296 Plato, *Republic* 5.455D, ejpi; pa`si de; aJsqenevsteron gunh; ajndrov", "yet for all a woman is weaker than a man," See also Philo, *Ebr*. 55.

297 Witherington, *Women in the Earliest Churches,* 47.

household codes from Hellenism down through Roman imperialism to the Christian literature. It also must have been unavoidable for the Christians in the first century CE to interact with the Jewish and Greco-Roman socio-religious, cultural and political influences. It is also important to note that the early Christian church had members, who converted from Greco-Roman religious background and thus brought in their cultural practices directly into their newly found faith.

V. Wife-Husband Relationship in the Writings of Early Christian Teachers

The literature of some early Christian teachers attest to the household duties assigned to the Christian families in the New Testament. The Household codes are found in *The Didache* 4:9-11, *The Letter of Barnabas* 19:5-7, *The First Epistle of Clement to the Corinthians* 1:3, 21:6-9, *The Epistle of Ignatius to Polycarp* 4:1-6:2, *The Epistle of Polycarp to the Philippians* 4:2-6:1. However, *The Didache*[298] and *The letter of Barnabas*[299] do not have household duties assigned to wives and husbands. The wife-husband relationship in the household codes in early Christian literature draws the attention of this research, mainly because they retain the hierarchical patriarchal modes of marital relationship. This indicates that they seem to have succumbed to the socio-political pressures of the Roman imperial government. Schussler Fiorenza comments that these later household

298 *Didache* 4.9-11 instructs parents to discipline their children, masters to treat their slaves reasonably and slaves to be subject to their masters. The reciprocity, the theme of submission and the motivation (the impartiality of God, who is over both master and slave) suggest a link with the tradition as used in Colossians and Ephesians.

299 *Barnabas* 19.5, 7 uses the same material as in The *Didache* with slight alterations, reversing the order of instructions to slaves first, then masters. In each case the household code material has been incorporated into the collection of traditions used to explain the Two Ways teaching (of "life and death," Did. 1.1; of "light and darkness," Barn. 18.1). The household and community relationship ethics implied by these sections are not applied in any discernible way to immediate situations. The material is simply included as orthodox.

codes reinstate "patriarchal submission to authority"[300] without critical evaluation of the Greco-Roman environment.

A. Marital Gender Norms in *The First Epistle of Clement to the Corinthians*

The major thrust of the first letter to Corinthians by Clement of Rome revolves around unity and harmony in the Corinthian church (*1 Clem.* 20:37–38, 46–48). There seemed to have been some threat to church stability by those who challenged ecclesiastical authority (1 Clem. 21:5; 44:1, 4; 47.6). The household codes in this letter (1:3; 21:6-9) "suggest that Clement urged a return to traditional family values as the key to harmony. Moreover, the authority of the male head of the house, central to Roman ethical thinking among the aristocracy, corresponded to Clement's views of ecclesiastical authority in the church."[301] In this manner, the pattern of the two codes in *1 Clement* suggests a preference for patriarchy in the Roman model of household codes.[302] The absence of instructions to the husbands or fathers suggests the main addressee is the male leader of the household. Nevertheless, they are praised for their role in keeping patriarchal house order intact in the past (1:3).

In *1 Clem.* 1:3, wives are exhorted to do all things with a blameless and pure conscience; to love their husbands dutifully; to live in the rule of obedience; to manage their households and to have discretionary power. The goal of such living pattern is mentioned in 2:1 that the Christian community ought to live in humility with a willingness to be in subjection in line with the household codes. Here the subjection is not commanded, but expected from an ideal Christian. In 1 Clem. 21:6-9, hortatory first person plural is used to address the marital gender norms attached to women: "let us direct our wives to that which is good. Let them exhibit the lovely habit of purity [in all their conduct]; let them show forth the sincere

300 Schussler Fiorenza, *In Memory of Her,* 293.

301 P. H. Towner, "Household Codes," in *Dictionary of the Later New Testament & Its Developments,* edited by Ralph P. Martin, Peter H. Davids (Downers Grove, Illinois: InterVarsity Press, 2000), CD-ROM.

302 Schussler Fiorenza, *In Memory of Her,* 291-2.

disposition of meekness; let them make manifest the command which they have of their tongue, by their manner of speaking; let them display their love, not by preferring one to another, but by showing equal affection to all that piously fear God."[303] Here the submission of wives is not only a God-given duty, but also a missionary strategy of the early Christian community.[304]

B. Marital Gender Norms in *The Epistle of Ignatius to Polycarp*

Ignatius, bishop of Antioch, in his *Letter to Polycarp* 4.1—5.2 introduces a church code that combines instructions concerning treatment of widows and slaves and reciprocal instructions to wives and husbands with instructions to Polycarp himself concerning ministry. This code of conduct is somewhat closer in tone and content to the NT codes than *1 Clement.*

The wives are particularly admonished to be satisfied with their husbands both in "the flesh and spirit" out of their love for the Lord. Similarly, the husbands have to love their wives, even as the Lord loves the Church (5:2). The marriage should be held with the approval of the Lord and the bishop, and not after their own lust (5:4). Here the Episcopal authority is reaffirmed in the Church, while male head holds authority in a household. Ignatius propagated that there should be "one God, one Bishop, One Church" in consonance with Roman monarchial rule, "One God, One Emperor, One Empire."[305] Such patristic advocacy for authority-submission binary relationship in the early church and household downplay the egalitarianism that Christianity could have achieved otherwise.

C. Marital Gender Norms in *The Epistle of Polycarp to the Philippians*

The Epistle of Polycarp to the Philippians 4.2—6.1 instructs the church—wives, widows, deacons, young men, young women, elders—to live their lives as pleasing to the Lord (cf. Pol. *Phil.* 5.2; 6.1; 4.1). The pattern of life described in the household or church code might

303 file:///G:/CCEL/FATHERS2/ANF01/ANF0105.HTM#P171_20841.

304 Osiek and Balch, *Families in the New Testament World,* 148.

305 Schussler Fiorenza, *In Memory of Her,* 293.

be applied to internal instability in the church at Philippi.[306] Like in *Ignatius' epistle to Polycarp* (4:1-3), here in 4:1-3 as well, one identifies patriarchal, ecclesiastical power and control of finances over against women (wives).

Pol. Phil. 4:4, the household codes regarding wives are explained. As per this verse, the male heads of the family should teach their wives "[to walk] in the faith given to them, and in love and purity tenderly loving their own husbands in all truth, and loving all [others] equally in all chastity; and to train up their children in the knowledge and fear of God." It is noticeable that no such exhortation is addressed to husbands. Unlike in Ephesians, each household group is not separately addressed, instead the author is in favor of presenting the literary *topos* of household management prevalent in Greco-Roman society, usually addressed to the male *paterfamilias.*[307]

Early Christian Marital Gender Norms: A Religious Subjection to Roman Imperial Household Norms

During the time span of 100 B.C.E. to 200 CE, Greco-Roman imperialism with Rome as the centre has gradually taken complete control over the Mediterranean region and religions, encompassing its power over all the subjected ethnic groups. Since Roman government considered family as the microcosm of the larger society, there was great emphasis on the proper management of households and rules and regulations in compliance with the imperial interests. The early Christians were a mixed group emanating from various regions, cultures and religious backgrounds consisting of both former Jews and non-Jews. This resembled the heterogeneity of the Asia Minor population.[308] It is hard to differentiate between Hellenistic Jewish and Hellenistic Gentile churches in the early century CE No single

306 P. H. Towner, "Household Codes," in Martin, Ralph P.; Davids, Peter H., *Dictionary of the Later New Testament & Its Developments* (Downers Grove, III: InterVarsity Press, 2000), CD-Rom.

307 Osiek and Balch, *Families in the New Testament World,* 146.

308 Elliott, *Home for the Homeless,* 65-66.

writing in the New Testament can be exclusively termed as either Jewish or Gentile, but only as mixed Jewish-Gentile.[309]

P. H. Towner comments that "the household codes of both the NT and the apostolic fathers reflect an awareness of the expectations of the Greco-Roman environment of the church. However, they also reveal some subtle differences in the way the church at different times and in different situations sought to interact with secular society."[310] The Patristic traditions have greatly legitimized the patriarchal household codes both theologically and christologically.[311] The New Testament household codes - which show sensitivity to imperial family rules by critically rationalizing theologically - aimed to direct Christians to a constructive middle ground, avoiding either the simple return to patriarchy or emancipation. In contrast, in the writings of the apostolic fathers, household codes are used without evidence of the critical reflection upon the church's responsibility in the world.[312] By the time of early Christian teachers, Christian ethic presumed that "careful control of contact between the sexes and the subordination of women were necessary ingredients in the Christian life."[313] Therefore, it may be assessed that the gradual adaptation to the patriarchal order of Greco-Roman society had tampered the Church's initial goal of making Christian faith, gender-egalitarian (cf. Gal. 3:28). We move on to investigate the disturbing portrayal of wives-husbands in the Ephesian household code to expose whether the struggle of the church at Ephesus retains the liberating elements of Christian faith in a dominant Roman imperial environment.

---

309 I. Howard Marshall, "Palestinian and Hellenistic Christianity: Some Critical comments," *New Testament Studies* 19 (1973): 286.

310 Towner, *Household Codes*, CD-Rom.

311 Schussler Fiorenza, *In Memory of Her*, 294,

312 Towner, *Household Codes*, CD-Rom.

313 Osiek and Balch, *Families in the New Testament World*, 146.

Chapter 4

Ephesians, Empire, and Egalitarianism

The portrayal of wife-husband relationship in Eph. 5:21-33 seems to provide an ambiguous picture of the early Christian understanding of marital equality. The passage begins with an exhortation to submit to one another (Eph. 5:21), which attests mutual relationships. But when it comes to the specific gender roles, husbands are asked to love their wives as Christ loved the church (Eph. 5:25) and wives to submit and to fear their husbands (Eph. 5:22, 33). Even though the exhortation to husbands stands as radically progressive in a hierarchical and imperial social environment, the exhortations to wives blur the liberative approach exhibited in exhorting the husbands. Further, the Christ-Church imagery seems to depict wives inferior to their husbands. Is the author of the letter to the Ephesians justifying Christologically the socio-cultural gender norms assigned to wives and husbands in a Roman imperial society? Another significant verse in this pericope is v. 31, where a quote from Gen. 2:24 is used ("For this reason a man will leave his father and mother and be joined to his wife, and the two will become one flesh."). This verse may suggest a mutual relationship of equality between wives and husbands in marriage. Therefore, the tension seems to remain between the concepts of mutuality and specific subordination of wives throughout this passage.

Historical and Literary Analysis of Ephesians

Traditionally, the letter to the Ephesians is attributed to Pauline authorship. The internal evidences in support of Pauline authorship are drawn from the implied author's allusions to apostolic authority (1:1) and suffering for the cause of Christ and his gospel and the Gentiles (3:1,13; 4:1; 6:19-20). The author calls himself Paul, a point which is sufficient in general case to approve the authenticity of the letter; nevertheless, critical research has shed suspicion on this claim of Pauline authorship. It is worth noting that the attestation of Pauline authorship of Ephesians draws strong support from the writings of early Christian Teachers as well.[314]

A majority of NT scholars is doubtful of Pauline authorship of the letter to Ephesians. Erasmus of Rotterdam initiated the critical study on the authorship of Ephesians in the 16th century (1519), followed by Edward Evanson (1792) and W. de Wette (1847). According to Evanson, the letter is very impersonal in its tone as the author says, "I have heard of your faith...and your love..." (Eph. 1:15), which is unlikely from a person who spent about a little more than two and a half years in Ephesus (cf. Acts. 18:18-21, 19:1-20:1). The author assumes that the addressees have most probably heard of his ministry (3:2). There are no individuals mentioned by name or greeted. Further, the epistle ends with a brief impersonal farewell.[315]

---

314 Clement of Rome, Ignatius, bishop of Antioch, Polycarp, bishop of Smyrna, Irenaeus, bishop of Lyons, Clement of Alexandria, and Tertullian of Carthage have quoted heavily from Ephesians authenticating as the words of the apostle Paul. See for a detailed explanation, Harold W. Hoehner, *Ephesians: An Exegetical commentary* (Grand Rapids, Michigan: Baker Academic, 2002), 2-4.

315 Edward Evanson, *The Dissonance of the Four Generally Received Evangelists and the Evidence of their Respective Authenticity Examined* (Ipswich, Engalnd: George Jermym, 1792), 261-62.; Hoehner counterargues that the lack of personal touch can be explained from the fact that this is a circular letter written to the churches at Ephesus and the surrounding places in western Asia Minor. Hoehner, *Ephesians*, 21.

The arguments against Pauline authorship postulated by Wilhelm Martin Leberecht de Wette are significant since they influenced the research ever after. He had highlighted three points: the literary dependence of Ephesians upon Colossians; the distinctive style of the epistle, and in particular the use of relative clauses, participles, prepositional phrases and genitival constructions; and the presence of certain expressions such as "on the foundation of the apostles and prophets" (Eph. 2:20) and "the holy apostles and prophets" (Eph. 3:5).[316] Thereafter, a number of scholars[317] questioned the authenticity of Pauline authorship.

A comprehensive discussion on the same is found in the work of C. L. Mitton (1951/1976)[318] Mitton has highlighted the new words and phrases in Ephesians which are lacking in the Pauline corpus[319]; the literary style (with long sentences); literary dependence on Colossians; and the different use of words like 'mystery' (1:9; 3:3; 5;32; 6:19), 'fulness' (1:10, 23; 3:19) and 'plan' (1:10; 3:2,9). He further points out the historical arguments, for instance, the issue of the place of Gentiles in Churches is replaced by the way the Gentiles have to treat Jews. This historical context refers to a later period than Paul himself.[320]

---

316 Wilhelm Martin Leberecht de Wette, An Historico-critical Introduction to the Canonical Books of the New Testament, trans. from the 5th ed. By Frederick Frothingham (Boston: Crosby, Nichols, 1858), 88-92, cited by Martin Kitchen, *Ephesians* (London and New York: Routledge, 1994), 5.

317 H. J. Holtzmann (1872), G. Bornkamm (1948), C. Maurer (1951), M. Dibelius (1953), D. E. Nineham (1956), E. Kasemann (1958), H. Conzelmann (1962), M. V. Abraham (2008), *Theology of St. Paul: An Introduction* (Thiruvalla: Christava Sahitya Samiti, 2008), 10-11.

318 C. L. Mitton, *The Epistle to the Ephesians: Its Authorship, Origin and Purpose* (Oxford: Oxford University Press, 1951), 11. C. L. Mitton, *Ephesians* (London: Oliphants, 1976), 15.

319 While Ephesians has the word, 'devil' (4:27; 6:11), Paul would be more likely to use the word, 'Satan'. The phrases such as 'in the heavenly places' (1:3,20; 2:6; 3:10; 6:12), 'the Father of glory' (1:17), 'before the foundation of the world' (1:4), 'be sure of this' (5:5) are untypical of Paul. The use of genitival formulations (1:6, 12, 14; 4: 16, 22) is also unlikely of Paul.

320 Mitton, *Ephesians,* 17, cited by Kitchen, *Ephesians,* 6.

Finally, Mitton sheds light on three doctrinal arguments: the reference to 'universal church' (1:22; 3:10, 21; 5:23, 24, 27) replacing the issue of circumcision by the unity of the church; apostles and prophets replace Christ (Eph. 3:5, cf. 1 Cor. 3:11) as the foundation of the church; and the denial of an imminent parousia (Eph. 2:7; 3:21; 4:13) resulting in household codes differing from Pauline teaching on marriage.[321]

From the various scholarly opinions discussed above, the arguments weigh more in favor of non-Pauline authorship of the letter to the Ephesians. This letter could be attributed to post-Pauline authorship on the basis of the lack of author's familiarity with the Ephesian church, the author's familiarity with the traditions of holy apostles and prophets (cf. 2:20, 3:5), non-Pauline literary style and vocabulary and the historical reality of Gentile Christians outnumbering Jewish Christians.

In line with the arguments favoring post-Pauline authorship, a date between 80 and 90 CE. might most probably be proposed as acceptable.[322] This would substantiate the Ephesian author's post-apostolic perspective and knowledge of Paul's letters. Further, the early Christian teachers' familiarity with the Ephesian text can also be rationalized.[323]

Eph. 1:1 mentions the destination of the letter as Ephesus. There are manuscripts that omit the name Ephesus in the text; however, they retain it in the title. The scholars who attribute the letter to Paul are against the Ephesian destination, for the reason that Paul stayed in Ephesus during his second missionary journey and he knew the church he founded very well (cf. Acts 19-20) contradicts the reference to Paul having heard of the faith of the addressees (1:15) and the addressees having known of Paul's mission (3:3).[324] But for those who opt for post-Pauline origin of the letter, Ephesus is undeniably the destination of the letter.

321 Mitton, *Ephesians,* 17, cited by Kitchen, *Ephesians,* 7.

322 W. G. Kummel, *Introduction to the New Testament,* edited and translated by H. C. Kee (Nashville; Abington Press, 1975), 366.

323 Andrew T. Lincoln, *Ephesians, Word Biblical Commentary, Vol. 42* (Nashville: Thomas Nelson Publishers, 1990), lxxiii.

324 Kitchen, *Ephesians,* 35.

The city of Ephesus has "a Greek connection as early as 1100 B.C.E. It was the chief of the twelve Ionian cities in Asia Minor's west coast. Croesus conquered it in 560 B.C.E., Antiochus captured it around 196 B.C.E., it was incorporated into the Roman province of Asia in 133 B.C.E., Mithridates had a brief stronghold there in 88 B.C.E., but it was returned to the Romans, and was eventually sacked by the Goths in 263 CE."[325] With an estimated population between 200,000 and 250,000 people, Ephesus stood as the third largest city in the Roman Empire behind Rome and Alexandria. It was the capital of the Roman province of Asia and the main port of its region. The temple for Artemis in Ephesus was considered as one of the seven wonders of the ancient world. This city was held with considerable importance for both Greek and Roman interests.[326]

As far as the origin and progress of Christianity is considered, Ephesus under Roman captivation played a significant role that scholars like Von Harnack calls it, the third capital of Christianity.[327] Emperor worship and Roman-imposed rules in Ephesus had tremendously influenced the life of Christians as well to the extent of incorporating Roman imperial social and moral codes into Christian ethic. The Roman government tried to bring about external political and economic unity; however, it was difficult to achieve social integration of all the cosmopolitan people lived under Roman imperialism.[328] In this monograph on Ephesians, the post-Pauline author of Ephesians is pre-supposed and therefore, the destination is invariably identified as the Ephesus.

---

325 http://www.novumtestamentum.com/acts/Ephesus/index.html viewed on 22nd October, 2008.

326 http://www.novumtestamentum.com/acts/Ephesus/index.html viewed on 22nd October, 2008.
http://ancienthistory.about.com/od/artarchaeologyarchitect/qt/Ephesus.html, viewed on 22nd October, 2008.

327 Adolf Von Harnack, *Marcion*: Das *Evangelium vom fremden Gott. Eine Monographie zur Geschichte der Grundlegung der Katholischen Kirche*, 2nd ed., edited by Adolf von Harnack and Carl Schmidt, vol. 45 (Leipzig: J. C. Hinrichs'sche Buchhandlung, 1924), cited by Ernst Best, *Essays in Ephesians* (Edinburgh: T & T Clark, 1997), 14.

328 Lincoln, *Ephesians,* lxxxiv.

The letter to the Ephesians retains its ambiguity regarding the purpose of its origin and the historical context even after many years of New Testament research. The absence of a definite purpose of writing this letter has made the popular theory of treating it as a circular letter, a view held mostly by those who propose Pauline authorship.[329]

E. J. Goodspeed in 1933 claimed that the Ephesians was written instigated by the book of Acts (since there is no reference to Paul's writings) as an introduction to the collected letters of Paul by a pupil of his. This author, being familiar with the Pauline letter to Colossians, probably because he himself was from Colossae, wrote the letter to the Ephesians with key terms and themes derived from that of Colossians.[330]

Mitton, despite his disapproval of Goodspeed's theory of treating Ephesians as an introduction to the Pauline corpus, ascertains the possibility of the author's relation with the Pauline letters and the intention of presenting the message of the collected writings of Paul to the communities of new believers.[331]

Andrew T. Lincoln (1990)[332] and R. Schnackenburg (1991)[333] have out rightly rejected the proposal of Goodspeed and Mitton mainly due to the difficulty involved in arguing for a single author's attempt in collecting all the letters of Paul while the possibility of gradual spreading of Pauline writings was realistic. Further Goodspeed's theory fails to address the pseudonymity of the letter.[334]

---

329 John Muddiman, *The Epistle to the Ephesians.* Black's New Testament Commentaries, edited by Morna D. Hooker (London and New York: Continuum, 2001), 12.

330 Edgar J. Goodspeed, *The Meaning of Ephesians* (Chicago: University of Chicago Press, 1933), 3-17, cited by Muddiman, *Ephesians*, 12, Margaret Y. MacDonald, *The Pauline Churches: A Socio-historical Study of Institutionalization in the Pauline and Deutero-Pauline Writings* (Cambridge: Cambridge University Press, 1988), 93.

331 Mitton, Ehesians, 17, cited by MacDonald, *The Pauline Churches,* 93.

332 Lincoln, *Ephesians,* xlvii-lxxiii.

333 Rudolf Schnackenburg, *Ephesians: A Commentary*, translated by Helen Heron (Edinburgh: T & T Clark, 1991), 24-37.

334 Muddiman, *Ephesians,* 13.

N. A. Dahl believes that Ephesians was written by Paul which was originally delivered as a homily for a baptismal occasion, instructing young Gentile Christians of the importance of their faith and baptism. Eph. 1:3ff can be best understood as a blessing on the Gentile believers before undergoing the rite of baptism.[335] G. Schille highlights the presence of a hymn of baptismal thanksgiving and catechesis in the letter attesting to its liturgical origin.[336] J. C. Kirby had done an elaborative study in the same stream of thought and concludes that the baptismal sermon in Ephesians has links with the festival of Pentecost influenced by Jewish liturgical traditions.[337]

A major stream of New Testament scholarship has dealt with the relation of Jewish and Gentile Christians mentioned in the letter of Ephesians (2:11-21). H. Chadwick proposed that this letter was an apologetic literature reiterating the antiquity of the Christian faith by linking church's continuity with the Judaistic roots. His interest was to show the church as universal so that the Christian church could be viewed as "a metaphysical entity encompassing all generations."[338] Ernst Kasemann suspected whether the Gentile Christians despised the Jewish Christian minority because of their majority in number.[339]

K. M. Fischer added an ecclesiastical crisis to the presumed Jewish-Gentile crisis. He argued that the letter responded to "a crisis of authority in the Church caused by the change from Pauline itinerant missionary structures… to the residential hierarchical organization

---

335 Nils Alstrup Dahl, "Gentiles, Christians, and Israelites in the Epistle to the Ephesians," *Harvard Theological Review* 79:1-3 (January/April/July 1986): 38.

336 G. Schille, *Fruhchristliche Hymnen* (Berlin: Evangelische Verlagsanstalt, 1965), cited by Muddiman, *Ephesians*, 14.

337 J. C. Kirby, *Ephesians: Baptism and Pentecost* (London: SPCK, 1968), cited by MacDonald, *The PaulineChurches*, 93.; Muddiman, *Ephesians*, 14.; Kitchen, *Ephesians*, 8.

338 H. Chadwick, "Die Absicht des Epheserbriefes" in ZNW 51 (1960): 145-53, cited by Lincoln, *Ephesians*, lxxx.

339 E. Kasemann, "Ephesians and Acts" in *Studies in Luke-Acts*, edited by L. E. Keck and J. L. Martyn (London: SPCK, 1968), 291, cited by Lincoln, *Ephesians*, lxxx.; MacDonald, *The Pauline Churches*, 94.

that is threatening to supplant them."[340] In his argument, the letter was written during the period when the new Episcopal order was promoted in the Gentile Christian congregations in Asia Minor.

The reference to "the foundation of the apostles and prophets" in 2:20 is a call to reverting to the charismatic structure of Pauline mission.[341] But MacDonald and Lincoln express their fear regarding the supposed crisis on the unity of Jewish and Gentile Christians.[342] It should be safeguarded that such speculation about the hostile attitude of Gentile Christians toward Jewish Christians does not edge out the research on understanding the implied social situation in Eph. 2:11-21.

A concern that emerges here is about the identity of the recipients of the letter. Are they exclusively Gentile Christians in composition? In that case, what is their relation to Jewish Christians? What is the socio-cultural and political necessity that persuaded the author to inculcate Jewish religious and cultural elements in the paraenesis of the letter? This needs urgent attention as to unravel the embedded Jewish nature of the letter. Dahl's comment is significant: the author does not seem to take into account the presence of Jewish Christians among the recipients of the letter. By doing this, despite the author's keen interest in the Jewish origin of the church, the letter fails to "show any concern for the relationship of his audience to contemporary Jews in or outside the church."[343] Therefore, the following section probes into the identity of the explicit reference in the letter to the Greek term, *ta ethne (literally means the nations, which is generally translated as gentiles in English versions).*

In Ephesians, the term, ta ethne (the nations) occurs thrice (2:11, 3:6 and 4:17), however the syntax of the same Greek word appears in 3:1 & 8 as well. The author uses the term ta ethne (the nations), to refer either to non-Jewish Christians or to non-Jews (3:1, 4:7). The phrase, ta ethne is generally translated in English as

340 K. M. Fischer, *Tendenz und Absicht des Epheserbriefs* (Gottingen: Vandenhoeck & Ruprecht, 1973), 21-25, cited by Muddiman, *Ephesians,* 14.

341 Fischer, *Tendenz und Absicht, 79-94,* cited by Lincoln, *Ephesians,* lxxx.

342 MacDonald, *The Pauline Churches,* 94.; Lincoln, *Ephesians,* lxxx.

343 Dahl, *Gentiles, Christians, and Israelites,* 31, cited by Lincoln, *Ephesians,* lxxxiv.

Gentiles, referring to nations other than Israel. Yet, it emphasizes the non-Jewish part of humanity instead of a collective plurality of nations.[344] From pre-Christian periods, ta ethne (the nations) had gained the significance of "nations other than one's own" mainly in contrast to Israel or church.[345] In a non-sociological sense, this word is used to refer to the people those who are not part of the chosen people of Israel.[346] Interestingly, Jews were not the only ones who used ethne to denote foreigners, but Greeks prior to Romans called the aliens to their nation as ethne in contrast to their national identity. The Greeks used it to mention non-Greek peoples in a disparaging sense.[347] So, it may be inferred that the term ethne is used in a derogatory sense.

In Ephesians, there is an overall negative impression about the Gentiles who are neither Jews nor Christians. In 2:1-3, the Gentiles are dead in their trespasses and sins and they remain as the followers of the ruler of the power of the air. They are the children of disobedience (cf. 5:6). And they follow the desires of flesh and senses. Further down in vv.11-13, they are referred to as Gentiles in flesh or by birth and uncircumcised. Here in v.12, an allusion is made to the Gentile Christian's way of life before they believed in Christ that they were aliens from the commonwealth (citizenship) of Israel, strangers to the covenants of promise and having no hope and without God in the world. The phrase, 'ones who are far off' (cf. 2:17) in v.13 is originally derived from Isa. 57:19, however, it is used here in the sense of exclusion in terms of sacred law rather

344 Dahl, *Gentiles, Christians, and Israelites,* 31-33.

345 D. R. de Lacey, "Gentiles," in *Dictionary of Paul and His Letters*, edited by Gerald F. Hawthorne, Ralph P. Martin, and Daniel G. Reid (Downer's Grove, Illinois: InterVarsity Press, 1993/1998), CD-Rom.

346 Bertram, "*Ethnos/Ethnikos,*" in *Theological Dictionary of the New Testament,* Vol. II, edited by Gerhard Kittel, translated and edited by Geoffrey W. Bromiley, 3rd print (Grand Rpaids, Michigan: William B. Eerdmans Publishing Company, 1968), 367.

347 Karl Ludwig Schmidt, "*Ethnos* in the NT," in *Theological Dictionary of the New Testament,* Vol. II, edited by Gerhard Kittel, translated and edited by Geoffrey W. Bromiley, 3rd print (Grand Rapids, Michigan: William B. Eerdmans Publishing Company, 1968), 371.

than geographical distance.[348] So, the Gentiles were far off from the privileges set for the Jews and the Jewish Christians.

Eph. 4: 17-19 mentions the general perception of Jews about Gentiles. The Gentiles live in the futility of their minds; they are darkened in their understanding; they are alienated from the life of God because of their ignorance and hardness of heart; they have lost all sensitivity and have abandoned themselves to licentiousness; and are greedy to practice every kind of impurity. The author of Ephesians also denotes the various characteristics of Gentiles in a subtle manner in 5:3-20. Moral integrity and sensitivity are expected from the recipients of the Ephesian letter in contrast to the behavior of Gentiles.

The letter to the Ephesians does not end with the hostile approach to Gentiles, but deal with the reconciliation of Gentiles with Jews through the salvific act of Jesus Christ. Especially, Eph. 2:14-22 narrates the reconciliatory act of Jesus, which transformed Gentiles from a state of being strangers and aliens to a state of being citizens with the saints and members of the household of God (cf. v. 19). Moreover, this united household of God is built upon the foundation of the apostles and prophets with Christ as the cornerstone (v. 20).

Jesus has abolished the hostility between Jews and Gentiles and created a new humanity beyond the liability of the Law. Because of the power of gospel, the Gentiles have now become fellow heirs, members of the same body, and sharers in the promise in Christ Jesus (Eph. 3:6). Therefore, the overall negative impression about non-believing Gentiles is changed once they believe in Christ and become members of the Church. For the author, this is a great mystery of God (3:9-12).

Interesting enough, there are no anti-Jewish sentiments expressed in this epistle.[349] Further, by the time of this epistle being written by the end of first century CE, the Churches were largely made of Christians of Gentile origin than of Jewish origin. This clearly indicates a social context of Jewish hostility toward Gentiles being replaced by Gentile domination over Jewish Christians in

348 Dahl, *Gentiles, Christians, and Israelites,* 32.

349 Dahl, *Gentiles, Christians, and Israelites,* 37.

the Churches. And by now, the Greek and Roman converts to Christianity would have outnumbered the Jewish Christians. Here the Gentile Christian majority needs not be viewed from a hostile point of view, but unlike the earlier communities of Christians, now the recent generations of Christians may not be aware of the Jewish roots. This view can be supported by the lack of anti-Semitic ideas and the presence of Jewish ideas embedded in the epistle.

The Church at Ephesus: A Colonized Community?

It is quite evident that the emperor worship in Rome and the imperial social codes have tremendously influenced the writing of the letter to the Ephesians as well. The Jews in Ephesus had been forced to absorb and affirm the socio-political hierarchical system that the Roman government had designed for the civil society in general. Over against their religious and moral codes of living, the Jews had to constantly negotiate with the demands of Roman administration, in order to foster a peaceful living.

Now as far as the Jewish Christians were concerned, there were clear indications of heresies creeping into Ephesian church (Eph. 4:17-32; 5:10-20) due to the overarching impact of Roman religions, imperial cult and their social codes of living.[350] The epistle to the Ephesians reflects overtones of imperial ideology as it struggles to keep the pressures from the colonial environment at a check. As far as the author is concerned, God's empire is in the heavenly realms with all the spiritual blessings (1:3), which in fact becomes the starting point for narrating the whole theology against the colonial backdrop. The superior power of God is manifested in raising Jesus from the dead and placing him at His right hand in the heavenly realms (1:20). The members of Ephesian ecclesial community are already seated with Christ in the heavenly realms (2:6). Pheme Perkins makes an interesting comment that the exalted Christ in Eph. 2:11-22, if read against the ideology of the Roman emperor

---

350 C. I. David Joy, *Revelation: A Post-colonial View Point* (Delhi: ISPCK, 2001), 7-10.

cult, resembles the emperor who was exalted through the speeches in favour of him.[351]

The empire of God's spiritual/heavenly realm is now incarnated into the household of God (2:19), where no one remains foreigner or alien but everyone is a fellow citizen with God's people. Interestingly the terms like 'citizen' or 'foreigner' or 'stranger' are all relevant in a political context of an empire.

A study on the ethnic, religious and linguistic groups in the multicultural Rome in first century CE supports that the Jewish and Christian communities were treated as 'foreign' to Roman culture and social life.[352] But, in the epistle to the Ephesians, the empire is replaced by the household, while retaining the other political terms. A household in a Roman society plays a significant role in that the social order is being established beginning from the smallest unit of the society. The concept of the household of God comprising all the members of Ephesian church links to the author's intention of making God's empire very much relevant for the church in a colonial environment.

The household of God is comprised of all those who were treated as aliens and foreigners, who have now become fellow citizens with God's people (Eph. 2: 19). This household is built on the foundation of the apostles and prophets, with Christ himself as the chief cornerstone. So, it is Christ who holds together the whole building of the household of God, making it a holy temple, in which God dwells by his Spirit (2:20-22).

All the members who were saved by the Gospel of Christ have been sealed with the mark of Holy Spirit (1:13). Jennifer G. Bird comments that once they are marked with the Hoy Spirit of promise, they are claimed by God and "are given the assurance that this counter-emperor will be true to the promise of redeeming them and offering them the inheritance of the empire of G(o)d. Instead of the emperor's gospel of salvation, we have the counter-gospel of a

351 Pheme Perkins, *Ephesians* (Abington New Testament Commentaries; Nashville: Abington Press, 1997), 51, cited by Bird, Ephesians, 267.

352 Beryl Rawson, "'The Roman family' in Recent Research: State of the Question" *Biblical Interpretation,* Vol. 11, no. 2 (2003): 131.

different deity, whose salvation is far greater than that offered by the Roman Empire."[353]

Therefore, one can easily identify the sealing of Holy Spirit as a subversive anti-colonial tact. For the seal of a king constantly reminds the subjects about him "as both the maintainer of justice and order and the source of authority; it also indirectly referred to the power of his kingdom, which sustained him in his role."[354] Now, the loyalty of a believing person is changed from the Roman emperor to the God almighty through the gospel of Jesus Christ and by the sealing of the Holy Spirit.

Does the Letter to the Ephesians Project a Counter-Empire?

"In the face of an empire that rules through military and economic control, what is the shape of a community that serves a ruler who brings reconciliation and peace by sacrificial death rather than military might? …How does a Christian community… live its life in empire?"[355] Generally, the letter to the Ephesians narrates a new movement in the sense of a counter-empire to the existing Roman imperial power. This is well manifested in the choice of terms like ecclesia, politeia, alients and strangers, and peace.

MacDonald reiterates that such terminologies highlight the points of contact of the letter with the imperial ideology; it could be of both appropriation and rejection. Unless the Ephesian church is a colonized community in itself, the thrust of the letter will not make sense to the readers.[356] It also should be noted that in the process of creating a counter-empire, the Ephesian church tends to become imperial by mimicking the strategies of the imperial power. The author's inclination to use Greco-Roman terminologies and concepts like Household, ecclesia, powers, authorities and the imagery of army/soldier in the letter to the Ephesians attests to this.

---

353 Bird, *Ephesians,* 269.

354 Irene J. Winter cited by Bird, *Ephesians,* 269.

355 Brian J. Walsh and Sylvia C. Keesmaat, *Colossians Remixed. Subverting the Empire* (Downers Grove, Illinois: InterVarsity Press, 2004), 61.

356 Margaret MacDonald, "The Politics of Identity in Ephesians," in *Journal for the Study of the New Testament* , Vol. 26 (2004): 422.

In general, colonial discourses were prominent during the colonial period as a means of propagation of knowledge, producing texts that were invariably "colonialist" in their endorsement and thus demanding conformity to the existing dominant imperial ideologies. These texts represented the social existence of colonial relations, which were shaped by dominant imperial notions of hierarchy, competency and absolute power and had the supreme target of consolidating the unity of the empire/imperialism.

The letter to the Ephesians is not different as it exhibits a tendency to write back to the empire adopting a colonial language and culture while at the same time intending to resist from a stand point of Christian ethical values. While there is cultural appropriation of colonial values in their socio-religious and political life, there are also elements of resistance to Roman imperial agenda. Therefore, the outcome is not just an exact imitation of colonial ideologies; instead there is a combination of acquiescence and resistance in relation to imperial agenda.

The Ephesian text itself is a weaving-together of different stands, which on the one side, yields to the pressing pressures from around the Roman socio-political powers, while on the other side attempts to deconstruct the reliance on a framework of hierarchical domination prevalent in the Roman colonial era. As such, colonial texts cannot be seen to express the dominant ideology alone because they are a tapestry of heterogeneous cultures and discourses. This is applicable for the letter to the Ephesians, written in a socio-political context of Roman imperialism.

The faith community portrayed in the letter to the Ephesians seems to project a " third space of enunciation,"[357] in which the hybridization of multi-cultures (Jewish, Greco-Roman and Christian) takes place and provides a trans-cultural space where the colonial domination has been continually challenged. This Christian document exhibits narrative ambivalence by which the reader encounters anti-imperial strategies of a fine blend of hybridity and colonial mimicry.

---

357 Bill Ashcroft, Gareth Griffiths and Helen Tiffin, *Key Concepts in Post-Colonial Studies* (London and New York: Routledge, 2004), 118.

The Origin and Background of Ephesian Household Codes

Christian household codes in general and Ephesian household codes in particular exhibit possibilities of a hybrid formulation of the prevalent household duties practiced from the time of Aristotle till Roman captivation. The imperial ideology of Roman government especially from the time of Augustus had implemented competition, hierarchy and patriarchy in the households as part of the larger Roman society.[358] It is possible that the New Testament authors have initiated the household pattern as we find it in the post-Pauline letters, drawing on a host of ethical material inherited both from Jewish heritage and possibly from the wider Greco-Roman milieu.[359]

Since the Ephesian letter indicates the presence of a majority of Gentile Christians, it would not have been difficult for them to adapt the Roman ethical codes in their Christian living. Further, the relation between the household codes and the household character of the Christian community in which and for which they are employed highlights the adaptive nature of the early Christian movement.[360] Since the household was viewed as the basic component of the Roman State, it was expected of all to manage household properly. Therefore, household management was a crucial socio-political concern and "any upsetting of the traditional hierarchical order of the household could be considered a potential threat to the order of society as a whole."[361] It would be appropriate at this juncture to analyze how *Pax Romana* and *Paterfamilias* functioned in the Roman society to understand the impact of Roman imperial ideology on Ephesian household codes.

Pax Romana

The significant aspect of God's household is that the enmity between Jews and Gentiles has been removed and are united as one body through the salvific act of Christ. Jesus Christ is projected as their 'peace,' which is a very important term as far as imperial rule is

---

358 Osiek and Balch, *Families in the New Testament World,* 119.

359 Witherington, *Women in the Earliest Churches,* 47.

360 Elliott, *A Home for the Homeless,* 211.

361 Lincoln, *Ephesians,* 358.

concerned. The *Pax Romana* instituted by Roman empire legitimized continued military oppression on the basis of their claim to establish cosmic peace, fertility and prosperity.

It is generally the emperor who brings about peace by imposing unity and order of all his subjects. Now, Christ as the ruler of all, becomess the peace of all those who are in enmity and assures them of reconciliation. The victory of the Roman emperor and Christ ensures peace as only a powerful can establish peace amidst adverse situations. Against this stream of thought, Bird's opinion is interesting to observe,

> Those who, as members of the cosmic *ekklesia*, presume to be memebrs of this new empire may be reassured by the dominance and rule of Christ, but it must be a fearsome thing for those 'outside'. The image constructed of those who continue to live in disobedience and ignorance (4. 17-22; 5. 5-8, 11-12) does not encourage including them but rather distancing oneself and one's group from others. So, the demonizing of the 'other' continues in this new empire – an act of intimidation at the very least – and sets the stage for violent military attacks once this *ekklesia* is also embraced by the emperor of this world.[362]

Bird's fear is valid as her opinion is historically correct. This is further re-iterated by Bird again:

> In Christ the law is removed, allowing for a new peace, one that is established much in the same way as the Pax Romana *(sic)* is given or established throughout the Roman Empire. In both cases, the act of pronouncing that peace has been won through victory which both makes the peace a reality and imposes the peace upon all. In both cases the 'peace' is won in a realm far removed from the lives of common people, making it an elusive abstraction that can be asserted or denied by those in power. All people are to bow before the Father (earthly and heavenly), from whom all peoples,

362 Bird, *Ephesians,* 272.

> families or nations receive their name (3:15) and through whom they are all unified. It is not that a new kind of order has been established, just a new version of the same.[363]

However, the peace assured by Christ for the Ephesian Christian community is not just a new version of the same old Roman imperial establishing of peace by military force, but an effort to establish reconciliation between Jews and Gentiles through the salvific death of a victim of the Roman imperial rule. Though the promise of this peace from Christ is ensured for the whole cosmos, it is never imposed upon anyone against their freedom of choice.

As perkins says, "despite their minority status in the world of first - century CE Asia Minor, Christians found themselves the centre of God's cosmic design because they belonged to the risen Lord who is exalted over all of the heavenly powers."[364] However, the peace of Christ's peace does not seem to involve terror, intimidation and military action unlike Roman rule, which would attack those who resist Roman rule and forcefully bring them to Roman regime of peace.[365]

The armour imagery in Eph. 6:11-18 indicates a spiritual warfare against the rulers, authorities, powers of darkness and spiritual forces in the heavenly realms; yet it never takes a violent mode of retaliation. So, what we see in the letter to the Ephesians is that it portrays socio-cultural and political mimicry of Roman imperialism resulting in a hybrid interweaving of heterogeneous cultures such as Jewish, Greco-Roman and Christian.

Paterfamilias: Roman Patriarchal Head

From the time of Augustus (as earliest as 9 CE), Roman emperors claimed universal power as '*pater patriae*' (father of the fatherland). Such a promise of "one big happy Roman family" on the approval of paternalism of emperors played a major role in constructing the colonial power. "Moreover, the established notion of an emperor as

363 Bird, *Ephesians,* 271.

364 Pheme Perkins, *Ephesians* (Abingdon New Testament Commentaries; Nashville: Abingdon Press, 1997), 44-45, cited by Bird, *Ephesians,* 270.

365 MacDonald, *The Politics of Identity in Ephesians,* 439.

father could be used to secure and insure the perpetual memory of a benevolent ruler (however despotic), the filial loyalty and subservience of subjects (however exploited), and even the reluctant obedience of imperial legislation where it was declared that the formula "patriotism=paternity" applied to emperor and empire alike."[366]

In other words, in the structure of the *paterfamilias* the emperor is the father supreme and the whole structure of society serves to secure his rule and authority.[367] This besets the background of household ideology being exploited to serve political cause in Roman empire.[368]

A household in a Roman society is defined by three main aspects: a hierarchical order-obedience structure, economic dependency, and marriage. The *paterfamilias* exercised a large measure of dominance over the other members of the family who were economically dependent on him. This list of subjugates included children, even adult sons, slaves, freed persons, clients and so on. The spouses of all the male members were also under the authority of the *paterfamilias.*[369] "Maintaining the system of the Roman empire, and of the subsystems within it, was made possible by hierarchical and patriarchal structures of domination on all levels of relationships, from the political institutions to the family."[370]

However, the wife of the *paterfamilias* exercised certain amount of freedom in her husband's household as she still belonged legally

---

366 Elliott, *Home for the Homeless,* 178

367 Walsh and Keesmaat, *Colossians Remixed,* 59.

368 The structured household code has its origin in Aristotle. Such household codes were historically reinforced by emperor Augustus as part of the "*pater patriae*" ideology. The classical Greek philosophers like Plato and Aristotle propose that "the man is intended by nature to rule as husband, father, and master, and that not to adhere to this proper hierarchy is detrimental not only to the household but also to the life of the state… The proper household management was generally regarded as a matter of crucial social and political concern and that any upsetting of the traditional hierarchical order of the household could be considered a potential threat to the order of society as a whole. See Lincoln, Ephesians, CD-Rom.

369 Sarah J. Tanzer, "Ephesians," in *Searching the Scriptures Volume Two: A Feminist Commentary* (London, Britain: SCM Press Limited, 1995), 328.

370 Sugirtharajah, *Postcolonial Biblical Interpretation,* 144.

to her father's household.[371] But this only placed her under the authority of her father, thus retaining her freedom still under the control of *paterfamilias*. It is interesting to highlight the comment made by Brian J. walsh and Sylvia C. Keesmaat in this context:

> Empires always guarantee the status quo of privilege and oppression through a centralization of power. In the Roman empire the *paterfamilias* – the patriarchal structure of marital, familial and economic relationships – was considered the empire's building block. In this "father-directed" hierarchy, power was centralized and the empire was socially encoded. The economic importance of women, children and slaves was carefully guarded in Roman law: the bulk of rulings regarding the guardianship of women and the various laws upholding the power fathers had over their sons was rooted in the practical necessity of safeguarding the family wealth.[372]

In response to Walsh and Keesmaat, it becomes conspicuous that the Ephesian household code does not have reference to finances. The absence of the reference to the economic activity of women in first century households clearly indicates that the Ephesian household code is a strategic one in that the economic productivity of women are subdued under the paternal authority. "The economic policies of Rome were designed to ensure that the lands they controlled would have no resources for resistance to the empire."[373] It is very tragic that the role of women and slaves in supporting the empire with economic resources is most subject to directives of control. Bird comments that "(t)he unspoken economic aspect... then, becomes part of the grander picture of imperial ideology that is co-opted by Ephesians and thus passed along to the churches thereafter."[374] In this way, the Ephesian household seems to mimic the Roman laws

---

371 Peter Lampe, "'Family' in Church and Society of New Testament Times," in *Affirmation* 5 (1992): 1-2, 15.

372 Walsh and Keesmaat, *Colossians Remixed,* 58.

373 Walsh and Keesmaat, *Colossians Remixed,* 60.

374 Bird, *Ephesians,*, 274.

that were formulated to restrict the economic importance of women, children and slaves and to safeguard family wealth within their own households.

It looks agreeable in this way to draw a Greco-Roman origin of the household codes including that of the letter to the Ephesians. But the question that arises at this point is that how the presence of Jewish cultural and religious elements in the Ephesian household codes can be understood against the backdrop of Greco-Roman household codes. This question deserves an in-depth study of the Jewish traditional material in the Ephesian household codes especially in connection to wife-husband relationship.

The Literary Relationship between Household Codes of the Colossians and the Ephesians

The syntax, grammar, style, language and theology of both the letters to Colossians and Ephesians reveal their pseudonymous nature. These two letters indicate that the author is, seemingly, trying to make the Pauline traditions relevant to his/her own audience. By now, there is a scholarly consensus that there is heavy dependence of Ephesians on Colossians. Margaret Y. MacDonald comments that "[t]he fact that the author of Ephesians could adopt so many ideas from Colossians suggests affinities between the communities underlying the writings. The communities may reflect similar stages of development."[375] For her, these two letters are basically meant to stabilize the community life of the late first century Christians.[376] She substantiates this point by highlighting the household codes in both Colossians and Ephesians. "The household code is the product of the institutionalization of norms determining what kind of behaviour is fitting for life in Christ."[377]

The Colossian *haustafel* presents the most primitive form of the material on household tables. Three pairs of relations, such as wives-

375 Margaret Y. MacDonald, *The Pauline Churches: A Socio-historical Study of Institutionalization in the Pauline and Deutero-Pauline Writings* (Cambridge: Cambridge University Press, 1988), 87.

376 MacDonald, *The Pauline, Churches,* 97.

377 MacDonald, *The Pauline Churches,* 105.

husbands, children-fathers and slaves-masters, are dealt with in Col. 3:18-4:1. These groups are arranged in a descending order from the closest to the least close relations.[378] Like in Ephesian *haustafel*, here in Colossians, it is the same person, i.e., the *paterfamilias*, who is referred to as the husband, father and master.

The household codes in Colossians, if taken out of the pericope, remain as a self-contained unit. Further, Col. 3:17 and 4:2 show the continuity, as they both refer to prayer. The Colossian household code (3:18-4:1) is noted for its brevity and emphasis on subordination and order, as well as mutual responsibility in the Lord.[379] It is evident from the fact that wives have to subject to their husbands (3:18); children have to obey their parents (3:20) and slaves to their masters (3:22). However, the exhortations to the dominant members of the households indicate that they were asked to moderate their control over their subordinates. The husbands are to love their wives in the light of the earlier imperative, "clothe yourselves with love" (Col. 3:14) and not to treat them harshly. In a similar manner, both fathers and masters are instilled with a non-abusive exercise of authority, as fathers should not provoke their children and masters should treat their slaves justly and fairly (3:21, 4:1). It seems to be that the household exhortations subvert the uncontrolled authority of *paterfamilias* by setting ethical Christian standards of love, compassion and humility.[380]

The Ephesian household codes form a longer pericope[381] than that of the Colossians with some 70 words same as in the latter one. The Ephesian *haustafel* is an expanded version of the Colossian one, including the exhortations on slaves-masters relation. Interestingly, the relation between wife-husband pair is treated disproportionately to the extent of sparing 13 verses (5:21-33) in comparison to the rest of the codes. "In Ephesians, Christ is drawn upon as a paradigm for

378 Ben Witherington III, *Women in the Earliest Churches,* 48.

379 MacDonald, *The Pauline Churches,* 111.

380 Suzanne watts Henderson, "Taking Liberties with the Text: The Colossian Household Code as Hermeneutical Paradigm" in *Interpretation,* October 2006, p. 425.

381 324 words in the haustafel in Ephesians in contrast to 117 in Colossians (as per the standard Greek Text).

husbands (5.25, 29) and for masters (6.9), whereas this was at most implicit in the Colossians' usage of"[382] 'in the Lord'. Further, there is material drawn from the Hebrew Scriptures in Ephesian *haustafel* (5:28, 29, 31). J. Paul Sampley, in his elaborate study on the traditional material used in Eph. 5:21-33, underscores that even though there are verbal similarities, the household codes in both Colossians and Ephesians show explicit independent development.[383]

Ephesians, Empire, and Egalitarianism

The fact that the author views the Church as household of God (2:19) is significant for the present study on household codes in Ephesians. As Ephesus and the surrounding places in the western Asia Minor were strongholds of Roman Empire in the second half of the first century CE and the Churches were predominantly comprised of Gentile Christians, it may be presumed that the ethical living of Christians were heavily influenced by the Roman imperial ideology. Roman laws, especially family laws were applicable to all Roman citizens anywhere in the Empire including the Greek speaking Jewish and Gentile Christians.[384] This raises questions regarding how the Christian Church maintained its identity amidst growing influences of the socio-political environment.

Since the letter to the Ephesians deals primarily with the 'household of God' (2:19), can it be proposed that the household codes are an effort to define the new identity of Church that is predominantly comprised of Gentile Christians amidst Roman political pressures? Gender plays a determining role in establishing the domination-subjugation order of the husband-wife relation in the Ephesian household codes. Can such male-privileged marital norms and relationship promote the unity of the household of God? While the Jew-Gentile harmony is envisioned in the epistle, it seems to be that the man-woman (apart from master-slave and parents-children pairs) harmony is sidelined in the ethical codes.

382 Ben Witherington, *Women in the Earliest Churches*, 54.

383 Sampley, *And the Two Shall Become One Flesh*, 23-27.

384 Carolyn Osiek, "The Family in Early Christianity: 'Family Values' Revisited," *The Catholic Bible Quarterly*, 58/1 (January, 1996): 10.

Why does the author fail to question the patriarchal customs of the then prevalent Greco-Roman household codes? Why does the author justify christologically the socio-cultural and political gender norms assigned to wives and husbands? What is the role of incorporating Jewish and Christian elements in the traditional Greco-Roman household ethical teachings? Does the reference to Gen. 2:24 in Eph. 5:31 propose equality or mutual submission between wives and husbands?

The pericope of Eph. 5:21-33 begins with an exhortation to the members of Ephesian church to submit to one another in the fear of Christ (5:21). The Greek word, *hupotasso* (to submit) is "a hierarchical term which stresses the relation to superiors,"[385] for instance, the submission of soldiers in an army to those of superior rank. This word, which belonged to the sphere of worldly order of state and politics, is used in Ephesians with a similar understanding of bringing order in the household.[386] This word connotes "to submit to the orders or directives of someone—'to obey, to submit to, obedience, submission'" or more forcefully, "to bring something under the firm control of someone—'to subject to, to bring under control.'"[387] Josephus uses *hupotasso* in the active voice to 'place under', 'subordinate', and in the middle voice to 'order oneself under' a leader (Jewish War 2:566, 578; 5:309). Helton affirms the notion of domination as he concedes that this verb presupposes hierarchical structure in which some people are in authority over others.[388] These references show that the verb *hupotasso* carries an overtone of authority and subjection or submission to it.[389]

---

385 Delling, "uJpotavssw," in *The Theological Dictionary of New Testament, Vol. VIII*, edited by Gerhard Friedrich (Grand Rapids: William B. Eerdmans Publishing Co., 1972), 41.

386 Delling, uJpotavssw, 45., Peter T. O' Brien, *The Letter to the Ephesians* (Leicester, Apollos, 1999), 399.

387 Johannes P. Louw and Eugene A. Nida, eds., *Greek-English Lexicon of the New Testament Based on Semantic Domains,* 2nd ed. (New York: United Bible Society, 1989), 92.

388 Stanley N. Helton, "Ephesians 5:21: A Longer Translation Note," *Restoration Quarterly, vol. 48, no.1* (2005): 37.

389 O'brien, Ephesians, 399.

While the author uses *hupotasso* to denote the submission of wives, it is the verb, *hupakouo*, (to obey) used for children (Eph. 6:1) and slaves (6:5). Mostly, the word *hupakouo* (to obey) is used in the Hellenistic Jewish and Greco-Roman contexts to refer to the submission of wives to their husbands. Therefore some scholars are of the opinion that *hupotasso* is uniquely used by the Christian author/ the community to place wives on equal basis with husbands.[390] Harold Hoehner raises three objections to such distinctions between the two verbs, *hupotasso* (to submit) and *hupakouo* (to obey). Firstly, he shows the historical use of *hupotasso* to denote a subordinate role of a person to another. Secondly, *hupotasso* is used for the slaves in the household codes in other writings of the New Testament (Titus 2:9, 1 Pet 2:18). In 1 Pet. 3:5-6, when Peter deals with wives in households, he uses *hupotasso* and *hupatouo* interchangeably. Thirdly and finally, Hoehner thinks that one who is subject to another is not qualitatively inferior.[391] Yet, *hupotasso* is a term strictly used for order, presuming a hierarchical social structure and reserving the first place for the man.[392]

Categorically, *hupotassomenoi* in this introductory verse in the pericope is understood in two ways, either as a participle dependent on the previous finite verb 'be filled' in v. 18 or as a participle in a paraenentic pericope with an imperative function (without dependence on any finite verb).[393] Andrew T. Lincoln suggests that this verse can be best understood as "transitional, completing the series of participles which are dependent on the verb 'be filled,' from v. 18, while itself providing the verbal form on which the first injunction in the following household code is dependent."[394] The filling of the believers with Holy Spirit is linked with mutual submission of believers. It may indicate an obliging behaviour to one another. Drawing cue from Eph. 4:2, Rudolf Schnackenburg suggests that the subordination or submission in v. 21 denotes "an embracing

390 Hoehner, *Ephesians,* 734.

391 Hoehner, *Ephesians,* 734-5.

392 Rudolf Schnackenburg, *The Epistle to the Ephesians: A Commentary,* translated by Helen Heron (Edinburgh: T & T Clark, 1991), 246.

393 Sampley, *And the Two Shall Become One Flesh,* 114.

394 Lincoln, *Ephesians,* CD-Rom.

expression for the behaviour of the Christians in community," or in other words, a "specificum of the early Christian Haustafel."[395] The call to mutual submission indicates readiness to renounce one's own will for the sake of others, and to give precedence to others.[396] Hence, the notion of subordination in this verse cannot be treated as an external legal demand, but an ethical exhortation to characterize their Christian living.

Following a variant reading, Wayne Walden suggests that *allelon* accompanied by the prepositions *eis, en, meta,* and *pros* could be translated "among yourselves/themselves" (cf. John 6:43, 52). This rendering is technically reflexive instead of reciprocal. According to him, the pronoun *allelon* basically denotes random or distributive activity among a group.[397] He translates v. 21 as "Out of reverence for Christ, be in subordination among yourselves. Therefore, in his opinion, this verse teaches "Obey whom you are supposed to," a general principle with examples following: wives (5:22-24), children (6:1), servants (6:5).[398] In a countering article to Walden, Stanley N. Helton comments that the reciprocal pronoun *allelon* (one another) in all the occurrences in Ephesians (4: 2, 25, 32 and 5:21) indicates reciprocity or mutuality. Helton analyses the semantics, syntax, literary structure, and the rhetoric intention of the passage to negate Walden's attempt to remove reciprocity/mutuality from the passage. For him, the level of reciprocity does not depend on the pronoun, but on the semantic limits of the verb and the prepositions.[399] Helton thus acknowledges the hierarchical thrust of the verb, *hupotasso.*

In other parts of the New Testament, submission is required only from women (1 Cor 14:34; Col 3:18; 1 Tim 2:11; Titus 2:5), children (1 Tim 3:4), and slaves (Titus 2:9, 1 Pet 2:18). It is required of believers elsewhere to the state as well (Rom 13:1, 5; Titus 3:1)

---

395 Schnackenburg, *Ephesians,* 245.

396 Lincoln, *Ephesians,* CD-Rom. See also Delling, *hupotasso,* 45.

397 Wayne warden, "Ephesians 5:21 – A translation Note," *Restoration Quarterly Vol. 45/no. 4* (2003): 254.

398 Walden, *Ephesians 5:21,* 254.; and idem, "Translating Ephesians 5:21," in *Restoration Quarterly,* Vol. 47, no. 3 (2005): 179-82.

399 Stanley N. Helton, "Ephesians 5:21: A Longer Translation Note," *Restoration Quarterly, Vol. 48, no.1* (2005): 34.

the church to her leaders (1 Pet 5:5; 1 Cor 16:16), the believer to God (Heb 12:9; Jas 4:7), Jesus' relationship to his earthly parents (Luke 2:51), demons to the disciples of the limited commission (Luke 10:17, 20) and even Christ's ultimate submission to the Father (1 Cor 15:28).[400] Helton bases his argument for mutual submission neither on the phrase, reciprocal pronoun of 'one another' nor on the verb, 'to submit',

> but in the *actual content* of Paul's argument developed under each paired relationship. Paul states, consistent with his culture, that wives should be subject to their husband and grounds this in an analogy of the church's submission to Christ. However in dealing with the obligations of husbands to wives, Paul *subverts* the notion of submission.[401]

From the various arguments of scholars in support of mutual submission in v. 21, it seems to be that the author clearly sets out the statement on mutual submission before the narration of household codes where submission to controlling authority is involved. Sampley comments on the same line that "Eph. 5:21 is to be understood not only as a specific injunction to be followed by all Christians but it is also a general introduction to the entire *Haustafel* form and therefore a rubric under which all of 5:22-6:9 is to be interpreted."[402]

The motivating force for mutual submission is drawn from the fear of Christ. The Hebrew Scriptures attest to the fear of the Lord as "the appropriate attitude of a creature to the Creator, producing obedience to his will."[403] The concept of 'fear of the Lord' (interchangeably with fear of Christ and fear of God) has strong allusions to Jewish concept of God as found in the Hebrew Scriptures.[404] The fear of the Lord is the fitting reaction to the

---

400 Schnackenburg, Ephesians, 244, n. 6., Lincoln, Ephesians, CD-Rom., Helton, *Ephesians 5:21: A Longer Translation Note*, 37.

401 Helton, *Ephesians 5:21: A Longer Translation Note,* 37-38.

402 Sampley, *Two Shall Become One Flesh,* 117.

403 Balz, *fovbo"*, in *Theological Dictionary of New Testament, Vol IX,* ed. Gerhard Friedrich (Grand Rapids: William B. Eerdmans Publsihing Co., 1974), 217-8.

404 Sampley, *Two Shall Become One Flesh,* 119.

awesome works of God. The same concept recurs in the Laws (Lev. 19:14, 32; Deut. 13:11, 17:13) and in the general piety of Israelites (Ps. 103:11, 13, 17; Prov. 1:7, 23:17).[405]

The household code in Col 3:22 has reference to "fearing the Lord" as a motivation for slaves, however, here the emphasis is laid on all. In cases of human relations, fear involves observance of the appropriate authority structures.[406] "Fear can denote the obedience demanded by the superior authority of masters or husbands as lords."[407] "In Paul's writings "fear of the Lord" or "fear of Christ" is virtually interchangeable with "fear of God." 2 Cor 5:11 sounds an eschatological note, "knowing the fear of the Lord, we persuade people," while 2 Cor 7:1 exhorts that holiness should be made perfect in the fear of God (cf: also Phil 2:12)."[408] The concept of fear in Phil. 2:12 bases on Paul's admonition to consider others better than oneself out of humility. Against this backdrop, the mutual submission is directly related to their attitude of fear of Christ. The issue at hand is that in the specific relationships within marriage, wives are particularly exhorted to fear Christ and husbands (cf. 5: 33).

Such a portrayal of the concept of fear in a supposedly love-relationship calls our attention to the prevailing Roman imperial ideology which demands all the Roman subjects to fear the emperors. Obviously, fear and control exist simultaneously. Jennifer G. Bird comments that "(f)earing the power of the emperor is one thing. (Re)importing such fear in the religious realm is simply ascribing the same dominant, and thus oppressive, position to the deity that the emperor has with the people."[409] It becomes all the more a dominant and oppressive concept when it is repeated in v. 33 as the rightful norm for a wife to fear her husband. Such a mimicking of imperial

---

405 O'Brien, *Ephesians,* 404.

406 Fear of citizens toward the State (cf. Rom 13:3,4,7), children to parents (*Barnabas* 19.5, *Didache* 4.9), slaves to masters (Eph. 6:5; 1 Pet 2:18; Did 4.11), or, as here, wives to husbands (cf. also 1 Pet 3:2).

407 Balz, *fovbo"*, 7-8.

408 Lincoln, *Ephesians,* CD-Rom.

409 Jennifer G. Bird, "The Letter to the Ephesians," in *A Postcolonial Commentary on the New Testament Writings,* edited by Fernando F. Segovia and R. S. Sugirtharajah (London: T & T Clark, 2007), 274.

ideology in the Christian household can only create havoc as far as the woman-man relationship is concerned.

Since Eph. 5:21 is an important verse deciding the theological thrust of the whole pericope dealing with the relationship between husbands and wives (5:21-33), it is necessary at this point to answer two questions before pursuing further. First, how does the phrase 'submit to one another' relate to the household codes assigned to wives and husbands in the following verses? If 'submit to one another' deals with the mutual submission, how will one understand the seemingly hierarchical relationship alluded in the wife-husband relation in vv. 21-33? There are mainly two streams of scholarship in this regard.

On the one hand, scholars are of the opinion that the whole pericope rests on an ethical perspective of mutual submission by all spirit-filled Christians in the household of God. So in all the relationships in a household, this general principle of mutual submission will nullify hierarchical relationships.[410] On the other hand, an alternate interpretation suggests that a general submission expected of spirit-filled Christians in v. 21 is different from particular ways in which Christians have to submit to various authorities.[411] It is difficult to endorse either one at this initial stage of reading the passage, however, this difficult question remains as to whether Eph. 5:21-33 deals with mutual submission of husbands and wives to one another or the submission of wives to the authority of their husbands.

The three verses of Eph. 5:22-24 deal with the submission of wives to their husbands. An imagery of Church-Christ relationship is highlighted to rationalize the subordinate position of wives to their husbands. The notion of 'head' or 'headship' is introduced here. Just like the Church is subordinate to the headship of Christ, wives have to subject themselves to the authority of their husbands. The structure of this section can be understood as: a household norm assigned to wives (22a) with a short comparative statement, 'as to the

410 Keener, *Paul, Women and Wives,* 168-72.

411 Andrew Lincoln and Peter O'Brien are of this opinion. O'Brien, *Ephesians,* 401.

Lord' (22b), a rationale for wives' household norm (23a), an analogy of Church-Christ relation (23b) with an additional phrase, 'he (is) savior of the body' (23c), a statement about Church-Christ analogy (24a) and finally a household norm to wives (24b).[412]

Eph. 5:21-33 starts with an exhortation to all 'saints' and 'faithful' (cf. Eph. 1:1) to submit to one another in the fear of Christ (5:21). This is followed by the exhortation to wives to submit to their husbands as to the Lord (5:22) and in everything as the Church submits to the Lord (5:24). Originally, Eph. 5:22 does not contain the verb, 'to submit to' (*hupotasso*), but it is carried over from the participle form in v. 21. Yet, the mood of the verb is understood as more of imperative, especially when it is translated into English. Similarly, in v. 24b the verb *hupotasso* is understood as implemented for wives from v. 24a.

Interestingly, the initial address to wives in the plural form is changed to singular in the comparative phrase, 'as to the Lord'. It may be understood as referring to husbands as lords, but the following verses show that this is a clear reference to Christ. Moreover the plural form of *kurios* is avoided. The shift from the initial plural address to singular till v. 24b highlights the author's concern for relating individual woman and man with Church and Christ.[413] The comparative statement 'as to the Lord' (22b) forms a link to the command to slaves in Eph. 6:5, where a reference to a similar phrase "as to Christ" is found. Does it indicate that wives and slaves are placed in a similar inferior position in a household? Scholars may immediately come to the rescue of the author of Ephesians to state that slaves and children are exhorted to obey rather than to submit (6:1 & 5).

Schnackenburg comments that subordination is an inclusive concept, which, by restricting to the members of Ephesian Church and to wives, cannot denote total subjugation in its strict sense.[414] Nevertheless, the submission meant for wives is toward their husbands and Christ, which certainly has implicit tones for subordination to

412 Sampley, *Two Shall Become One Flesh*, 122.

413 Sampley, *Two Shall Become One Flesh*, 122.

414 Schnackenburg, *Ephesians*, 245.

a higher authority. As it is related to the subordination of church to Christ, as in Hoehner's words, submission to the husband becomes a by-product of her submission to Christ.[415]

Since the word, submission or subordination, can make considerably different meanings according to the person in a household to whom it is applied to, it certainly highlights a hierarchical structure within a family, where the man of the house decides for others. It is relevant to accord to the opinion of Schnackenburg once again that even though the household norms deal with a social order with responsibilities, more of a moral code than a legal one, "behind it lies a conception of society which reserves the first place for the man."[416]

Elisabeth Schussler Fiorenza would identify the comparative statement 'as to the Lord' (22b) as a *kyriarchal* one attesting to the master or the Lord. Such texts, according to her, reveal the interlocking structures of domination controlled predominantly by elite masters of huge households.[417] The power structures that control women or wives in Ephesians revolve around the power epitome of Lord or *kurios*.

Interesting enough, v. 23 highlights the correlation between two masculine words, *aner* (husband) and *Christos* (Christ), and two feminine words, *gunaikos* (wife) and *ekklesia* (church). The use of a causal clause *hoti* at the beginning of the verse, underscores the reason for wife's submission to her husband. Just like Christ is the head of the church, so is the man of his wife. Sampley's comment in this regard is remarkable:

> While v. 23 a provides a basis upon which one can justify the demand placed upon women by the haustafel injunction to them, it also provides the occasion for the author of Ephesians to move, by means of the correlative conjunction

---

415 Hoehner, *Ephesians,* 738.

416 Schnackenburg, *Ephesians,* 246.

417 Elisabeth Schussler Fiorenza, *But She Said: Feminist Practices of Biblical Interpretation* (Boston: Beacon, 1992), 8, 117.

ώς and the emphatic καί to a similar statement about Christ's headship of the church.[418]

In 1 Cor. 11:3, Paul uses the same expression that husband is the head of his wife. In Greek understanding, *kephale* (generally translated as 'head') has many figurative meanings like 'origin', 'starting point', and 'completion'.[419] The word *kephale* appears twice in v. 23, in both cases, referring to the authority of the masculine noun over the feminine one. *Kephale* is used in connection with the husband and wife relationship only in 1 Cor. 11:3 and Eph. 5:23.[420] The reference of Christ as the head of the church appears earlier in Eph. 1:22-23, where Christ is made as the head of his body, the church. Further in Eph. 4:16-17, the same idea is repeated. This imagery "reinforces the picture of the absolute authority conveyed to Christ over all things, including the church."[421]

However, Hoehner is of the opinion that such a rationale for women's submission due to the headship of husband is contrary to the family structure of the then Roman society. He explains,

> ...when a woman married in the early Roman Republic it involved manus, the husband's authority over his wife just like patria postestas. However, in the later Republic and in the early Roman Empire (Paul's day), there was trend toward the bride entering sine manus, that is, the father, not the husband, had authority over her as long as she lived. Therefore, she was independent from and not legally subject to her husband, she could seek divorce from him in

418 Sampley, *Two Shall Become One Flesh,* 123.

419 Pauline Chakkalakal, "Must Women cover their Heads?" in *Envisioning a New Heaven and New Earth,* edited by Lalrinawmi Ralte and others (Delhi: SPCK, 1998), 184., Hoehner, 739.

420 Chakkalakal, *Must Women cover their Heads?,* 184. In other passages, kefalh refers to the head of a human being. The body is spoken of as growing from the head (Eph. 4:16, Col. 2:19). In Col.2:9-10, Christ is the head of every ruler and authority.

421 Sampley, *Two Shall Become One Flesh,* 124.

conjunction with his father, and, in fact, the father could even initiate a divorce.[422]

How can this be understood? Is it a Christian subversion of Roman household codes which subject women to both fathers and husbands? In any case, the basic patriarchal system goes unchecked.

Eph. 5:23 presents the metaphor of head to underline the authority of Christ and husbands. It forms a parenthetical statement, in Sampley's words, when headship of man over his wife is placed parallel to the headship of Christ over the church. However, a strong contrast is inserted with the emphatic pronoun, autos (he) in v. 23c (he (is) savior of the body), by which the author makes clear that "there is no power or authority co-extensive with that of Christ."[423]

Eph. 5:23c, (he (is) savior of the body), is an additional clause found only here in the New Testament. Scholars like Schlier and Fischer find some allusion to the Gnostic concept of the redeemer myth, "where the first man (Urmensch) fell, saved himself, and became both the redeemer/savior and head of the entire universe which is his body."[424] But this explanation does not fit in the literary context. Probably, the reference to Christ as the head of the church has immediately been connected to the concept of body as well.

Earlier, in Eph. 1:22 and 4:15, the church, over which Christ exercises authority, is treated as his body. It is Christ, the head, from whom the whole body has been grown. Hoehner contends the idea of connecting this clause to both Christ and husbands:[425] first, the personal pronoun, 'he' is in apposition to 'Christ' and can refer only to the one precedes immediately to it. Second, even though husbands have to love their wives as their own bodies as in v. 28 and they become one flesh (v. 31), there is no direct reference to wife as the body of husband. Third, a spouse can only be an instrument in bringing salvation to the other and not the saviour by himself

422 Hoehner, *Ephesians,* 741.

423 Sampley, *Two Shall Become One Flesh,* 125.

424 Heinrich Schlier, *Der Brief an die Epheser* (Dusseldorf: Patmos, 1971), 254-255, and Fischer, *Tenenz und Absicht,* 181-200, cited by Hoehner, *Ephesians,* 743.

425 Hoehner, *Ephesians,* 742-3.

(cf. 1 Cor. 7:16). Fourthly, the word soter (saviour) is never used for human beings and is exclusively reserved for Christ or God in the New Testament. In short, it may be understood as a contrast between Christ and husbands in general as Christ alone is the saviour of humanity including women.

Since v. 23c, (he (is) savior of the body), is a slight deviation from the comparison between wife-husband and church-Christ imagery, the author returns to the statement on Christ and church in v. 24 by using hos (as) following the adversative conjunction alla (but). Just like the church submits to Christ, wives have to submit to their husbands. The expectation of submission is emphasized by the prepositional phrase, 'in everything'. Strangely, even though the authority of husband is not equivalent to that of Christ, the level of submission expected of wife is to the extent of church's response to the authority of Christ.

In other words, "(t)he limitation of the husband's authority (v. 23) does not limit the wife's submission (έν παντί, v. 24b)."[426] Further, unlike husbands who follow the model of Christ to love their wives, there is no reference to "loving subordination"[427] of wives to their husbands. If the Church is the recipient of the benevolent love of Christ, then it automatically places Church in an unequal position to Christ, similarly, placing wives in a receiving end to husbands' love.

The use of 'in everything' in this verse creates a controversial tone in the exhortation. Elsewhere, children have to obey their parents 'in everything' (Col. 3:20) and slaves, their masters (Col. 3:22). Does it not indicate that a wife has to subordinate to her husband in every aspect of her life? It may not as easy, as it is said, to accept S. B. Clark's explanation that "(n)o part of her life should be outside of her relationship to her husband and outside of subordination to him."[428] It is also difficult to endorse similar notions, which promote such submission of wives as necessary for the unity in family and in church.

---

426 Sampley, *Two Shall Become One Flesh,* 126.

427 Schnackenburg, *Ephesians,* 246.

428 S. B. Clark cited by O'Brien, *Ephesians,* 417.

The very analogies of Christ-is-to-Church as husband-is-to-wife indicates the inferior position of wives to husbands, since the Church is not equal in its position and role to Christ in any way. Even though husband is not the saviour of his wife, and does not have the same authority over his wife as Christ has over the church, wife is nevertheless to be obedient to him "in all things."[429] It is all the more fascinating to note that the role of Christ as saviour of the Church is something that human husbands can scarcely assume on their wives' behalf.

Nevertheless, one may find the admonitions to husbands form a larger section within the pericope (5:25-32). It can be divided into two sub-sections: vv. 25-27 and vv. 28-32. In the first section (vv. 25-27), after the initial command to husbands to love their wives (25a), the author places emphasis on the relation between Christ and church (25b-27). The second section, Eph. 5:28-32, projects the role of husbands in the household, especially in relation to their wives. The imagery of Christ's sacrificial love for the church is now projected as the basic norm for the husbands to follow in their attitude and approach to their marital relationship.

Unlike in Colossians, the author of Ephesians highlights the requirement of love as a willful act from husbands by referring to the radical notion of love through the analogy of Christ's love for the church.[430] The verb, 'to love' *(agapao)* appears six times in the pericope and is used as a command for husbands thrice in vv. 25, 28 and 33. This exhortation to love their wives does not find parallel in the Hebrew Scriptures, Rabbinic literature or in the Greco-Roman household codes. It seems to be that the patriarchal domination is radically challenged by the analogy of "paradigmatic love relationship of Christ to the church."[431]

In Ephesians, Christ's death plays a major role in the development of the whole theology. Christ's love is measured by his sacrificial death for the redemption of the church. And this is evident from

---

429 Sampley, *Two Shall Become One Flesh,* 126, C. A. Newsome & Sharon H. Ringe (eds.), *Women's Bible Commentary* (Louisville: Westminster John Knox Press, 1998), 431.

430 Lincoln, *Ephesians,* 374.

431 Schussler Fiorenza, *In Memory of Her,* 269-70.

the two verbs, 'loved' and 'gave up', which are in fact repeated from 5:2, "Christ loved us and gave himself up for us, a fragrant offering and sacrifice to God." In Eph. 1:20, God raised Christ from the dead and seated him at his right hand in the heavenly places. In 2:5-6, the death and resurrection of Christ has promised the same privilege for the believers to be raised and seated up with Christ in the heavenly places. V. 2:13 assures that the blood of Christ has brought the believers closer to God.

In this way, Christ's sacrificial death plays a significant role in highlighting the marriage relationship.[432] In fact, Christ's love for church is manifested in the giving up of himself for the same. The effect of Christ's death on the church is followed by three sub-clauses. In the first two clauses, Christ is the subject acting upon the church (26a and 27a), and in the third clause (27c), Church is the subject showing the result of Christ's action. The love of Christ for church is now getting elaborated. Christ sanctifies the church (v. 26), which serves as a technical term to mean 'to separate out for oneself, namely in the sense of marriage.'[433] The occurrence of 'her' before the verb 'to sanctify' in Greek text, for some scholars like Schlier, indicates the emphasis that the author wants to place on church as the sole object of Christ's sanctification.[434] Or it could be that the verb 'to sanctify' and the participle 'having cleansed' are closely related now and thus Christ remains the subject of both the verb and the participle.[435] Christ sanctifies the church because he has cleansed it by his sacrificial death. It must be reaffirmed that both the acts of sanctification and cleansing occurs at the same time. The verb, 'to cleanse' is generally used of cleansing of food (Mk. 7:19; Acts 10: 15, 11:9), of ceremonial cleansing (Mt. 23:25-26), and of

432 In Ephesians, Christ's death plays a major role in the development of the whole theology. In Eph. 1:20, God raised Christ from the dead and seated him at his right hand in the heavenly places. In 2:5-6, the death and resurrection of Christ has promised the same privilege for the believers to be raised and seated up with Christ in the heavenly places. V. 2:13 assures that the blood of Christ has brought the believers closer to God.

433 Sampley, *Two Shall Become One Flesh*, 129.

434 Schlier, *Epheser*, 264-76, *cited by Sampley, Two Shall Become One Flesh*, 129.

435 Sampley, *Two Shall Become One Flesh*, 129.

the moral cleansing of the people (1 Cor. 6:11, 2 Cor. 7:1, Titus 2:14, Heb. 9:14).[436] Against the backdrop of the use of the word in New Testament, it could be suitable to identify the moral cleansing of the church in the Ephesian passage.

The phrase, 'by the washing of the water appears only in Eph. 5:26 and Titus 3:5. This phrase suggests a "metaphorical expression of redemption with the imagery of the bridal bath practiced in the first century."[437] This phrase has created discussion among scholars on baptism. Since the reference here is made with the entire church, it would probably not refer to baptism, but rather to the purification of church by the sacrificial act of Christ.[438] But the sacrificial death of Christ becomes relevant to Christian church through the confessional act of baptism. As the husband-wife relationship is in the center of this passage, the custom of pre-nuptial bath in Jewish and Greek might have evoked the author's mind.

Sampley suggests that there is a close affinity between this passage and Ezek. 16:8ff., "in that both reflect a *hieros gamos* (YHWH-Jerusalem, Christ-church) in which the groom cleanses his bride by a washing with water and in which the result is a strong emphasis on the beauty and purity of the bride."[439] In Ezek. 16:9, bathing of Israel with water is mentioned, which according to Sampley, could have influenced the author of Ephesians to use the phrase 'by the washing of the water'.

The church is sanctified not only by the washing by water, but also in the word. Even if baptism is taken into account here, the sanctifying and cleansing act of Christ finds completion in the word or the gospel message as well.[440] Sampley attests to the sanctifying act of Christ bringing about "purification of the church as the bride of Christ by analogy from the cleansing of Israel; and that it is made relevant to the reader by turning it to speak of baptism, the means by which each of the readers became incorporated into the church."[441]

436 Hoener, *Ephesians,* 751-2.

437 Hoehner, *Ephesians,* 753.

438 Erdmann, *Der Brief an die Epheser,* 45, *cited by Hoehner, Ephesians,* 753.

439 Sampley, *Two Shall Become One Flesh,* 43.

440 Lincoln, *Ephesians,* 376.

441 Sampley, *Two Shall Become One Flesh,* 133.

The second sub-clause (27a) directs to the effort of Christ in presenting the church "in splendor, without spot or wrinkle or any such thing" to himself. This has strong allusion to Ezek 16:10-14, where Yahweh adorns Israel in royal splendor. Here the author refers back to the earlier citation of church as God's glorious inheritance in Eph. 1:18 and as a realm where God's glory is revealed (3:21).[442] In v. 27a, Christ remains the subject and the emphasis upon Christ's action is underlined by the use of 'to himself' as the indirect object of the verb 'he might present.'[443] Sampley identifies the tone of sacrificial purity in the use of the verb, 'he might present' which refers to Christ rendering her glorious before him, or transforming her a sacrifice that is without blemish or spot.[444]

The use of terms like 'spot' and 'wrinkle' indicates the purity of the bride, i.e. the church, synonym to the image of a young and beautiful bride. However, the beauty intended here is that of moral perfection as the third sub-clause indicates: 'but that she might be holy and blameless'. In fact, Christ has called the church to be "holy and blameless" even before the foundation of the world (Eph. 1:4). The purity of the church is a serious concern in the letter to Ephesians as impurity clearly sets the characteristic of outsiders of the church (cf. Eph. 4:19; 5:3).[445]

V.27c, though starts with an adversative conjunction, *alla* (but), does not contradict with the preceding clauses, but only distinguishes third clause from the other two. Here the subject of the sub-clause is the church herself, which has become holy and blameless by the sacrificial act of Christ.

In the Jewish practices of cultic and ethical purity, there was no difference between the purity expected of priests and that of brides. Thus, v. 27c signifies the religious and ethical purity of the church in relation with Christ and symbolizes the marital bond between wives and husbands. Hoehner believes that the hope of presenting church as holy and blameless to Christ is not only an allusion to

442 Lincoln, *Ephesians,* 377.

443 Sampley, *Two Shall Become One Flesh,* 134.

444 Sampley, *Two Shall Become One Flesh,* 136.

445 Lincoln, *Ephesians,* 377.

the immediate context but also to the climax of the theology of the whole letter to the Ephesians.[446]

Moving to v. 28, one finds the adverbial conjunction 'therefore' referring back to the sacrificial love of Christ towards the church. In a similar manner, now the husbands have to love their wives. The author's primary intention of highlighting the relationship between the church and Christ is now translated into its impact on wife-husband relationship. The verb, *opheilousin* (must) followed by an infinitive *agapan* (to love) denotes the obligation emphasized on the role of husbands to love their wives. Apart from the rationale of Christ's love for the church, now another reason is spelt out, that is, to love their wives as their own bodies. If they love their wives, that will only affirm their love for their own selves.

Sampley considers that the exhortation to husbands to love their wives as their own bodies is a formulation drawing ideas from the last part of Gen. 2:24 ("and the two shall become one flesh") and Lev. 19:18 ("you shall love your neighbour as yourself"). It is made relevant for husbands to love their wives as their bodies since they have become one flesh in marriage.[447] If this argument is acceptable, then it unfolds the incorporation of Jewish Scriptural understanding of marriage into the Christian adaptation of Greco-Roman *haustafel.* But, are they not selfish motives in comparison to Christ's selfless sacrificial love towards the church? Is it to highlight the humanness of husbands over against the divine love of Christ?

The second part of v. 28 shows a shift from the plural to singular as now it deals with the love to one's wife as denoting love to one's self. The intensity of love in a marital bond is now further emphasized, but by dealing with the opposite of it in stating that "no one ever hates his flesh" (v. 29). It is interesting to note the variances used from 28a through 29a. In 28a, it is as their bodies that the husbands have to love their wives. In 28b, it is as to himself that their love for their wives to be portrayed. And in v. 29a, the allusion is to love their wives as they love their flesh. This further links to v. 31, where Gen 2:24 is quoted that "the two shall become one flesh."

446 Hoehner, *Ephesians,* 761.

447 Sampley, *Two Shall Become One Flesh,* 141.

As far as the author of the letter to Ephesians is concerned, it comes in a synonymous manner that husbands love their wives as their body and flesh. The subject and object of all the three verbs (to hate, to nourish, to cherish) in v. 29 remain the same. Both the verbs, *ektrephei* and *thalpei* (nourishes, cherishes) are in present tense, indicating nature of action as a continuous one. Both the verbs are generally used in the context of taking care of children (cf. Eph. 6:4, 1 Thess. 2:7). This characteristic of nourishing and cherishing one's own flesh is also applied to Christ as he does the same for the church (29b), as the church is his body. The reference to collective plural (we are) in v. 30 indicates that all the saints in the Ephesian church are included in the body of Christ as members.

V. 31 is a direct quotation of Gen. 2:24 from the Septuagint with two alterations. [448] Marriage is considered as a divine ordinance in Judaism.[449] Jesus quotes Gen. 2:24 when he answers Pharisees to their question on divorce in Mk. 10:2ff (parallel in Matt. 19:3ff). Paul uses Gen. 2:24 in 1 Cor. 6:16 to warn the Corinthian church against adultery. The fact that the man has to leave his father and mother and cleave to his wife sets a marital norm that is contradictory to the social custom in most cultures, where it was expected of the woman to leave her parents and join the husband's family. In general, this verse is a justifying statement to overcome domination in marital relationships.

Annette Merz comments that "in 5:25-32 the underlying axiom that the woman is the flesh/body of the man is justified in terms of creation theology by means of the 'one flesh'(*sic*) idea from Gen. 2. 24; at the same time, this is presented as the image of the relationship between Christ and the *Ekklesia*, rooted in Christ's gift of himself and his loving care for his bride/body."[450] In this way,

448 The phrase, 'because of this' is used here in Ephesians. Further, the possessive pronoun 'his' which appears after father and the mother in LXX is omitted in the Ephesian text. Lincoln, *Ephesians,* 380.

449 Sampley, *Two Shall Become One Flesh,* 56.

450 Annette Merz, "Why did the Pure Bride of Christ (2 Cor 11:2) become a Wedded Wife (Eph. 5.22-33)? Theses about the Intertextual Transformation of an Ecclesiological Metaphor," *Journal for the Study of the New Testament* 79 (2000): 137.

Merz highlights the Christ-church relationship as a normative and universal criterion of the relationship between the sexes. Here we see the substantiating argument for the exhortation for husbands to love their wives as their own flesh. But for Klara Butting, the idea of reconciliation stands out in the interpolation of Gen. 2:24 into the Ephesian household code. In a *haustafel*, dominated by the patriarchal marriage, the concept of husband and wife becoming one flesh marks the possibilities of reconciliation between unequally treated marriage partners. She connects Eph. 2:14-15 with the wife-husband relationship, in that, the reconciliation promised for the circumcised and the uncircumcised at the beginning of the letter is applicable even for the broken (hierarchical) relationship between spouses.[451]

Stephen Francis Miletic claims that the marital norms attached to husbands and wives in Eph. 2:21-33 should be viewed as part of the author's intention to develop a new creation theology on the basis of vv. 31-32.[452] For him, both the roles of wives and husbands are "christological, both roles demand total self-renunciation and both roles contribute to the soteriological process, manifesting the 'one flesh' unity of Christ and the church, the New Adam and Eve of the New Creation."[453] Mary Ann Getty comments further on the same line that "The unity of the husband's and wife's love relationship realizes the goal of the unity of all things in Christ. As a representation of the new creation achieved through Christ's love of the church, the Christian husband/wife relationship necessarily rejects any dehumanizing elements (e.g., domination, control) in androcentric culture."[454]

---

451 Klara Butting, "Pauline Variations on Genesis 2. 24: Speaking of the Body of Christ in the Context of the Discussion of Life Styles," *Journal for the Study of New Testament* 79 (2000), 88-89.

452 Miletic works with the presupposition that Paul is the author of the letter to the Ephesians. Stephen Francis Miletic, *Óne Flesh": Eph. 5. 22-24, 5.31. Marriage and the New Creation* (Anchor Bible 115; Rome: Biblical institute, 1988), 111.

453 Miletic, *Óne Flesh,* 111.

454 Mary Ann Getty, Review of *Óne Flesh": Eph. 5. 22-24, 5.31. Marriage and the New Creation,* by Stephen Francis Miletic, *The Catholic Biblical Quarterly* 52 (1990): 761.

V. 32 reveals the mind of the author in placing Gen. 2:24 in v. 31 to bring to light not only the marital bond between husband and wife but also the relationship between Christ and the church. However, the use of mystery in v. 32 has created hermeneutical confusion among the scholars. The use of the adjective, 'great', has been translated and interpreted in both attributive and predicative senses. Nevertheless, only the predicate adjective does justice to the immediate context drawing attention back to v. 31. This is further attested by author's use of 'but I say to Christ and to the church'. The adversative particle 'but' functions as a conjunction indicating a general contrast, providing a link between v. 32b and the interpretation of Gen. 2:24. Here the author's intention to emphasize his idea of relation between Christ and the church is evident. This makes many scholars think that the author of Ephesians is making his opinion explicitly different from the existing interpretations of Gen. 2: 24.[455] Sampley comments that even before Gen. 2:24 is quoted in v. 31, the ideas are inherent in vv. 21-30.

The concluding statement of the whole pericope of Eph. 5:21-32, starts with an adversative (however), which indicates the shift from the new creation theology of Gen. 2:24 to practical advice to the husbands and wives. The husband is addressed first, probably as a

455 Martin Dibelius believes that v. 32b was to show that others also have interpreted OT quotation as mysterious, but the reference to Christ and the church may be uniquely of the author (Martin Dibelius, *An die Kolosser Epheser an Philemon* (Tubingen: J. C. B. Mohr (John Siebeck, 1953), 95). Gunther Bornkamm thinks that the interpretation introduced by ejgw; de; levgw is to express opposition to other interpretations which also find a musthvrion in the text but different from Ephesian context (Gunther Bornkamm, "musthvrion", in *Theologisches Worterbuch zum Neuen Testament*, edited by Gerhard Kittel (Stuttgart: W. Kohlhammer Verlag. iv) 823). R. E. Brown states that the use of ejgw; de; levgw by the author need not indicate existence of opposing interpretations, but goes beyond the explicit meaning of the passage (Raymond E. Brown, "The Semitic Background of the New Testament Mysterion (II)" in *Biblica*, 40, 74-84). Morton Smith also has highlighted that ejgw; de; levgw is a standard form derived from Judaism to oppose established interpretations of scripture. Morton Smith, *Tannaitic Parallels to the Gospels (The Journal of Biblical Literature Monograph Series, vol. vi)* (Philadelphia: The Society of Biblical Literature, 1951), 28. See Sampley, Two shall become *OneFflesh*, 87-89 for elaborate discussion.

continuation of his admonitions to husbands in the previous verses. And both the addressees are given in singular, which is a unique feature found only in this verse. That is to say, only in this verse, the addressees are addressed in singular number in all over the New Testament household codes.

Here the author recapitulates the exhortations to wives and husbands in a Christian household, but adding the verb, 'to fear' most probably from v. 21. The subjunctive mood of *phobetai* with *hina* attests to the hortatory function expected of the wife. The critical question that one needs to answer is whether the fear expected of wives toward their husbands is similar to that of Christians to Christ in v. 21. In cases of human relations, fear involves observance of the appropriate authority structures.[456] "Fear can denote the obedience demanded by the superior authority of masters or husbands as lords."[457] The syntax with *hina* and the subjunctive *phobetai* replaces a command or imperative. It functions more as a wish. Many English and vernacular translations substitute 'respect' or 'obey' for 'fear' in 5:33 and thus attempt to make the writer less patriarchal and more agreeable to modern readers. But this translation cannot mean exactly the same as that in Greek. The author justifies that since the fear of Christ (v. 21) is Ephesian saints' appropriate response to Christ's overwhelming love and power, the wife's fear is her appropriate response to her husband's headship. The form and content of this verse highlights the text's masculine prejudice and its acceptance of a patriarchal structure. Here the text itself seems to be sexist in its approach to the marital norms attached to wives.

Conclusion

The exegetical study of Eph. 5:21-33 unravels the historical and literary context of the letter to the Ephesians briefly to highlight the fact that the Ephesian *haustafel* has depended collaboratively on Jewish, Greek, Roman and Christian ethical codes. The

456 Fear of citizens toward the State (cf. Rom 13:3,4,7), children to parents (*Barnabas* 19.5, *Didache* 4.9), slaves to masters (Eph. 6:5; 1 Pet 2:18; Did 4.11), or, as here, wives to husbands (cf. also 1 Pet 3:2).

457 Balz, *fovbo*", 217-8.

Ephesian passage on wife-husband relationship has been developed significantly from that of the Colossian passage. Though it is impossible to draw a fixed household code from which the author of Ephesians was depending on, it may be appropriate to say that the Ephesian household code is a hybrid formulation of the prevalent household duties practiced from the time of Aristotle till Roman captivation.

Like any other New Testament authors, the author of Ephesians also had drawn from a host of ethical material inherited both from their Jewish heritage and possibly from their wider Greco-Roman milieu.[458] The Hellenistic Judaism might have probably played a major role in the transport of household codes from Hellenism down through Roman imperialism to the Christian literature. The relation between the household codes and the household character of the Christian community in Ephesus for which they are employed highlights the adaptive nature of the early Christian movement.[459]

It is quite evident to recognize the nexus between colonial and patriarchal elements incorporated into the Ephesian household code, especially in connection to the relationship between wives and husbands. The primary command to wives to submit to their husbands is a direct interpolation possible from the commanding terms of Roman army as similar words are used to denote the action of soldiers of inferior rank. Since the word, *hupotasso* carries overtones of order or domination; it also intends to bring order in a household in the Ephesian church. Thus, it is a word carrying a heavy connotation of authority and submission or subordination to it. Even though, the Greek word *hupotasso* may be interchangeably used with *hupakouo*, the hierarchical social structure inherent in the former term cannot be sidelined.

Despite the fact that v. 21 deals with mutual submission of the believers, there is no clarity regarding what submission means. It is mainly because of the fact that the apparent mutuality in v. 21 is totally negated by the hierarchical relation that follows. However, the scholars who argue strongly for mutual submission in the whole

458 Witherington, *Women in the Earliest Churches,* 47.

459 Elliott, *A Home for the Homeless,* 211.

pericope views v. 21 as a special injunction deliberately added to nullify the narration of household codes where wife's submission to husband's controlling authority is involved. In this sense, v. 21 could be viewed as a Christian effort to adapt the existing Roman household code into the Christian community while at the same time highlighting a Christian ethic of mutual submission, which may resist the other. Yet, the unequal portrayal of the marital norms of wives and husbands fails to endorse such a high Christian ideal of mutual submission, which in fact originates from reverence for Christ. In my opinion, v. 21 has created a tension within the pericope of Eph. 5:21-33 as to laying a moral responsibility over the members of Ephesian church to chose between the two, which will in turn reveal what their spiritual stand is, especially in relation to day-to-day Christian living as wives and husbands.

"The fear of Christ" has strong allusions to the Jewish term, "the fear of the Lord." This phrase particularly denotes the Jewish origin of Christianity, probably to high light a Jewish motive for a Christian ethic over against a Roman colonial household code. The fear of the Lord is the fitting reaction to the awesome works of God. The concept of 'fear of the Lord' (interchangeably with fear of Christ and fear of God) has strong allusions to Jewish concept of God as found in the Hebrew Scriptures. Once the motivating force for mutual submission is drawn from the fear of Christ, and then it is certainly not the loyalty to the emperor or the Roman empire that decides their adaptation of the Roman household code.

The imagery of Church-Christ relationship tends to rationalize the specific subordinate role of wives to their husbands within the marital bond. The exhortation to wives to submit to their husbands as to the Lord emphasizes the authority attached to the role not only of Christ but also of husbands. The reference to husbands as head of their wives underlines the authority of them over their wives. Just like the Church submits to Christ, the wives are advised to submit to their husbands. If wife's submission to husbands is treated as a by-product of their submission to Christ, then husbands also need to follow the model of Church in submitting to Christ. In this way, husbands are not exempted from imitating the attitude of the Church, which they are also part of.

Further, Christ is different from husbands, as the power or authority Christ holds is not shared with the husbands. This is evident from the contrasting statement (v. 23c) that Christ is the saviour of the body. That means husband cannot share in the salvific authority of Christ. Or in other words, husbands just like wives, as members of Church, are to be submissive to the salvific role of Christ. This certainly distinguishes Christ from husbands despite the use of Church-Christ imagery to highlight the marital relation between wives and husbands. In fact, the role of Christ as saviour of the Church is something that human husbands could hardly assume. Even when husband is not the saviour of his wife, and does not share in the authority over his wife as Christ has over the Church, wife is nevertheless expected to submit to him in everything or all things (v. 24). Therefore, the analogy of Church-Christ in relation to wife-husband indicates the inferior position of wives to husbands, since the Church can never be equated in its position and role to Christ.

Categorically, a major section of the admonitions is directed to the husbands delegating eight verses in the pericope. This section is dominated with the concept of love. Christ's self-sacrificial love is the ultimate goal for husbands in fulfilling the marital obligation toward their wives. The concept of love appears as a radical notion as it requires a willful agreement from the side of husbands. It is interesting to not that this command to love is found anywhere else in the contemporary literature or in the possible background literature like the Hebrew Scriptures, rabbinic literature or in the Greco-Roman household codes. Therefore, it could be treated as a very unique Christian contribution to the theology marriage. This, in turn, shows the possibilities of challenging the imperial patriarchal domination. This kind of interpretation is validated by the paradigmatic love relationship of Christ to the Church. Such a paradigmatic love relationship is elaborated in vv. 25b-27.

Christ loved and gave himself up for the sake of Church so that three goals would be achieved. First of all, his sacrificial love sanctifies the Church. The verb, 'to sanctify', is used simultaneously with the verb, to 'cleanse'. The Church is purified in terms of pre-nuptial bath in Israel, which refers to the purification of the Church as the bride of Christ. Secondly, the sacrificial love of Christ aims at presenting the Church without blemish in royal splendor to himself. Thirdly, Christ makes the Church holy and blameless. The kind of beauty attributed to the Church indicates moral perfection and spiritual purity. In fact, these verses denoting the relation between Christ and Church become the climax of the theology of the letter to the Ephesians.

Having portrayed the ultimate goals of Christ's sacrificial love, the author now pushes the case for husbands to follow the same model for loving their wives. Apart from the rationale of Christ's love for the Church, there is one more emphasis given, that is to love their wives as their own bodies (v. 28). This addition finds another expression in vv. 29-30 that husbands ought to love their wives as their own flesh as no one hates his own flesh. This could be possible due to the fact that both husbands and wives become one flesh in marriage. The husbands ought to nourish and cherish their wives just like they do to their own bodies. This also derives inspiration from Christ as the church is constantly nourished and cherished by the love of Christ.

The hortatory section to husbands finds culmination in the quote from the Septuagint version of Gen. 2:24. The 'one-flesh' marital bond is a challenging interpolation to a Greco-Roman household code driven by patriarchal marriage. The concept of wife and husband becoming one flesh marks the clear possibilities for reconciliation between unequally treated marriage partners. This in turn creates unity of wives and husbands realizing the unity of all believers in Christ. Such a new creation theology does away with all dehumanizing patriarchal elements involved in a marital union.

In general, the marital norm of husbands is exhibiting a high ideal, which paves way for an ideal marital union. However, the harmonious tone in vv. 25-32 is again ruptured by the final verse in the pericope, where the author recapitulates the marital norms attached to both husbands and wives. Here, in v. 33, while a husband loves his wife, a wife has to fear her husband. It seems to be that the fear of the Lord in v. 21 is replaced by the fear of one's husband becomes the fundamental motivation for following household codes. The form and content of this verse draws the readers back to the masculine prejudice embedded in the text.

The marital norms attached to both wives and husbands highlight various theological nuances such as Christological and soteriological, manifesting a new creation theology of 'one-flesh' union of Christ and Church. There is much scope for analyzing these varying theological nuances, which would most probably expose the hybrid formulations of Christian household ethics, which have in fact drawn insights from a pool of differing religious and socio-political elements in the first century CE. The distinctively Jewish, Hellenistic Jewish and Greco-Roman elements in the Ephesian passage of the present study reveals the overlapping of opposing concepts, which tend to blur the borders of their differences.

Chapter 5

The Mutual "One-Flesh" Relationship
A Third Space of Enunciation

A theological appraisal of colonial and feminist nuances in the Ephesian passage (5:21-33) exposes the complexities of the hybrid interactions of both the Roman imperial government and the colonized Ephesian community. The elements of colonial appropriation and the confrontation are intrinsically embedded here. However, the patriarchal notions take precedence over establishing an egalitarian wife-husband relationship. In Eph. 5:21-33, the gender norms tend to sustain hegemony within marriage. As we have seen in the previous exegetical study, there is a constant tension between mutual submission between wives and husbands (as among believers, cf. 5:21) and a subjugate – dominant relation of wife - husband (5:22-33). Furthermore, the marital norms differ for both wives and husbands that wives have to submit and to fear their husbands while husbands have to love their wives. In a mutual relationship, it cannot be practiced this way. It should probably be the same norm for both wife and husband, that they love each other and submit to each other. Perhaps, a detailed theological evaluation using the literary critical tools from postcolonial and feminist hermeneutics will unravel the nexus between colonial and patriarchal nuances embedded in

Eph. 5:21-33. It becomes inevitable to start with a discussion on theoretical framework of gender norms functioning within any patriarchal marriage in order to critically analyze the colonial and patriarchal nuances embedded in the Ephesian passage.

Gender Norms in Wife-Husband Relationship

The portrayal of wife-husband relationship in Eph. 5:21-33 reflects the gender norms prevailed in the first century CE. There existed various socio-cultural gender notions, as understood from the background study of Mediterranean cultures including Jewish, Hellenistic and Roman. There were mutual exchange of ideas and ideologies among these different cultures and that resulted in many 'trans-cultural hybrid' spaces of identities. It was observed that Greco-Roman culture itself had a complex mix of gender norms imbibed from the surrounding nations.

In helping us to understand what constitutes gender norms, Lisa Isherwood says,

> Far from being a God-given difference, gender is a social construction based on dominance and submission, unhealthy foundational aspects for any fully functioning sense of self. Gender is not simply about knowing the difference but also about making the difference, a difference that can be harshly felt in the lives of women and men.[460]

Gender is not just making distinct differences of women and men, but it determines how they live as human beings in a community. "It is kept in place by rigid systems, one of which is the practice of heteropatriarchal sexuality and another is the compounding of that through the expectations on Christian marriage."[461] This explanation of gender provides an analytical tool for gender norms in Eph. 5:21-33.

---

460 Lisa Isherwood, "The Violence of Gender: Christian Marriage as Test Case," in *Weep not for Your Children: Essays on Religion and Violence,* edited by Lisa Isherwood and Rosemary Radford Ruether (London: Equinox, 2008), 54.

461 Isherwood, *The Violence of Gender,* 57.w

As far as the gender notions are considered, strangely enough, while wives are asked to submit to their husbands and to fear them in a marital relationship, husbands are supposed to love their wives. Though the concept of husbands loving their wives gains popular appreciation, it undergoes critical evaluation under feminist scrutiny. Mary Daly calls it, "the patriarchalism of love."[462] It is always a matter of wonder how a positive command 'to love' emerges as an agent of male domination and oppression, which could probably be understood as something to do with the patriarchal bias prevalent in the text and the interpretive society or community. How can it be justified, if wives are expected to fear their husbands in a passage where all the believers are to submit to one another out of reverence for Christ? The gender norms like 'submitting' and 'fearing' meant only for wives project a negative approach in comparison to that of husbands. A woman's sex and sexuality is manipulated to govern her loyalty to her husband by such gender norms.

Isherwood in another essay comments that "Sex and sexuality are central aspects of how we police gender."[463] In this way, the institution of marriage successfully maintains the non-egalitarian gender norms. This is evident from the kind of gender norms attached to wives and husbands in the Ephesian passage. The biased portrayal of the gender roles of wives becomes more visible when one compares them with the gender role assigned to husbands. The attitudes of submission and fear in wives would naturally make them subject to authority structures. If domestic violence in marriage is analyzed, one encounters two major aspects: the authority the husband has over his wife and the service he expects to get from his wife.[464]

At this juncture, it would be appropriate to analyze the gender logic that is coined and popularized by Western (Euro-American) philosophy of hermeneutics. According to the Western interpretation, gender is understood as categories of 'male' and 'female' and there

---

462 Mary Daly, *Beyond God the Father* (Great Britain: The Women's Press, 1973), 139.

463 Lisa Isherwood, *Erotic Celebacy: Queering Heteropatriarchy (*London: T & T Clark, 2006), 56.

464 Anne Borrowdale, *Distorted Images: Christian Attitudes to Women, Men and Sex* (London: SPCK, 1991), 107.

is always the predominance of 'masculinity' over femininity'. In order to establish their "first principles" (their grounding claims about reality) in the forms of argumentation (reasoning), Western philosophers like Plato, Aristotle and Descartes defined a principle by reference to what it is not. "It must have an 'other' to establish the borders of its own existence. This 'other' serves as the conceptual point of difference that makes not only the birth of the principle but also its continued existence."[465] Luce Irigaray points out that 'this other' is the typical gendered female while the central point it defines is characterized as male.

For Western philosophy, the first principle needs to be self-evident without any origin, and therefore, having defined the parameters of the male first principle by means of the 'other', they deny the feminine 'other's very existence.[466] Thus, the feminine 'other' ceases to exist. She further suggests, "this dynamic repression not only structures our thoughts; it is also linked to pervasive social practices that follow similar patterns of exclusion and silence."[467] The symbolic exclusion of the 'other' may be evident in the field of biblical interpretation in general, and is very apparent in the Ephesian passage of our study. In a household, where man or husband is considered as the major principle that carries out the functions, the existence of wife tends to be rendered insignificant.

Any gender study needs to challenge conventional ideas concerning the constitution of human nature, the grounds of reliable knowledge and the foundations of social relations, language and culture.[468] Categorically, the notion of gender undergoes 'historicizing' and 'particularizing' with respect to culture. Sheila Briggs comments that the women of the present century are not the gender to which the Ephesian passage admonished submission and

---

465 S. Jones, "Bounded Openness: Postmodernism, Feminism, and the Church Today," in *Interpretation* 55.1 (January, 2001): 53.

466 Luce Irigaray, *This Sex Which is not One*, translated by Catherine Porter (New York: Cornell University, 1985), cited by Jones, *Bounded Openness*: 53.

467 Irigaray, *This Sex Which is not One, cited by Jones, Bounded Openness:* 53.

468 E. Graham, "Gender," in *An A to Z of Feminist Theology*, edited by Lisa Isherwood and Dorothea McEvan (Sheffield: Sheffield Academic Press, 1996), 79.

fear toward their husbands. Gender is not only a historically varied and discontinuous category; it also does not affect all women in the same way or any woman in the same way all the time. Therefore the modern notions of gender formulations ought to critically analyze all unequal power relations between man and woman.[469] Since the Ephesian passage exhibits the kind of patriarchal gender roles prevalent in the Greco-Roman society, the modern interpreter ought to approach the text with critical faculties to decode them as relevant for the contemporary situations.

> "Gender then is no innocent natural phenomena, it is part of a much wider and pervasive problem, it is in reality the root of much of the violence both personal and public that we live under. Christian marriage, if we are to continue with it, needs then to be the nurturing ground of people who live outside the all pervasive confines of gender construction, who challenge the status quo from a base of just love and mutuality which rejoices in the as yet untapped fullness of the human/divine reality."[470]

Significantly, the Christian virtues underlying marital gender norms need to be remolded to incorporate justice in an ethic of love. This calls for serious redress of unequal gender relations within marriage.

Marriage Under Postcolonial Feminist Lens

Like any other empire, the Roman empire also strove to exercise its authority over its subjects by means of politics, culture and religion. Further, the local cultures and religions were promoted or at least tolerated in order to establish a peaceful rule of Roman government (*Pax Romana*). Since the household was a micro unit of the larger macro unit of *Pax Romana*, the imperial cultural influences on the household affairs were very prominent. The Jews, Greeks, and Romans

---

469 Sheila Briggs, *The Spiritual Body Politic* (Atlanta, Georgia: Emory University, 1988), cited by G. Aichele, *et. al, The Postmodern Bible* (London: Yale University Press, 1995), 237.

470 Isherwood, *The Violence of Gender,* 64.

had their own distinct modes of living, however, there were many overlapping to the point of creating hybrid spaces of identities. Since the first century Ephesian Christians were predominantly converts from either Jewish or Greco-Roman religio-cultural background, the Christian social and familial existence reflected much of the hybrid identities of the time. Marriage is a significant social institution, which reflects the impact of the surrounding cultures. The author of Ephesians gives a vivid picture of the Christians' effort to establish a unique understanding and theology of marriage in the context of growing influence of Roman cultural and ethical values.

Marital concord was a great ideal for Roman families as we see such images reflected in the art (especially funerary art), inscriptions and literature of Rome from the late republic onward. The speeches of emperors, political rhetoricians and Roman moralists indicate that civic harmony is closely associated with marital harmony. The marriage imagery in Ephesians 5 represents "an image of unbreakable order that the pagan world could understand."[471]

That the metaphor of marriage is used to explain the relationship between Christ and the church foreshadows the larger Greco-Roman society to treat the married couple as an ideal microcosm of the society as a whole.[472] Even if frequently viewed as a symbol of accommodation to the world, and deeply embedded in Greco-Roman ethics, the author of Ephesians presents household code as an institution, which will ultimately set Christians at Ephesus a distinct community.[473] Even though there is no explicit polemical attitude prevalent in the letter to the Ephesians, the way the author sets out his own position indicates that he is aware of the competing positions. Especially, the phrase, εγώ δέ λέγω denotes that the interpretation of Gen. 2.24 as speaking of Christ and the church is set in contrast to other expositions.

471 Peter Brown, *The Body and Society: Men, Women and Sexual Renunciation in Early Christianity* (London: Faber and Faber, 1988), 57. Peter Brown cited by Osiek and MacDonald, *A Woman's Place*, 120.

472 Osiek and MacDonald, *A Woman's Place,* 120.

473 Osiek and MacDonald, *A Woman's Place,* 122.

Annette Merz thinks,

> this verse is proof that the author assumes the familiarity of his addressees with deviant positions (or indeed their sympathy with such positions). Verse 29a makes it likely that he has in mind tendencies that were critical of marriage: the affirmation that no one has ever hated (ἐμίσησεν) his own flesh (σαρξ), which according to v. 28 designates both one's own body and one's wife) must be understood as indicating an anti-ascetic position."[474]

Therefore, according to Merz, the paraenesis on marriage in Eph. 5.21-33 has an anti-ascetic motivation. When hierarchically structured marriage is presented as the image of that relationship between Christ and the church, which is established in creation (Gen. 2.24) and redemption, it appears as the normative lifestyle.[475]

Paul J. Sampley links the Christ-church marriage imagery back to the sacred marriage (*hieros gamos*) traditions in Judaism. The term, *hieros gamos* could refer to "the union between divine or celestial beings, the union between a divine being and earthly one, the union of the representatives of the divine and the earthly, or the ritual enactment of the union of celestial beings in the sexual union of two humans."[476] Yahweh's covenantal relation with Israelites is often treated as a sacred marriage between a divine and an earthly one.[477] Even though the Ephesian marriage imagery shows similarity with the concept of sacred marriage in Judaism, it seems that it moves much beyond the Jewish imagery in making the Christ-church imagery a model for the husband-wife relationship.

There are also allusions to connect the milieu of Ephesians with the influences from (Hellenistic) Jewish Gnosticism, which deal with

---

474 Annette Merz, "Why did the Pure Bride of Christ (2 Cor. 11:2) become a wedded wife (Eph. 5:22-33)? Theses about the Intertextual transformation of an Eschatological Metaphor," *Journal for the Study of New Testament* 79 (2000): 136.

475 Annette Merz, *Why did the Pure Bride of Christ,* 139.

476 Lincoln, *Ephesians,* 362.

477 Cf. Isa. 54:1, 5, 6; 62:4,5; Jer. 2:2, 3, 32; Ezek. 16:23; Hos. 2:19, 20; Mal. 2:14.

the sacred marriages as prototype of human marriages.[478] In Mystery Religions, "the marriage of Zeus and Hera was thought of as a pattern for human marriage in terms of procreation and fecundity, and where the sacred marriage could be enacted in a human ritual."[479]

Schussler Fiorenza had understood the presence of Jewish, Greco-Roman and Christian characteristics in New Testament household codes as an effort of the authors to christianize the patriarchal Aristotelian ethics and to institutionalize submission-dominance model at the expense of an early vision of the discipleship of equals.[480] However, the use of Jewish elements in Eph. 5:21-33 is also an attempt to remind the readers of the Jewish origin of Christian ethical codes.

As far as Schussler Fiorenza is concerned, the discipleship of equals in early Christian missionary movement allowed women to exercise leadership in Christianity, which might have challenged the Roman patriarchal household for the conversions of women and slaves happened independently at least to a certain extent. The argument that the Christian communities projected a threat to the Roman patriarchal household would have certainly forced the early Christian church to demonstrate a continuity of Christian ethics to the Roman household codes.[481] But what actually lacks in Schussler Fiorenza's argument is that it does not address the amount of threat still prevails in the Christian elements of the household codes, for instance the model of Christ in Christian household codes could easily and directly replace the Roman emperor.

It could be that the author was influenced by the existing religious ideologies; however, the author modifies such knowledge in the light of the Christian faith. To be sure, all these differing opinions highlight

---

478 Lincoln, *Ephesians,* 362.

479 W. K. C. Guthrie, *Orpheus and Greek Religion* (London: Methuen, 1952), cited by Lincoln, *Ephesians*, 362.

480 Elisabeth Schussler Fiorenza, *Bread Not Stone: The Challenge of Feminist Biblical Interpretation* (Boston: Beacon Press, 1985), 74-77.

481 Schussler Fiorenza, *Bread Not Stone,* 74-77. Schussler Fiorenza, *Bread Not Stone*, 74-77, cited by Sarah J. Tanzer, "Ephesians," in *Searching the Scriptures Volume Two: A Feminist Commentary* (London, Britain: SCM Press Limited, 1995), 331.

the fact that the author is aware of the contemporary religious and philosophical trends in the teachings on marriage. Here again, the idea of marriage exhibits hybridity as it reflects the influence of differing religious faiths that existed simultaneously overlapping with one another.

Christian marriage, as inferred from Eph. 5:21-33, is based on the imagery of the Christ-church model, which explicitly addresses the unity motif. This is particularly evident in v. 31, where the wife and husband are treated as one flesh in marriage union. Since the roles of wives and husbands are Christologically oriented, they would probably indicate rejection of selfish motives.

This is what is highlighted by Stephen Francis Miletic, when he says that the marital gender roles attached to wives and husbands in Ephesians are "Christological, both roles demand total self-renunciation and both roles contribute to the soteriological process, manifesting the 'one flesh' unity of Christ and the church."[482] In this way, the marriage motif could be understood as an egalitarian one, which culminates in unity of both.

In fact, the unity of wife and husband directs our attention to the unity of all things in Christ. "As a representation of the new creation achieved through Christ's love of the church, the Christian husband/wife relationship necessarily rejects any dehumanizing elements (e.g. domination, control) in androcentric culture."[483]

Klara Butting brings in the notion of reconciliation to understand the interpolation of Gen. 2:24 into Eph. 5:31. Against the backdrop of a patriarchal household code, the concept of wife and husband becoming one flesh marks the possibilities of reconciliation between unequally treated marriage partners. She thinks that the marital gender roles in Eph. 5:21-33 could better be understood if reconciliation between Jews and gentiles in Eph. 2: 14-15 is applied

---

482 Stephen Francis Miletic, "*One Flesh": Eph. 5.22-24, 5.31. Marriage and the New Creation* (Anchor Bible 115; Rome: Biblical Institute, 1988), 111.

483 Mary Ann Getty, Book review of Stephen Francis Miletic, "*One Flesh": Eph. 5.22-24, 5.31. Marriage and the New Creation* (Anchor Bible 115; Rome: Biblical Institute, 1988) in *The Catholic Biblical Quarterly* 52 (1990): 761.

for the broken hierarchical relationship between the spouses.[484] In this way, marriage could be viewed as representing the relationship between Christ and church, to the point of imitating Christ's self-sacrificial death and loving care for his bride/body, i.e. the church.

However, there are differing opinions about the way marriage is treated in the Ephesian passage. For Letty M. Russell, such kind of imagery,

> gives divine sanction to the idea of female dependence as bride and wife and to the idea of headship as the model for all marriage. In such a structure of subordination, it is true that two become one, but the one is the husband who absorbs the identity and name of the woman. Unlike Jew and Gentile, male and female find their unity by a process of absorption and assimilation rather than equal partnership.[485]

This idea cannot be sidelined, since in many cultures, the model of domination-subjugation between husband-wife is evolved from the same passage.

If husband is equated to Christ in marriage imagery, then the questions that arise are: is a woman without a husband incapable of existence, as the church cannot exist without Christ? Why is it that the husbands are exhorted to love their wives as their own bodies while Jesus loved Church without a selfish motive and with sacrificial attitude? Why does a marital relationship deal with different gender norms such as loving for husbands and submitting for wives? Why does it not talk about mutuality even though there is mutual submission among the believers as mentioned in 5:21?

Exegeting Eph 5:21-33 infers that mutuality and subordination exist side by side in constant tension. What is the role of interpolating

---

484 Klara Butting, "Pauline Variations on Genesis 2.24: Speaking of the Body of Christ in the Context of the Discussion of Life Styles," *Journal for the Study of the New Testament* 79 (2000): 88-89.

485 Letty M.Russell, *Imitators of God: A Study Book on Ephesians* (New York: Mission Education and Cultivation Program Department of the United Methodist Church, 1984), 103. Russell, *Imitators of God*, cited by Sarah J. Tanzer, "Ephesians," in *Searching the Scriptures Volume Two: A Feminist Commentary* (London, Britain: SCM Press Limited, 1995), 340.

Gen. 2:24 in v. 31? How does this quote from Genesis help in affirming 'the mutual "one flesh" relationship as more authentic than a domination-subjugation model? [486] Yusak Budi Setyawan comments that the author of Ephesians brings in the Jewish cosmology by incorporating Gen. 2:24. Woman and man are one flesh in the creation stories, which in turn, indicates that they are "one". This notion, of course, might disturb both Jews with their religious belief and Greeks with their philosophical idea of woman and man. Both Jewish religion and Greek philosophy treat a woman only in terms of a man's possession.[487]

Gen. 2:24 serves the purpose of underscoring the original will of God in establishing marriage as a relationship of husband and wife as one flesh, which further in vv. 28-29 is highlighted by the exhortation for husbands to love their wives as their own flesh. By using the introductory phrase, 'for this reason,' this author emphasizes the significance of 'mutual one flesh relationship' of wives and husbands. Probably the following verse (v. 32) raises suspicion about the validity of this interpretation. However, it has to be understood as a valid argument in support of God's original intention of marriage as 'mutual one flesh relationship'. Merz supports this idea when she says,

> The disclosure of the 'great mystery' which follows, that is the interpretation of the words from Genesis as speaking of Christ and the church (v. 32), does not in the least invalidate the interpretation in terms of marriage. Rather, its validity is reinforced in the sense of an analogy between the first age and the last. No longer do Adam and Eve function as imperfect models; now, the models are Christ the second Adam and his spotless wife the church, for in the context of Ephesians, where salvation is understood as something present here and now, it is only the reality of the redemption that can possess normative character. This model leaves no

486 Lincoln, *Ephesians,* 361.

487 Yusak Budi Setyawan "Be Subject to Your Husband as You are to the Lord" in Ephesians 5:21-33 - Illuminated by An Indonesian (Javanese)," *Asia Journal of Theology* April 2007, Vol. 21 Issue 1 (April 2007): 60-61.

> niche free for an unmarried imitation of Christ that would possess the same value as marriage.[488]

There has been a lack of consensus among scholars regarding how the 'mystery' in v. 32 can be understood in the overall context of Eph. 5:21-33. There are mainly three opinions. According to the first one, the word, mystery refers exclusively to the human marriage relationship since the whole passage deals with the human marriage as one flesh relationship. The Christ-church model functions only to support the author's arguments on human marriage. The second opinion refers exclusively to the union of Christ and the church.

> Within the structure of 5:22-33 there is a shift in emphasis (esp. in vv. 28a-32) to the church as the body of Christ, while the immediate antecedent of the Genesis 2:24 quotation is the clause 'for we are members of his body' (v. 30). Further, the demonstrative pronoun in the expression '*this* mystery' probably points to 'a certain aspect of the marital union', that is, 'the two shall become one flesh', which ties in with the Christ-church relationship.[489]

However, the more reliable one is the third opinion, which states the relationship between Christ and the church as a typology of marriage.

Raymond C. Ortlund[490], G. W. Dawes[491] and Peter T. O'Brien[492] have observed that the parallels between Christ-church and husband-wife run through the whole passage and therefore, the word mystery could refer to both the relations. In the given pericope, Christ-church imagery is used to underscore the relation between husband-wife pair and thus to evolve a theology of marriage that will mark the distinct identity of Christians amidst the Roman imperial culture.

---

488 Annette Merz, *Why did the Pure Bride of Christ,* 139.

489 O'Brien, *Ephesians,* 431.

490 R. C, Ortlund, *Whoredom: God's Unfaithful Wife in Biblical Theology* (Leicester/ Grand Rapids: Apollos/Eerdmans, 1996), 156.

491 G. W. Dawes, *The Body in Question: Metaphor and Meaning in the Interpretation of Ephesians 5:21-33* (Leiden: Brill, 1998), 175-85.

492 O'Brien, *Ephesians,* 432.

As inferred from v. 31, the love of both the first Adam and the last Adam toward their body/bride, grounded in primeval human origins support the argument that "Christ and the church in a loving relationship is the paradigm for the Christian husband and wife."[493] Ortlund proposes thus: the mystery in v. 32 denotes the line of thought running through the whole passage than just the preceding verse (v. 31).[494] Therefore, the mystery is referring to the union of Christ and the Church which is expected in reality to be reflected in the marital union of humans.

It seems that the author of Ephesians is concerned about formulating a theology of marital union incorporating the teachings of both Judaism and Christianity. The marital union is not a contractual relationship as the Roman society would think of, but a sacramental union, to the extent of becoming one flesh, enhancing mutuality. Despite the criticisms raised by feminist interpreters, there is a great sense of mutuality envisioned in such a 'one flesh' relationship. The issue at hand could be how the interpreter redeems the text from the overarching tone of subordination and highlights the significant aspect of mutuality overtaking subordination in the whole pericope. In this whole process of evaluating the tension between subordination and mutuality in marriage in Eph. 5:21-33, the encounter with the dominant notions of patriarchal and imperial hierarchy is quite disturbing.

Christological and Ecclesiological Nuances: A Counter-Culture to Roman Household Codes

Since the Ephesian household code and especially the wife-husband pair directly link to the Ephesian understanding of Christology and ecclesiology, it would be appropriate to subject them under postcolonial feminist theological lens. The analogy between Christ and husband and wife and church begins in v. 23 and continues throughout the passage.

---

493 O'Brien, *Ephesians,* 433.

494 Ortlund, *Whoredom,* 156, cited by O'Brien, *Ephesians,* 433.

> It could be argued that the Christ-church analogy to the relationship of husbands and wives can be a case of mutual illumination, reciprocity in the way one relationship sheds light on the other, especially on the basis of v. 21. But because the Christ-church analogy is used to provide motive and theological justification for the exhortation to wives and in later verses, to husbands, the balance is more lopsided than mutual.[495]

Here, husband is head of wife not by nature but out of reverence to Christ. The author is not interested in demonstrating why it is to be husband over wife rather than wife over husband. If wife is "in Christ" as fully as husband is "in Christ," it is not apparent how the relationship with Christ entitles either to headship over the other. What becomes predominant here is that, on the basis of verse 21, each one should submit to the other. "However tempered, no sound exegesis can fully overcome the subordination of wife to husband explicit in the Ephesian *Haustafel.* It probably is best understood as representing a cultural and cultic pattern already established, the Ephesian code being one attempt to Christianize it."[496]

In contrast to the one verse allocation to husbands' role in Col. 3:19, ("Husbands, love your wives and never treat them harshly" NRSV), here in Ephesian household code, husbands' duties are expanded into six verses (25-30). In the Christological metaphor, love and sacrifice are combined together. Christ's love for the Church led him to give up his own life, which means that love is unconditional even to the point of death.

Muddimann understands Christ's love in terms of his surrendering to the church. This is derived from 5:2, where Christians are to live in love on the model of Christ, who "loved us and gave himself up for us, a fragrant offering and sacrifice to God." The concept of sacrifice has clear links to complete

---

495 R. Schnackenburg, *Ephesians: A Commentary* (Edinburgh: T & T Clark, 1991), and C. L. Mitton, *Ephesians* (London: Oliphants, 1976), cited by Tanzer, *Ephesians*, 334.

496 Frank Stagg, The Domestic Code and Final Appeal Ephesians 5:21-6:24, *The Review and the Expositor,*(vol. 76, no. 4, Fall 1979): 545.

surrendering.[497] This explanation raises the possibilities of understanding the household duty of husbands in terms of subordination or submission similar to the duty of wives. Even though it is not clearly spelt out as in the case of wives, it is implicit in v. 25 that husbands are also required to exhibit such a great Christian virtue of sacrifice or submission as a matter of Christian living. If then, one probably may identify some space to accommodate the mutual relationship of love and submission between wives and husbands.

The author of Ephesians, by asking the husbands to love their wives, is actually setting a resistant tone to the then prevailing Greco-Roman household codes. It was by no means conventional in the imperial Roman society to expect of husbands to love their wives. The marriage relationship is generally viewed as a contractual bond, which can be broken legally at any time by divorce. Since wives continued to live under the patriarchal control of their fathers even after their marriage, the husbands were actually not enjoying much legal control over their wives in Roman society.

In such a context of lacking emotional bond between wives and husbands in a conventional Roman society, it would be radical and revolutionary to demand from husbands love toward their wives. It raises the question whether such an exhortation challenges the patriarchal domination safeguarded by the imperial powers. Despite the conventional understanding of patriarchal domination in the Ephesian passage, it nevertheless exhibits a kind of constant resistance to the norms of the world outside the Church. Can this kind of approach be called a defensive strategy in developing a unique Christian identity different from those who live outside the Church in the Roman captivated world? The argument of Carolyn Osiek and Margaret McDonald answers thus:

> The household code of Ephesians represents a defensive strategy in the sense that it promulgates a vision of marriage that is integral to an emerging identity in opposition to those on the outside. What is ironic about the social

---

497 Muddimann, *Ephesians,* 264.

> impact of the exhortations, however, is that they do not in fact create a visibly distinct identity in the social realm. Understood as shaped by "reverence for Christ" (Eph. 5:21), but nevertheless providing concrete patterns for daily life that are conventional, the household code provides a type of balance between flight from society and confrontation with society. The code ties the community defensively to a social structure that has the power to render members fairly invisible among their neighbours. But lest anyone misunderstand the overarching program, the author of Ephesians moves immediately from the code imbued with the socio-political agenda of traditional household management to a call to do battle with evil (Eph. 6:10-20). This strategy for survival often manifests itself outwardly in highly conventional terms, but it is rooted in the conviction that there is no compromise to be made with a profoundly evil world.[498]

Their argument explains how the Ephesian household code struggles to strike a balance between the social demands of the Roman imperial society and the pressing need to have a distinct Christian identity. The resistance to the imperial power system is inherent in the Ephesian household, but masked by the resemblance to the social codes of surrounding society.

Soteriology

Salvation is a central theme in the letter to the Ephesians. God's plan for salvation is worked out before 'the foundation of the world' (1:4). This highlights the fact that the elect are chosen before the creation of the world. Christ, unlike the husband, not only is the head of his body (the church) but its saviour as well. ""Saviour" acts as a kind of code word for Christ's whole work of redemption, out of which the church lives. The church derives not only her origins from Christ but also her continuing saved existence."[499] When the author shifts

498 Osiek and MacDonald, *A Woman's Place,* 122-23.

499 Schnackenburg, *Ephesians,* and Mitton, *Ephesians,* cited by Tanzer, *Ephesians,* 334.

from Christ as "head of the church" to "savior of the body" it is not apparent whether his primary concern continues with the wife/husband relationship or reverts to the letter's earlier preoccupation with the church as the body of Christ. In what follows, there is oscillation between both concerns (v. 32).

A major question that arises here is whether the saviour concept is applied only to Christ-church relationship. Is husband also understood to be the saviour of the wife? A similar concern is found in 1 Cor. 7:12-16, where a husband might save his wife, in case of the marriage between a believer husband and a non-believer wife. Similarly, a believing wife might save her unbelieving husband. However, the Corinthian context is entirely different from that of Ephesians, where both husband and wife are apparently believers. "Saviour as a christological title is rare in Paul, occurring only at Phil. 3:20; but it becomes more frequent in the deutero-pauline letters (2 Tim. 1.10; Titus 1.4; 2.13; 3.6) and in post-Pauline literature from Asia Minor (2 Pet. 1.1 etc.; John 4.42; 1 John 4.14). It is a regular designation for Yahweh in the LXX (cf. Isa. 45.15)."[500]

Lincoln draws insights from the story of Tobias and Sarah in Tobit 6 that Tobias' marriage to Sarah will save her from the demonic power. Lincoln thinks that the term saviour "should be taken in general sense of protector or provider for welfare and order in the way it would have been applied to the emperor in its Hellenistic usage."[501] Lincoln is not strictly exploring the imperial background of the term, 'saviour'. But he has initiated a conversation by drawing our attention to Hellenistic understanding of the same. Muddimann's comment is significant at this point:

> The initial reluctance on the part of early Christian writers to use it of Christ is surprising; it may have been caused by the associations of the title with the cult of the Roman Emperor as *Salvator Mundi.* However, as the conflict between the Church and the Roman state intensified towards the end of the first century and became more official, Christians more

500 Muddimann, *Ephesians,* 262

501 Lincoln, *Ephesians,* 370.

> and more claimed the title, polemically, for Christ rather than Caesar as the real saviour of the world. [502]

Attributing the title of 'saviour' to Christ certainly has serious political implications, which direct the focus to the anti-imperial elements in the Christian form of Greco-Roman household codes.

Realized Eschatology

The author of Ephesians bases the theology of marriage on the realized eschatological connotations. The imagery of Christ-church relationship highlights the present continuing relationship, which is different from that of futuristic eschatology by which the marriage between Christ and church was treated as an end time event. Lincoln comments that this shift in the theology of end time and marriage could be directed to address the ascetic tendencies within the church.[503] Merz supports this argument further that

> ...the addressees of Ephesians actually included persons who advocated an existence free of marriage. This probability is increased by the clear option taken by the letter for a realized eschatology, which would lead to the same general distance vis-a-vis earthly ties, and the enthusiastic desire to lead an angelic life...[504]

Therefore, the intention of the author is to justify the institution of marriage as a continuing relation of Christ-church model so that the Ephesian community would opt for a stabilized notion of marriage and family.

In Eph. 5:25-26, Christ sanctifies the church, moving it toward its ultimate splendor and perfection. It is a present continuous action

---

502 Muddimann, *Ephesians*, 262. The older view that the phrase 'saviour of the body' reflects gnostic speculations about the redeemer who saves fallen Sophia ... has seemed less plausible to recent commentators, both because of the chronology of the surviving identifiably gnostic evidence, and also because of the likelihood that such speculations were themselves dependent on a particular misreading of texts in the Pauline letters.

503 Lincoln, *Ephesians,* 363.

504 Annette Merz, *Why did the Pure Bride of Christ,* 135.

which is already realized in the present world even as the believers are still waiting for the consummation. Christ, by his act of 'cleansing with the washing of water in word', manifests his love and self-giving to the church and his efforts to bring church to her glorious fulfillment.

By using 'in word' *(rema),* the author probably refers to the word of God or Christ's word as in Eph. 6:17. God's word is a creative word; it accomplishes and does not just express.[505] Therefore, the reference to 'in word' certainly goes beyond the external washing to a continuous cleansing through the continuing work of the Scriptures in believers' lives.

A Theology of Creation

In the letter to the Ephesians, Christ is pictured as the head of both creation and the Church. Christ is the one in whom all things are summed up (1:10) and in whom the elect are chosen from the creation of the world (1:4). Muddimann feels that in 1. 22-3, Christ is the 'head over all things for the Church, his body', which in fact shows how the themes of creation and ecclesiology are intertwined.[506]

The reference to husband as the head of the wife echoes Pauline theology of creation from 1 Cor. 11:2-16. 1 Cor. 11:3 states that "husband is the head of his wife." Augustinian theology patronizes this patriarchal argument. According to him, only the male possesses the image of God; women are included in the image of God only 'under the male' as their head (husband). Femaleness, for him, does not reflect God but reflects the bodily creation that the human male is given to rule over.[507]

The traditional hierarchy maintained in the interpretation of creation stories is justified in Ephesians by blending it well with Christology, soteriology and ecclesiology. Merz identifies this:

---

505 Stagg, *The Domestic Code and Final Appeal,* 546. The term "baptism" is not employed, and there is no way to determine usage here. Baptism naturally comes to mind, because of its dominance as initiation rite.

506 Muddimann, *Ephesians,* 261.

507 Augustine, *De Trinitate* 7.7.10 cited by Ruether, *Redemption in Christian Feminism*, 84.

> … in 5.25-32 the underlying axiom that the woman is the flesh/body of the man is justified in terms of creation theology by means of the μία-σάρξ idea from Gen 2.24; at the same time, this is presented as the image of the relationship between Christ and the *Ekklêsia,* rooted in Christ's gift of himself and his loving care for his bride/body. These justifications show that marriage is the *only lifestyle* which does justice to the will of the Creator and to the event of redemption.[508]

In the Septuagint, *kephale* is used to translate the Hebrew term, *rosh*, which indicates "the notion of authority being connected with that of priority."[509] The terms like 'head' and 'body' appear together in Eph. 1:22 apart from 5:22-24. Even though such combination is missing in Septuagint, the same is found in Greco-Roman imperial literature, "where the city or state was depicted as a body, the ruler could be seen as "head" of the body."[510]

The Greek God Zeus is often referred to as head of the cosmos, "pervading it with his power as it lies in his mighty body."[511] Referring to Christ as *kephale* in Eph. 1:22 denotes Christ's authority over the whole cosmos. In 4:15, the church is expected to grow up unto Christ, the head, which may highlight the use of *kephale* as the source or origin. The same combination of 'head' and 'body' appears in 5:22-24, where husband is referred to as the head of his wife. Now the question is whether the term *kephale* is used for husband in the same sense as ruler or source or as a combination of both.

Given the Greco-Roman context of patriarchal household relations, it may be easy to understand the role of husband as that

---

508 Annette Merz, *Why did the Pure Bride of Christ,* 137.

509 Lincoln, *Ephesians*, 67. The connotations of the Hebrew *rosh* lies behind kefalh; and mean that in some places kefalh; is synonimous with arch and has the force of determinative source or origin; this llows for the development of thought whereby the body is not only in subjection to the head as its authoritative "overlord" but also derives its growth and development from its head. See Lincoln, *Ephesians*, 69-70.

510 Cf. Tacitus, Plutarch, Curtius Rufus, Philo use the combination of head and body in this sense in their literature. See Lincoln, *Ephesians,* 69.

511 Lincoln, *Ephesians,* 69.

of a ruler or someone holding authority over the whole household. Aristotle says, "The rule of the household is a monarchy, for every house is under one head."[512] However, the use of *kephale* in terms of source or origin at this point is implicit if 1 Cor. 11:1-16 is taken into account, where the author is arguing for the headship of husband from the creation story where Eve is created from Adam. The role of *paterfamilias* in a Roman household attests to an enormous amount of authority by virtue of his position in the family. In such a context, the Christian ethics based on such a hierarchical concept is against the spirit of Christian egalitarianism.

Apart from the implicit reference to creation in the notion of headship in vv. 22-24, there is also a clear quotation from Gen. 2:24 in Eph. 5:31. The use of the Jewish understanding of marriage in a Greco-Roman social context, especially in a Christian epistle, highlights a kind of overlapping of spaces as possible in a colonial context. There are clear pressures from the surrounding Greco-Roman culture to adapt their social norms into Christian living. However, the author of Ephesians is trying to negotiate with them in order to create an exclusive identity of their own. The household code duties in Eph. 5:21-33 though resemble the surrounding social norms, express a clear-cut resistance to the same by incorporating ethical values form the Jewish and Christian ways of life. By quoting from Gen. 2:24, the author is trying to show the readers that their understanding of marital obligations does not base on the Greco-Roman social norms, but on their ancestral roots of religious living. Nevertheless, the tension continues as the reader identifies an androcentric bias in v. 33, where wives have to fear their husbands.

The Mutual "One-Flesh" Relationship: A Third Space of Enunciation

Eph. 5:21-33 highlights 'mutuality' and 'headship', two seemingly contradictory concepts within the context of marital relationships. The pericope starts with the notion of 'mutuality' in v. 21 where all the saints or the believers of the Ephesian church are called to

512 Aristotle, *Politics,* 1255 b, cited by Lincoln, *Ephesians,* 69.

submit to one another out of reverence for Christ. Here, there is no disparity or distinction between members of the Ephesian christian community and submission is portrayed as a characteristic of Spirit-filled life.

But, in the immediately succeeding verses, i.e., vv. 22-24, the headship of husbands over wives is emphasized along with wives' subordination to their husbands. This domination-subjugation model is again replaced by mutuality in vv. 28-31, where the wife-husband relationship is considered as the mutual "one-flesh" relationship.[513] And the final verse in this pericope, v. 33, is the recapitulation of the hierarchical stand of the author by reinstating love and fear (submission) as the key gender norms of husband and wife respectively. In such a context of overlapping presence of mutuality and headship in Eph. 5:21-33, how can headship-subordination be understood in connection with mutuality in marriage? Can these two concepts exist simultaneously in a marital relationship? How can it be justified theologically to hold both mutuality and headship in the Ephesian passage?

It has already been explained in the second chapter that the Ephesian passage heavily draws its material from the surrounding Greco-Roman culture, especially from the Roman household-duties. In Greco-Roman contexts, the content of the household codes predominantly revolves around structures of authority and order between wife-husband, children-father and slave-master pairs of relationships.

Even though there are a variety of household codes such as Aristotelian, Stoic, and Neo-Platonic household codes in the Hellenistic culture, it is the Aristotelian tradition of household norms that prevailed in the New Testament literature, produced during Roman imperialism. Aristotle's literature plays a significant role in deciding the kind of gender norms pertaining to Roman social codes. It would be appropriate at this point to evaluate whether the author of Ephesians uncritically incorporates the Roman household duties.

513 Andrew T. Lincoln calls the kind of relation between wife and husband in Eph. 5:21-33, the mutual "one flesh" relationship. Lincoln, *Ephesians,* 361.

Aristotle is concerned about the "proportional equity between husband and wife ("the man rules in accordance with his worth") and a constitutional aristocracy of the husband over the wife based on this superior worth."[514] This is strictly contradictory to the idea of mutual submission expected of wife and husband in v. 21, where they are exhorted to submit to one another out of reverence for Christ.

Further Aristotle is commending on the superiority of men on the basis of the order of nature. He feels that man is by nature fitter for command than women. In this way he attests to the proportional equity of husbands and wives in the "alleged higher deliberative powers of males."[515] But the author of Ephesians places the motivation for mutual submission on their reverence for Christ. It is neither the fear of Roman empire nor of the emperor that motivates the Christian community in Ephesus to opt for an imperial notion like submission, which would send waves of terror in an imperial context.

It is further contradictory to the kind of imperial notion of power and hegemony that the role of husband is equated to Christ, a role model for self-sacrificing love. Aristotle attaches more of social honour and power to husbands as he believes that men deserve the best in home and society by virtue of their manhood.[516] Here it becomes necessary to look into the male honour-shame values of Greco-Roman society.

Is Christianity in general compromising on the concept of egalitarian Christian family by succumbing to the honor-shame values of the imperial environment? It gets Scholarly approval that

> although primitive Christianity never completely escaped the honor-shame codes of Roman Hellenism, it did fracture or partially undermine them. The early church required Christian men to restrict their sexual activity to their wives. The church also rejected the agnostic challenge-riposte pattern of the Greco-Roman male-honor code.[517]

514 Aristotle cited by Lincoln, *Ephesians, 7.*

515 Aristotle (Politics 1.12.) cited by Lincoln, *Ephesians, 7.*

516 Aristotle (Nicomachean Ethics 8.11) cited by Lincoln, *Ephesians, 7.*

517 Lincoln, *Ephesians,* 69.

John W. Miller comments that the New Testament household codes including the Ephesian one do not undermine, subvert or destroy their patriarchal counterparts in the wider Roman Hellenistic society, rather they modify "by curtailing male promiscuity and establishing males in caring husband/father roles in families."[518]

The mutual "one flesh" marital relationship in Eph. 5:31 negates all possibilities of treating wife as the 'other' and nullifies any kind of domination over the other's body. In a marital bond, where husband treats his wife as his own body or flesh, there is no room for subjugation of the other's emotions and will. This may resonate the egalitarian *kerygma* of the early Jesus movement, which has been defeated in the course of time. This is re-iterated further that,

> The pervasive patriarchal attitudes of the ancient world presented a formidable cultural fact for Christians trying to be respectable citizens and to integrate into Greco-Roman society. ...the New Testament codes represent early accommodations and compromises to mainstream Hellenistic culture; in other words, in the post-Pauline period, Christians caved into cultural pressures and abandoned the egalitarian thrust of the gospel in order to meet the expectations of the dominant patriarchal order.[519]

Therefore, there must have been some negotiations with the Roman gender norms in the process of the political subversion of the household codes. However, further inquiry into the concept of mutuality appearing side by side with headship-subjugation model reveals the tension that still persists in the wife-husband relationship in Eph. 5:21-33.

The Ephesian household projects a new set of household codes exclusively for the Ephesian Christian community which will challenge the surrounding imperial norms. However, in doing this, the author does not clearly demarcate the differences envisioned for the Ephesian community. Instead, there is a silent outplay of

518 John W. Miller, *Calling God "Father": Essays on the Bible, Fatherhood and Culture* (New Jersey: Paulist Press, 1926), cited by Lincoln, Ephesians, 69.

519 Lincoln, *Ephesians,* 96.

traditional Roman expectations about its subjugates by incorporating traditions of sacred marriages and Hebrew spousal relationships between Yahweh and Israel.

John Paul II highlights "a conspirational egalitarian *Kerygma*" by which "the gospel does not disown lay cultures but engages them in their historical particularity and presses for their re-creation. The strategy for social reform is to enter into everyday relationships and to effect "transformation from within" by inserting radically new theological leaven that subverts the inner core of patriarchal codes."[520] From this argument, it can be inferred that even though the Roman patriarchal notions generally go unchallenged, there is an attempt to ensure a transformation from within towards establishing egalitarian marriage.

The analogy of husband as head of wife and Christ as head of church is a symbol of biblical vision for an egalitarian marital bond. If such an imagery is overemphasized beyond the original context of Roman imperialism and early Christian church, it can become a dangerous metaphor of marriage demeaning the full personhood of wives or women in general. The comparison of husband to Christ is only an analogy and not a literal statement. Pope John Paul II comments on this analogy that "whereas in the relationship between Christ and the Church the subjection is only on the part of the Church, in the relationship between husband and wife the 'subjection' is not one-sided but mutual."[521] This kind of mutuality is based on Christ's self-sacrificing love which is modeled for both wife and husband. Therefore, the mutual "one flesh" relationship moves beyond the exclusive gender norms assigned for wives to submit to husbands and for husbands to love their wives. It now becomes imperative in a mutual relationship to love each other and to submit to each other.

Bhabha's idea of 'third space of enunciation' makes a remarkable contribution to understand the contradictory presence of the two notions of mutuality and headship in Eph. 5:21-33. The concept of

---

520 John Paul II, *On the Dignity and Vocation of Women* (United States Catholic Conference: Washington, D.C., 1988), 9.

521 John Paul II, *On the Dignity and Vocation of Women,* no. 24.

submission of wives to their husbands is radically challenged by the exhortation to husbands to love their wives. The self-sacrificial love remains inconsistent with the hierarchy between wife and husband. It seems that the Ephesian marital norms exhibit the struggle on the part of the author to do away with the Greco-Roman ideology while at the same time actively interacting with them. This presents what they hoped for: "mutuality negates the hierarchical nature of the imperial process."[522] Further the Ephesian household code is developed by the author by incorporating Jewish and Christian religious values into an imperial set of marital codes. Such interpolations alter the original form and function of Greco-Roman household codes. In this way, the Ephesian household code stands out as a constant threat to the imperial and patriarchal hegemony.

The inherent Resistance to Imperial and patriarchal hegemony in the Ephesian text is not necessarily an overt act of confrontation, but one that can be decoded from the ambivalent attitude of presenting mutuality and headship simultaneously in the text. This text, highlighting the conflict between dominant ideology and the ideology of the marginalized Christian community at Ephesus, provides space for resistance and subversion because the hegemony of the dominant is constantly challenged by such discourses. In this way, the Ephesian household code continues to renegotiate the power-claims of imperialism by mimicking "almost the same, but not quite."

It is the paradoxical status of wives and husbands in Eph. 5:21-33 that highlights the 'almost the same, but not quite' portrayal of the marital bond. The new paradoxical status in Christ challenges the patriarchal and imperial notions embedded in the Roman household norms. The husband is expected to love his wife as her head just like Christ loves the church. Christ's headship is characterized by the power of love, which is paradoxically revealed in the weakness of his sacrificial death. Similarly, the mutual submission expected of all believers in v. 21 continues to remain applicable for husbands as well, even though they are metaphorically equated to Christ. Further, a husband's headship is evaluated by the amount of love manifested in

522 Ashcroft, *Post-Colonial Studies,* 119.

his sacrificial attitude to his wife. Therefore, the Ephesian household code, and especially the marital gender norms continuously negotiate with the power structures of the Roman marital codes, by which the passage remains resistant to the imperial power notions of the hegemony of Roman imperialism.

Summary of Findings

In this chapter, the literary critical tools proposed by postcolonial and feminist biblical hermeneutics help to evaluate the imperial and patriarchal nuances identified in the exegetical study of Eph. 5:21-33, done in the previous chapter.

Marriage as an institution, successfully maintains the non-egalitarian gender norms. This is evident from the kind of gender norms attached to wives and husbands in the Ephesian passage. Attitudes of submission and fear in wives would unsurprisingly make them subject to authority structures. This calls for a re-reading of the gender norms through a postcolonial lens to analyze how imperial and patriarchal ideologies are intertwined to maintain a hierarchical system. However, the imagery of Christ stands as an exemplary model for husbands to love their wives sacrificially to the point of risking their lives to death. Nevertheless, domestic violence in many marriages is caused by the authoritarian attitude of husbands which unduly expect the wives to render selfless service.

A postcolonial feminist reading of the gender norms questions the binaries created by the popularized Western philosophy. According to the Western interpretation, gender is understood as categories of 'male' and 'female' and there is always the predominance of 'masculinity' over femininity'. But in Christian marriages, the marital gender norms need to be remolded to incorporate justice in an ethic of love.

Eph. 5:21-33 plays a significant role in the theological formulations of Christianity especially in relation to marriage. The author of Ephesians gives a vivid picture of the Christians' effort to establish a unique theology of marriage in the context of growing influence of Roman cultural and ethical values. Since the first century Ephesian Christians were predominantly converts from either Jewish or Greco-Roman religio-cultural background, the Christian social and familial existence reflected much of the hybrid identities of the time. Marriage is a significant social institution, which reflects the impact of the surrounding cultures.

The unity motif prevails through the Ephesians, which also appears in Eph. 5:21-33. If wife and husband are to be treated as 'one-flesh', then there is no room for domination in marital relationship. The notion of reconciliation helps in understanding the interpolation of Gen. 2:24 into Eph. 5:31. The concept of wife and husband becoming one flesh over against a patriarchal context marks the possibilities of reconciliation between unequally treated marriage partners. Therefore, the marital gender roles in Eph. 5:21-33 could better be understood if reconciliation between Jews and gentiles in Eph. 2:14-15 is applied for the broken hierarchical relationship between the spouses.

However, there have been very disturbing dimensions of the kind of marital relationship envisioned in the Ephesian passage. For instance, the question of whose identity prevails in the one-flesh relationship raises serious challenges to the growing cases of domestic violence in patriarchal societies. Such challenges raised by feminist interpreters inspire to explore the complexity inherent in the two contradictory concepts like mutuality and hierarchy appearing together in the same passage.

The Roman society would probably think of marital union as a contractual relationship. But for the author of the letter to the Ephesians, it is more like a sacramental union, to the extent of wife and husband becoming one flesh enhancing mutuality. There is a great sense of mutuality envisioned in such a 'one flesh' relationship. Nevertheless, the text constantly reveals a tension between a mutual relationship and a hierarchical one. Only deliberate theological attempts could bring about a desirable change by redeeming the text from the overarching tone of subordination.

It could be argued that the Christ-church imagery is used in Eph. 5:21-33 to underscore the relation between husband-wife pair and thus to evolve a theology of marriage that will mark the distinct identity of Christians amidst the Roman imperial culture. The analogy between Christ and husband and the church and wife is a unique feature to the Ephesian household codes. Even though the metaphor of Christ-Church has certain limitations, it tends to pose resistance to the Greco-Roman household codes. It is by no means conventional in the imperial Roman society to expect of husbands to love their wives. The marriage is generally viewed as a relation on contractual bond, which can be broken legally at any time by divorce. Since wives continued to live under the patriarchal control of their fathers even after their marriage, the husbands were actually not enjoying much legal control over their wives in Roman society. In such a context of lacking emotional bond between wives and husbands in a conventional Roman society, it would be radical and revolutionary to demand husbands to love their wives.

In trying to develop a soteriology from Eph. 5:21-33, it is recognized that there was initial reluctance on the part of early Christian writers to use the title 'saviour' for Jesus Christ. This title has close associations with the cult of the Roman Emperor as *Salvator Mundi.* However, as the conflict between the Church and the Roman state intensified towards the end of the first century and became more official, Christians began to claim the title, polemically, for Christ rather than Caesar as the real saviour of the world.

Despite Christ-Church metaphor links to husband-wife relationship, the 'saviour' concept refers exclusively to salvific role of Christ. A husband can never take upon himself the role of a saviour. The soteriological formulations are closely related to the eschatological propositions as well. The imagery of Christ-church relationship highlights the present continuing relationship, which is different from that of futuristic eschatology by which the marriage between Christ and church was treated as an end time event.

The Ephesian passage of our study also provides pointers to the Jewish theology of creation from the book of Genesis, which has been incorporated into the Greco-Roman household codes to create a distinct Christian dependence on Hebrew Scriptures. Having incorporated ethical values from the Jewish and Christian ways of life, the author tries to project resistance to the surrounding dominant Greco-Roman culture. The implicit reference to Creation in the notion of headship in vv. 22-24 and the direct quotation from Gen. 2:24 in Eph. 5:31 serve the purpose of showing the readers that their understanding of marital obligations do not base on the Greco-Roman social norms, but on their ancestral roots of religious living.

Finally, the pericope starts with the notion of 'mutuality' in v. 21 and ensures no disparity or distinction between any member of the Ephesian Christian community and submission as a characteristic of Spirit-filled life, nevertheless, the concept of headship lingers around in husband's attitude to wife. In the relationship between Christ and the Church, the subjection is only on the part of the Church, whereas, in the relationship between husband and wife the 'subjection' is not one-sided but mutual. This kind of mutuality is based on Christ's self-sacrificing love which is modeled for both wife and husband.

Therefore, the mutual "one flesh" relationship moves beyond the exclusive gender norms assigned for wives to submit to husbands and for husbands to love their wives. It now becomes imperative in a mutual relationship to love each other and to submit to each other. The mutual "one flesh" marital relationship in Eph. 5:31 negates all possibilities of treating wife as the 'other' and nullifies any kind of domination over the other's body. In a marital bond, where husband treats his wife as his own body or flesh, there is no room for subjugation of the other's emotions and will.

Conclusion

To conclude, the methodological framework developed from Bhabha's 'Third Space of Enunciation' helps to identify the Ephesian passage on wife-husband relationship as a site for postcolonial and feminist theological formulations. Since Ephesus itself is a colonized city and a prominent centre of Christianity in the first century Roman imperial era, it is quite appropriate to have explored the impact of Greco-Roman religion, ideology and ethics on the Christian living in its early stages of development. The Church at Ephesus existed in a multicultural context of Jewish, Greco-Roman and Christian socio-religious and cultural values. It is inevitable that Christianity in its initial stages of establishment had negotiated with the dominant imperial values to sustain its existence.

Christianity, until the destruction of the Jerusalem Temple in 70 CE and the canonization of Hebrew Scriptures at Jamnia in 85 CE, continued to live in the shadow of the legacy of Jewish ancestry. Therefore, in the struggle to establish an exclusive and unique identity for Christianity, there could have been many points of contacts with the surrounding cultures and religions. This would have created trans-cultural spaces of mutual cultural exchange nullifying hierarchical purity of cultures.

Due to the hybridization of Jewish, Greco-Roman and Christian ideas of religion and culture, the letter to the Ephesians tend to portray a narrative ambivalence as a literature. Thus, the reader encounters anti-imperial strategies in such literature not in an explicit manner, but in a subtle way in the form of hybridity and colonial mimicry.

In the portrayal of wife-husband relationship in Eph. 5:21-33, the author mimics the Greco-Roman household codes for Christians. However, the imperial household norms are not adapted just as they are; instead they undergo tremendous modifications on the basis of both Jewish and Christian ethical values. This, in fact, creates a hybridized identity for the Christian Church at Ephesus. It may look superficially that the Ephesian Church is imitating the dominant imperial social ideologies, however, an in-depth analysis unravels the overlapping identities, which in turn pose threats to the dominant ideologies.

Thus, in the Ephesian marital norms, a reader identifies two way interaction of the Roman Empire, the colonizers and the Ephesian Church, the colonized towards creating something new, in Bhabha's words, "third space of enunciation." As it is evident, the colonial mimicry of Roman household codes highlights that in spite of the adoption of the Greco-Roman cultural habits, assumptions, institutions and values, the result is simply not a mere imitation. Therefore, the kind of threat inherent in mimicking the Roman household codes does not pose an overt resistance, but continually projects a new identity different from the surrounding Roman society. This kind of tension is what expressed when Bhabha says, "almost the same, but not quite." Therefore, the wife-husband relationship narrated in Eph. 5:21-33 would demand the readers to recognize the hybridized 'one-flesh mutual relationship' which surpasses a subjugate-dominant marital bond.

Chapter 6

Conclusion

This book emerged by identifying a problem of the submission of wives to the husbands in the household code of Eph. 5:21-33. This becomes an issue when it is viewed against the mutual submission mentioned in Eph. 5:21. While the radical exhortation stands out in this passage for husbands to love their wives just like Christ loved the Church and gave himself up for the same, the household duties attached to wives to submit to their husbands in everything (cf. v. 24) and to fear them (cf. v. 33) pose a challenge to the Christian egalitarian norms of gender justice. However, the analogies drawn from the Church-Christ model indicate the possibilities of challenging the traditional patriarchal norms, which were prevalent in the then Greco-Roman colonized Palestine or specifically in Ephesus. The present research explored the passage of study with the hypothesis that the Ephesian household code was heavily influenced by the Greco-Roman household codes, which most probably had been brought to contact with Christian homes through Hellenistic Judaism and Greco-Roman converts to Christianity.

A theological evaluation of the imperial and patriarchal nuances in Eph. 5:21-33 resonates with the postcolonial postulation of Homi Bhabha, i.e., a 'third space of enunciation,' in that the hybridization of multi-cultures (Jewish, Greco-Roman and Christian) leads into a trans-cultural space where the colonial domination has been continually challenged. The outcome of colonial exchange between the colonizer and the colonized always end up in innovative arenas of social existence.

Emperor worship and Roman-imposed rules in Ephesus had considerably influenced the life of Christians as well, to the extent of incorporating Roman imperial social and moral codes into Christian ethic. The Jews in Ephesus had been forced to absorb and affirm the socio-political hierarchical system that the Roman government had designed for the civil society in general. Over against their religious and moral codes of living, the Jews had to constantly negotiate with the demands of Roman administration, in order to foster a peaceful living. Now as far as the Jewish Christians were concerned, there were clear indications of heresies creeping into Ephesian church (Eph. 4:17-32; 5:10-20) due to the overarching impact of Roman religions, imperial cult and their social codes of living. And for the Gentile Christians, it was very much in line with their earlier social customs to adapt a Greco-Roman household code into their Christian homes. This is well attested by the presence of Jewish and Christian values in the imperial set of marital codes found in the letter to the Ephesians. Such interpolations in fact alter the original form and function of Greco-Roman household codes. In this way, the Ephesian household code stands out as a constant threat to the imperial and patriarchal hegemony.

The inherent resistance to imperial and patriarchal hegemony in the Ephesian text is not necessarily an overt act of confrontation, but one that can be decoded from the ambivalent attitude of presenting mutuality and headship simultaneously in the text. This text, highlighting the conflict between dominant ideology and the ideology of the marginalized Christian community at Ephesus, provides space for resistance and subversion because the hegemony of the dominant is constantly challenged by such discourses. In this way, the Ephesian household code continues to renegotiate the power-claims of imperialism by mimicking "almost the same, but not quite".

Bhabha's idea of 'third space of enunciation' makes a remarkable contribution to understand the contradictory presence of the two notions of mutuality and headship in Eph. 5:21-33. The concept of submission of wives to their husbands is radically challenged by the exhortation to husbands to love their wives. The self-sacrificial love remains inconsistent with the hierarchy between wife and husband. It seems that the Ephesian marital norms exhibit the struggle on the part of the author to do away with the Greco-Roman ideology while at the same time actively interacting with them. This presents what they hoped for: "mutuality negates the hierarchical nature of the imperial process."[523]

When femaleness is assumed to be less than maleness, a relationship of dominance and submission results as is evident in Eph. 5:21-33. Since husbands are projected as persons of superior nature within marriage in connection with their gender roles, they may tend to develop a superior self-image. This leads to treating women as private property, "to be battered and used accordingly,"[524] as is evident in the dowry system and bride burning especially in India.

The social nurturing of male domination starts right from the natal home by the practical assumption that boys are superior to girls and they are physically and mentally stronger. This ultimately leads to a higher share in the resources such as health care, nutrition, education and material assets. Such an oppressive familial ideology fosters a fertile soil to cultivate self-conscious and oppressive ego in a male psyche. This is strongly interwoven in the societal fabric that it restricts women to exercise their legitimate freedom within marital relationships.

Wives are ideally expected to obey their husbands in 'everything' and this eventually calls for a silent bearing of all the atrocities inflicted upon them. Women remain silent mainly because the social system forces them to ignore domestic violence in order to save the honour of their families. This kind of attitude is enhanced by the shame-honor binaries of ethical living in many societies.

---

523 Ashcroft, *Post-Colonial Studies,* 119.

524 Rosemary Radford Reuther, Women's Liberation in Historical and Theological Perspective," in *Women's Liberation and the Church,* edited by Sarah Bentley Doely (New York: Association Press, 1970).

Sexual violence or harassment has existed in families for ages, but it has been concealed in the silence of wives because of the dependent and subservient gender roles attached to them. Since an ideal wife is projected as a stereotype of tolerance and submissiveness to her husband, victims of domestic violence do not share their struggles with others, thereby giving a way of escape to their guilty husbands. Moreover, there exists a fear of being rejected apart from the shame of being humiliated by the society.

Against the background of growing domestic violence against women in their marital homes, the study of Eph. 5:21-33 encounters various challenges. Selected anti-women biblical passages like 1 Tim. 2:11-15, Titus 2:5, 1 Pet. 3:1, and Eph. 5:22-23, 33 are interpreted from an andro-centric perspective to propagate marriage of unequal partners. According to these passages, wives cannot have authority over their husbands and they need to remain submissive to their husbands. Wives are weaker vessels in relation to their husbands. Further, uncritical readings of such passages and their interpretation especially during matrimonial services have confused the Christian minds regarding marriage.[525] A marital bond based on fear and submission ends up in broken relationships.

A postcolonial feminist reading of Eph. 5:21-33 undertaken in the present study exposes possibilities of re-reading the most misinterpreted and manipulated biblical passages. Christian marriage, as inferred from Eph. 5:21-33, is based on the imagery of the Christ-church model, which explicitly addresses the unity motif. This is particularly evident in v. 31, where the wife and husband are treated as one flesh in marriage union. Since the roles of wives and husbands

525 The marriage services in the Church of South India use older order of Worship in which husbands make a vow to "love, cherish, and protect" their wives. Whereas wives vow to "love, cherish, and obey" their husbands (See *The Book of Common Worship* (1967), 176-77). Though the Revised version has adopted an inclusive approach to marital vows, it is not widely used. The recital of Eph. 5:21-28 excluding the mystery of marriage (vv. 29-32) holds an inevitable part in the marriage worship order of Malankara Marthoma Church (See *Malankara Marthoma Suriyani Christhianikallude Shrushrushakramam* (2000), 48-49). The reading of Eph. 5. 21-33 and the marital vows based on that passage also hold a prominent place in the order of marriage in the *Lutheran Agenda* (See 36-37, 43, 4, 49, 54, 55).

are Christologically oriented, they would probably indicate rejection of selfish motives. Against the backdrop of a patriarchal household code, the concept of wife and husband becoming one flesh marks the possibilities of reconciliation between unequally treated marriage partners.

Both concepts of mutuality and subordination exist in Eph. 5:21-33 side by side in constant tension. However, it becomes self-evident that by interpolating Gen. 2:24 in v. 31, the author affirms 'the mutual "one flesh" relationship as more authentic than a domination-subjugation model for a Christian marriage. Gen. 2:24 in Eph. 5:31 serves as the great mystery of the union of wife and husband in comparison with the union of Church and Christ.

The 'mystery' highlighted in New Testament times is the once-hidden purpose of God, now revealed in and through Christ. Now in Christ, the great mystery calls for a mutual relationship that will exist between wife and husband (Eph. 5:32). Since the author of Ephesians uses 'flesh' and 'body' synonymously in 5:28 and 29a, it is clear that both wife and husband are treated as 'one body' or 'one flesh' in marriage. Earlier, husbands were asked to love their wives as their own body (v. 28), or flesh (v. 29a) and now interestingly enough, in v. 31, wife has become one body or flesh with the husband. This interpretation poses a challenge to the domestic violence in marital homes. As the husband moves towards his wife for mutual 'one-flesh' union, it becomes anomalous if he exerts violence upon the wife, who is his own body or flesh.

In such a consummation of mutual 'one-flesh' union, while the distinctiveness of both the sexes is cherished, the dichotomy of gender ceases to exist. This denotes an ideal rejection of gender dichotomy, and in turn, of gendered sexes. Therefore, a liberative marital union with mutual co-existence of wife and husband as one flesh can become a reality. Such an understanding of marriage calls for mutuality in submission as in Eph. 5:21. "The notion of the permanent 'one flesh' union provides the ground for replacing the hierarchical gender roles to a marital relationship of justice and love where "the justice will require that traditional male dominance cannot be tolerated and love will assure that the relationship does not degenerate into a sterile competition for control."[526] Such re-reading of Eph. 5:21-33 may unravel a possible alternate reading of biblical passages to move towards a mutual 'one-flesh' marital union. Such interpretations will further enable addressing the social issue like domestic violence from an egalitarian biblical perspective.

526 A. T. Lincoln and A. J. M. Wedderburn, *The Theology of the Later Pauline Letters* (Cambridge: Cambridge University Press, 1993), 162.

Bibliography

I. Primary Sources

A. Texts and Translations

Aland, Barbara, *et.al.*, eds. *The Greek New Testament, Fourth Revised Edition.* Stuttgart: United Bible Societies, 1994.

Grant, Robert M. *The Apostolic Fathers, Vol. 1.* New York: Thomas Nelson & Sons, 1964.

The Holy Bible. The New Revised Standard Version. Catholic Edition for India. Bangalore: Thomas Nelson, Inc., 1990.

The Septuagint Version of the Old Testament. London: Samuel Bagster and Sons Limited.

B. Lexicons

Arndt, William F. and F. Wilbur Gingrich. *Greek-English Lexicon of the New Testament and other Early Christian Literature.* Chicago: University of Chicago Press, 1957.

Louw, Johannes P. and Eugene A. Nida, eds. *Greek-English Lexicon of the New Testament Based on Semantic Domains.* 2nd ed. New York: United Bible Society, 1989.

Smith, G. Abbott. *A Manual Greek Lexicon of the New Testament.* Edinburgh: T & T Clark, 1937.

Thayer, Joseph Henry. *A Greek-English Lexicon of the New Testament.* New York: Harper & Brothers, 1887.

The Analytical Greek Lexicon. London: S. B. & Sons Ltd., 1794.

C. Dictionaries

Balz. "fovbo"." *Theological Dictionary of New Testament*, Vol IX. Edited by Gerhard Friedrich. Grand Rapids: William B. Eerdmans Publsihing Company, 1974, CD-ROM.

Bertram. "*Ethnos/Ethnikos.*" *Theological Dictionary of the New Testament*, Vol. II. Edited by Gerhard Kittel, translated and edited by Geoffrey W. Bromiley. Grand Rapids, Michigan: William B. Eerdmans Publishing Company, 1968. 364-369.

Delling. "uJpotavssw." *The Theological Dictionary of New Testament*, vol. VIII. Edited by Gerhard Friedrich. Grand Rapids: William B. Eerdmans Publishing Company, 1972.

Freedman, David Noel, et al, eds. *Anchor Bible Dictionary*. Vols. 1-6. New York: Doubleday, 1992.

Hawthorne, Gerald F. and Ralph P. Martin, eds. *Dictionary of Paul and his Letters*. Illinois: InterVarsity Press, 1993.

Isherwood, Lisa and Dorothea McEwan, eds. *An A to Z of Feminist Theology*. Sheffield: Sheffield Academic Press, 1996.

Keener, C. S. "Marriage." *Dictionary of New Testament Background*, Edited by Craig A. Evans and Stanley E. Porter. Illinois: InterVarsity Press, 2000.

Kroeger, C. C. "Women in Greco-Roman World and Judaism." *Dictionary of New Testament Background*. Edited by Craig A. Evans and Stanley E. Porter. Illinois: InterVarsity Press, 2000.

Martin, Ralph P. and Peter H. Davids, eds. *Dictionary of the Later New Testament and its Developments*. Illinois: Intervaristy Press, 1997.

Ryken, Leland James C. Wilhoit and Tremper Longmon III, eds. *Dictionary of Biblical Imagery*. USA: InterVarsity Press, 2002.

Schmidt, Karl Ludwig. "*Ethnos* in the NT," in *Theological Dictionary of the New Testament*, Vol. II. Edited by Gerhard Kittel, translated and edited by Geoffrey W. Bromiley, Grand Rapids, Michigan: William B. Eerdmans Publishing Company, 1968.

D. Commentaries

Barrett, C. K. *The First Epistle to the Corinthians.* London: Adam & Charles Black, 1971.

Fee, Gordon D. *The First Epistle to the Corinthians.* Grand Rapids: William B. Eerdmans Publishing Company, 1987.

Hoehner, Harold W. *Ephesians. An Exegetical Commentary.* Grand Rapids: Baker Academic, 2002.

Kitchen, Martin. *Ephesians.* London and New York: Routledge, 1994.

Lincoln, Andrew T. *Ephesians: Word Biblical Commentary*, Vol. 42. Dallas, TX: Word Books, 1998.

Lohse, Eduard. *A Commentary on the Epistles to the Colossians and Philemon.* Translated by W. R. Poehlmann and R. J. Karris. Philadelphia: Fortress Press, 1971.

Mitton, C. L. *The Epistle to the Ephesians: Its Authorship, Origin and Purpose.* Oxford: Oxford University Press, 1951.

Newsom, Carol A. and Sharon H. Ringe. *Women's Bible Commentary.* Louisville: Westminster John Knox Press, 1998.

O'Brien, Peter T. *The Letter to the Ephesians.* Leicester: Apollos, 1999.

Perkins, Pheme. *Ephesians.* Nashville: Abingdon Press, 1997.

Schnackenburg, Rudolf. *The Epistle to the Ephesians: A Commentary.* Translated by Helen Heron. Edinburgh: T & T Clark, 1991.

Segovia, Fernando F. and R. S. Sugirtharajah, eds. *A Postcolonial Commentary on the New Testament Writings.* New York: T & T Clark, 2009.

Thurston, Bonnie. *Reading Colossians, Ephesians, and 2 Thessalonians: A Literary and Theological Commentary.* New York: Crossroad, 1995.

II. Secondary Sources

A. Books

Abraham, M. V. *Theology of St. Paul: An Introduction. Tiruvalla: Christava Sahitya Samiti,* 2008.

Ashcroft, Bill, Gareth Griffiths and Helen Tiffin. *Key Concepts in Post-Colonial Studies*. London and New York: Routledge, 2004.

Balch, David L. *Let Wives be Submissive. The Domestic Code in 1 Peter.* Chicago, CA: Scholars Press, 1981.

Balch, David. *Let Wives be Submissive. The Domestic Code in 1 Peter*. Chicago, CA: Scholars Press, 1981.

Best, Ernst. *Essays in Ephesians*. Edinburgh: T & T Clark, 1997.

Bhabha, Homi K. *The Location of Culture*. London: Routledge, 1994.

Bird, Phyllis. *Missing Persons and Mistaken Identities: Women and Gender in Ancient Israel.* Minneapolis: Fortress Press, 1997.

Borrowdale, Anne. *Distorted Images: Christian Attitudes to Women, Men and Sex*. London: SPCK, 1991.

Brown, Peter. *The Body and Society: Men, Women and Sexual Renunciation in Early Christianity*. London: Faber and Faber, 1988.

Ceresko, Anthony R. *The Old Testament: A Liberation Perspective*. Bombay: St. Paul's, 1993.

Corbett, P. E. *The Roman Law of Marriage*. Oxford: Clarendon, 1969.

Crouch, James E. *The Origin and Intention of the Colossian Haustafel.* Gottingen: Vandenhoek, 1972.

Dube, Musa W. *Postcolonial Feminist Interpretation of the Bible*. St. Louis, Missouri: Chalice Press, 2000.

Ebeling, Jennie R. *Women's Lives in Biblical Times*. London & New York: T & T Clark International, 2010.

Edersheim, Alfred. *Sketches of Jewish Social Life*, 3rd Print. U.S.A: Hendrickson Publishers, 1996.

Evanson, Edward. *The Dissonance of the Four Generally Received Evangelists and the Evidence of their Respective Authenticity Examined.* Ipswich, Engalnd: George Jermym, 1792.

Ferguson, Everett. *Backgrounds of Early Christianity*. Grand Rapids: William B. Eerdmans Publishing Company, 1993.

Fiorenza, Elisabeth Schussler. *Bread Not Stone: The Challenge of Feminist Biblical Interpretation*. Boston: Beacon Press, 1985.

Fiorenza, Elisabeth Schussler. *But She Said: Feminist Practices of Biblical Interpretation*. Boston: Beacon, 1992.

Fiorenza, Elisabeth Schussler. *In Memory of Her: A Feminist Theological Reconstruction of Christian Origins*. London: SCM Press Ltd., 1983.

Fiorenza, Elisabeth Schussler. *Wisdom Ways: Introducing Biblical Interpretation*. Maryknoll, New York: Orbis Books, 2001.

Garnsey, Peter and Richard Saller. *The Roman Empire: Economy, Society and Culture*. U.S.A: University of California Press, 1987.

Gritz, Sharon H. *Paul, Women Teachers, and the Mother Goddess at Ephesus*. A Study of 1 Timothy 2:9-15 in Light of the Religious and Cultural Milieu of the First Century. Lanham: University Press of America, 1991.

Hayter, Mary. *The New Eve in Christ*. London: SPCK, 1987.

Hurley, James B. *Man and Woman in Biblical Perspective: A Study in Role Relationships and Authority*. England: InterVarsity Press, 1981.

Isherwood, Lisa. *Erotic Celebacy: Queering Heteropatriarchy*. London: T & T Clark, 2006.

Jeremias, Joachim. *Jerusalem in the Time of Jesus*. Philadelphia: Fortress, 1969.

Joy, C. I. David. *Revelation: A Post-Colonial View Point*. Delhi: ISPCK, 2001.

Keener, C. S. *Paul, Women and Wives: Marriage and Women's Ministry in the Letters of Paul*. Peabody, MA: Hendrickson, 1992.

Keener, Kraig S. *Paul, Women and Wives: Marriage and Women's Ministry in the Letters of Paul*. U.S.A: Hendrickson Publishers, 2007.

Kelly, Liam. *Sacraments Revisited: What do they Mean Today?* London: Darton, Longman and Todd Ltd., 1998.

Kummel, W. G. *Introduction to the New Testament*. Edited and translated by H. C. Kee. Nashville; Abingdon Press, 1975.

Lincoln A. T. and A. J. M. Wedderburn. *The Theology of the Later Pauline Letters*. Cambridge: Cambridge University Press, 1993.

Llewelyn, S. R. and R. A. Kearsley. *New Documents Illustrating Early Christianity. A Review of the Greek Inscriptions and Papyri Published in 1980-81*. Australia: The Ancient History Documentary Research Centre, Macquarie University, 1992.

Loewe, Raphael. *The Position of Women in Judaism*. London: SPCK, 1966.

MacDonald, Margaret Y. *The Pauline Churches: A Socio-Historical Study of Institutionalization in the Pauline and Deutero-Pauline Writings*. Cambridge: Cambridge University Press, 1988.

Meeks, Wayne A. *The First Urban Christians: The Social World of the Apostle Paul.* New Haven and London: Yale University Press, 1983.

Miletic, Stephen Francis. *"One Flesh": Eph. 5.22-24, 5.31. Marriage and the New Creation.* Anchor Bible 115; Rome: Biblical Institute, 1988.

Mollenkott, Virginia R. *Women, Men and the Bible.* Nashville: Abingdon Press, 1977.

Moore, George Foot. *Judaism. In the First Centuries of the Christian Era, the Age of the Tannaim, Vol. II.* Cambridge: Harvard University Press, 1950.

Osiek, Carolyn and David L. Balch. *Families in the New Testament World. Households and House Churches.* Louisville: Westminister John Knox Press, 1997.

Osiek, Carolyn and Margaret Y. MacDonald with Janet H. Tulloch. *A Woman's Place: House Churches in Earliest Christianity.* Minneapolis: Fortress Press, 2006.

Pilcher, Jane and Imelda Whelehan. *Fifty Key Concepts in Gender Studies*. London: Sage, 2004.

Pui-lan, Kwok. *Postcolonial Imagination and Feminist Theology.* Louisville: WJK, 2005.

Rhee, Helen. *Early Christian Literature: Christ and Culture in the Second and Third Centuries*. London & New York: Routledge, 2005.

Russell, Letty M. *Imitators of God: A Study Book on Ephesians.* New York: Mission Education and Cultivation Program Department of the United Methodist Church, 1984.

Sampley J. Paul. *And the Two Shall Become One Flesh: A Study of Traditions in Ephesians 5:21-33.* Cambridge: University Press, 1971.

Samuel, Simon. *A Postcolonial Reading of Mark's Story of Jesus.* London: T & T Clark, 2007.

Sawyer, Deborah F. *Women and Religion in the First Christian Centuries.* London and New York: Routledge, 1996.

Schnackenburg, Rudolf. *The Epistle to the Ephesians: A Commentary.* Translated by Helen Heron. Edinburgh: T & T Clark, 1991.

Stegemann, E. W. and W. Stegemann. *The Jesus Movement: A Social History of its First Century.* Translated by O. C. Dean, Jr. Minneapolis: Fortress Press, 1995.

Sugirtharajah, R. S. *Postcolonial Criticism and Biblical Interpretation.* Oxford: Oxford University Press, 2002.

Sugirtharajah, R. S. *Postcolonial Reconfigurations: An Alternative Way of Reading the Bible and Doing Theology.* London: SCM Press, 2003.

Theissen, Gerd. *Essays on Corinth: The Social Setting of Pauline Christianity.* Edited and Translated by John H. Schutz. Edinburgh, T & T Clarke, 1982.

Theissen, Gerd. *Sociology of Early Palestinian Christianity.* Philadelphia: Fortress Press, 1978.

Verner, David C. *The Household of God: The Social World of the Pastoral Epistles.* Chico, California: Scholars Press, 1983.

Walsh, Brian J. and Sylvia C. Keesmaat. *Colossians Remixed: Subverting the Empire.* Downers Grove, Illinois: InterVarsity Press, 2004.

Yamaguchi, Satoko. *Mary and Martha. Women in the World of Jesus.* Maryknoll, New York: Orbis Books, 2002.

Yee, Tet-Lim N. *Jews, Gentiles and Ethnic Reconciliation: Paul's Jewish Identity and Ephesians.* Cambridge: Cambridge University Press, 2005.

B. Articles in Books

Balch, David L. "Household Codes." In *Greco-Roman Literature and the New Testament.* Edited by David. E. Aune. Atlanta, GA: Scholars Press, 1988.

Bird, Jennifer G. "The Letter to the Ephesians." In *A Postcolonial Commentary on the New Testament Writings.* Edited by Fernando F. Segovia and R. S. Sugirtharajah. London: T & T Clark, 2007.

Chakkalakal, Pauline. "Must Women cover their Heads?" In *Envisioning A New Heaven and New Earth.* Edited by Lalrinawmi Ralte and others. Delhi: SPCK, 1998.

Chakkalakal, Pauline. "Paul a Friend or a Foe of Women?" In *Feminist Theology: Perspectives and Praxis.* Edited by Prasanna Kumari. GSI: Madras, 1998.

Dixon, Suzanne. "Sex and the Married Woman in Ancient Rome." In *Early Christian Families in Context: An Interdisciplinary Dialogue.* Edited by David l. Balch and Carolyn Osiek. Grand Rapids, Michigan/Cambridge, U.K.: William B. Eerdmans Publishing Company, 2003.

Graham, E. "Gender." In *An A to Z of Feminist Theology.* Edited by Lisa Isherwood and Dorothea McEvan. Sheffield: Sheffield Academic Press.

Hallett, Judith P. "Women's Lives in the Ancient Mediterranean." In *Women and Christian Origins.* Edited by Ross Shepard Kraemer and Mary Rose D'Angelo. New York/Oxford: Oxford University Press, 1999.

Hengel, Martin. "The Interpenetration of Judaism and Hellenism in the Pre-Maccabean Period." In *The Cambridge History of Judaism, Vol. 2. The Hellenistic Age.* Edited by W. D. Davies and Louis Finkelstein. Great Britain: Cambridge University Press, 1989.

Horbury, William. "Women in the Synagogue." In *The Cambridge History of Judaism, Vol. 3. The Early Roman Period.* Edited by William Horbury, W. D. Davies and John Sturdy. Great Britain: Cambridge University Press, 2001.

Isherwood, Lisa. "The Violence of Gender: Christian Marriage as Test Case." In *Weep not for Your Children: Essays on Religion and Violence*. Edited by Lisa Isherwood and Rosemary Radford Ruether. London: Equinox, 2008.

Kraemer, Ross S. "Jewish Women and Women's Judaism(s) at the Beginning of Christianity.' In *Women and Christian Origins*. Edited by Ross Shepard Kraemer and Mary Rose D'Angelo. Oxford: Oxford University Press, 1999.

MacDonald, Margaret Y. "Rereading Paul. Early Interpreters of Paul on Women and Gender." In *Women and Christian Origins*. Edited by Ross Shepard Kraemer and Mary Rose D' Angelo. New York/ Oxford: Oxford University Press, 1999.

MacDonald, Margaret Y. "Was Celsus Right? The Role of Women in Expansion in Early Christianity." In *Early Christian Families in Context: An Interdisciplinary Dialogue*. Edited by David L. Balch and Carolyn Osiek. Grand Rapids, Michigan/Cambridge, U.K.: William B. Eerdmans Publishing Company, 2003.

Minh-ha, Trinh T. "Writing Postcoloniality and Feminism," In *The Post-Colonial Studies Reader*. Edited by Bill Ashcroft, Gareth Griffiths and Helen Tiffin. London: Routledge; 1995.

Mohanty, Chandra. "Under Western Eyes," In *Colonial Discourse and Postcolonial Theory*: A Reader. Edited by Patrick Williams and Laura Chrisman. New York: Columbia University Press, 1994.

Pui-lan, Kwok. "Postcolonialism, Feminism and Biblical Interpretation." In *Scripture, Community and Mission*. Edited by Philip L. Wickeri. HongKong: CCA & CWM, 2002.

Reuther, Rosemary Radford. "Women's Liberation in Historical and Theological Perspective." In *Women's Liberation and the Church*. Edited by Sarah Bentley Doely. New York: Association Press, 1970.

Saller, Richard. "Women, Slaves and the Economy of the Roman Household." In *Early Christian Families in Context: An Interdisciplinary Dialogue*. Edited by David L. Balch and Carolyn Osiek. Grand Rapids, Michigan/Cambridge, U.K.: William B. Eerdmans Publishing Company, 2003.

Schweizer, E. "Traditional Ethical Patterns in the Pauline and Post-Pauline Letters and their Development (Lists of Vices and

Housetables)." In *Text and Interpretation*. Edited by E. Best and R. M. Wilson. Cambridge: Cambridge University Press, 1979.

Tanzer, Sarah J. "Ephesians." In *Searching the Scriptures, Volume Two: A Feminist Commentary*. Edited by Elisabeth Schussler Fiorenza. London, Britain: SCM Press Limited, 1995.

C. Articles in Journals

Balch, David L. "1 Cor 7:32-35 and Stoic Debates about Marriage, Anxiety, and Distraction." *Journal of Biblical Literature* 102/3 (1983): 429-439.

Bauman-Martin, Betsy J. "Women on the Edge: New Perspectives on Women in the Petrine *Haustafel.*" *Journal of Biblical Literature* 123/2 (2004):253-279.

Butting, Klara. "Pauline Variations on Genesis 2. 24: Speaking of the Body of Christ in the Context of the Discussion of Life Styles." *Journal for the Study of the New Testament* 79 (2000): 79-90.

Campbell-Reed, Eileen R. "Should Wives "Submit Graciously" A Feminist Approach to Interpreting Ephesians 5:21-33." *Review and Expositor* 98 (2001): 263-276.

Dahl, Nils Alstrup. "Gentiles, Christians, and Israelites in the Epistle to the Ephesians." *Harvard Theological Review* 79: 1-3 (January/April/July 1986): 31-39.

George, Michele. "Domestic Architecture and Household Relations: Pompeii and Roman Ephesos." *Journal for the Study of the New Testament* 27.1 (2004): 7-25.

Getty, Mary Ann. Review of *Óne Flesh": Eph. 5. 22-24, 5.31. Marriage and the New Creation* by Stephen Francis Miletic. *The Catholic Biblical Quarterly* 52 (1990): 760-762.

Helton, Stanley N. "Ephesians 5:21: A Longer Translation Note." *Restoration Quarterly* 48/1 (2005): 33-41.

Henderson, Suzanne watts. "Taking Liberties with the Text: The Colossian Household Code as Hermeneutical Paradigm." *Interpretation* (October 2006): 420-432.

Hezser, Catherine. "The Impact of *Household Slaves on the Jewish* Family in Roman Palestine." *Journal for the Study of Judaism* 34/4 (November 2003): 375-424.

Jones, Serene. "Bounded Openness: Postmodernism, Feminism, and the Church Today." *Interpretation* 55/1 (January 2001): 49-59.

Lampe, Peter. "'Family' in Church and Society of New Testament Times." *Affirmation* 5 (1992): 1-20.

Lillie, W. "The Pauline House-Tables." *Expository Times* 86 (1975): 179-183.

Lincoln, Andrew T. "The Household Code and Wisdom Mode of Colossians." *Journal for the Study of the New Testament* 74 (1999): 93-112.

MacDonald, Margaret Y. "The Politics of Identity in Ephesians." *Journal for the Study of the New Testament* 26/4 (2004): 419-44.

MacDonald, Margaret Y. "Domestic Space and Families in Early Christianity: Editor's Introduction." *Journal for the Study of the New Testament* 27.1 (2004): 3-6.

Mangatt, George. "Jesus' Teaching on Marriage and Divorce," *Bible Bhashyam* (1994): 100-105.

Marshall, I. Howard. "Palestinian and Hellenistic Christianity: Some Critical Comments." *New Testament Studies* 19 (1973): 271-87.

McFarland, Ian A. "A Canonical Reading of Ephesians 5:21-33. Theological Gleanings." *Theology Today*, 57/3 (2000): 344-356.

Mercy, K. J. "Mutuality and Interdependence of man and Woman: An Exegetical Study of 1 Cor 11, 11-12." *Bible Bhashyam* XXVI/3 (September 2000): 197-8.

Merz, Annette. "Why did the Pure Bride of Christ (2 Cor. 11:2) become a wedded wife (Eph. 5:22-33)? Theses about the Intertextual Transformation of an Eschatological Metaphor" *Journal for the Study of the New Testament* 79 (2000): 131-147.

Morrell, Samuel. "An Equal or Ward: How Independent is a Married Woman according to the Rabbinic Law?" *Jewish Social Studies* 44/3 and 4 (1982): 189-210.

Nigam, S. "Asserting Women's Rights at the Domestic Front: Problems and Challenges." *Women's Link* 7/1 (January-March 2001): 43-47.

Osiek, Carolyn. "The Family in early Christianity: 'Family Values' Revisited." *The Catholic Biblical Quarterly* 58/1 (January 1996): 1-25.

Pezhumkattil, Abraham. "Husband-Wife Relationship in the Wisdom Literature." *Bible Bhashyam* XX/2 (June, 1994).

Rawson, Beryl. "'The Roman Family' in Recent Research: State of the Question." *Biblical Interpretation* 11/2 (2003): 119-138.

Setyawan, Yusak Budi. "'Be Subject to Your Husband as You are to the Lord' in Ephesians 5:21-33 - Illuminated by An Indonesian (Javanese)." *Asia Journal of Theology* 21/1 (April 2007): 50-68.

Stagg, Frank. "The Domestic Code and Final Appeal Ephesians 5:21-6:24." *The Review and the Expositor* 76/4 (Fall 1979): 541-552.

Standhartinger, Angela. "The Origin and Intention of the Household Code in the Letter to the Colossians." *Journal for the Study of the New Testament* 79 (2000): 117-130.

Wayne warden. "Ephesians 5:21 – A Translation Note." *Restoration Quarterly* 45/4 (2003): 254.

Wayne Warden. "Translating Ephesians 5:21." *Restoration Quarterly* 47/3 (2005): 179-82.

III. Electronic Sources

Drane, J. W. "Family," *New Dictionary of Biblical Theology*. Edited by Alexander, T. Desmond and Brian S. Rosner. Downers Grove, Illinois: InterVarsity Press, 2000. CD-Rom.

Dunn, James D. G. *Word Biblical Commentary.* Volume 38a, *Romans* 1-8. Dallas, Texas: Word Books, Publisher, 1998. CD-Rom.

Hagner, Donald A. *Word Biblical Commentary*. Volume 33a, *Matthew* 1-13. Dallas, Texas: Word Books, Publisher, 1998. CD-Rom

Lacey, D. R. de. "Gentiles." *Dictionary of Paul and His Letters.* Edited by Gerald F. Hawthorne, Ralph P. Martin, and Daniel G. Reid. Downer's Grove, Illinois: InterVarsity Press, 1993/1998. CD-Rom.

Lincoln, Andrew T. *Word Biblical Commentary.* Vol. 42, *Ephesians.* Dallas, TX: Word Books, 1998. CD-Rom.

Michaels, J. R., *Word Biblical Commentary.* Vol. 49, *1 Peter*. Dallas, Texas: Word Books, Publisher, 1998. CD-Rom.

O'Brien, Peter T. *Word Biblical Commentary*. Vol. 44, *Colossians, Philemon.* Dallas, Texas: Word Books, Publisher, 1998. CD-Rom.

Ortlund, R. C. Jr. "Marriage." *New Dictionary of Biblical Theology.* Edited by Alexander, T. Desmond and Brian S. Rosner. Downers Grove, Illinois: InterVarsity Press, 2000. CD-Rom.

Towner, P. H. "Household Codes." *Dictionary of the Later New Testament & Its Developments.* Edited by Ralph P. Martin and Peter H. Davids. Downers Grove, Illinois: InterVarsity Press, 2000. CD-Rom.